THE SIXTH GUN

BOOK 6: GHOST DANCE

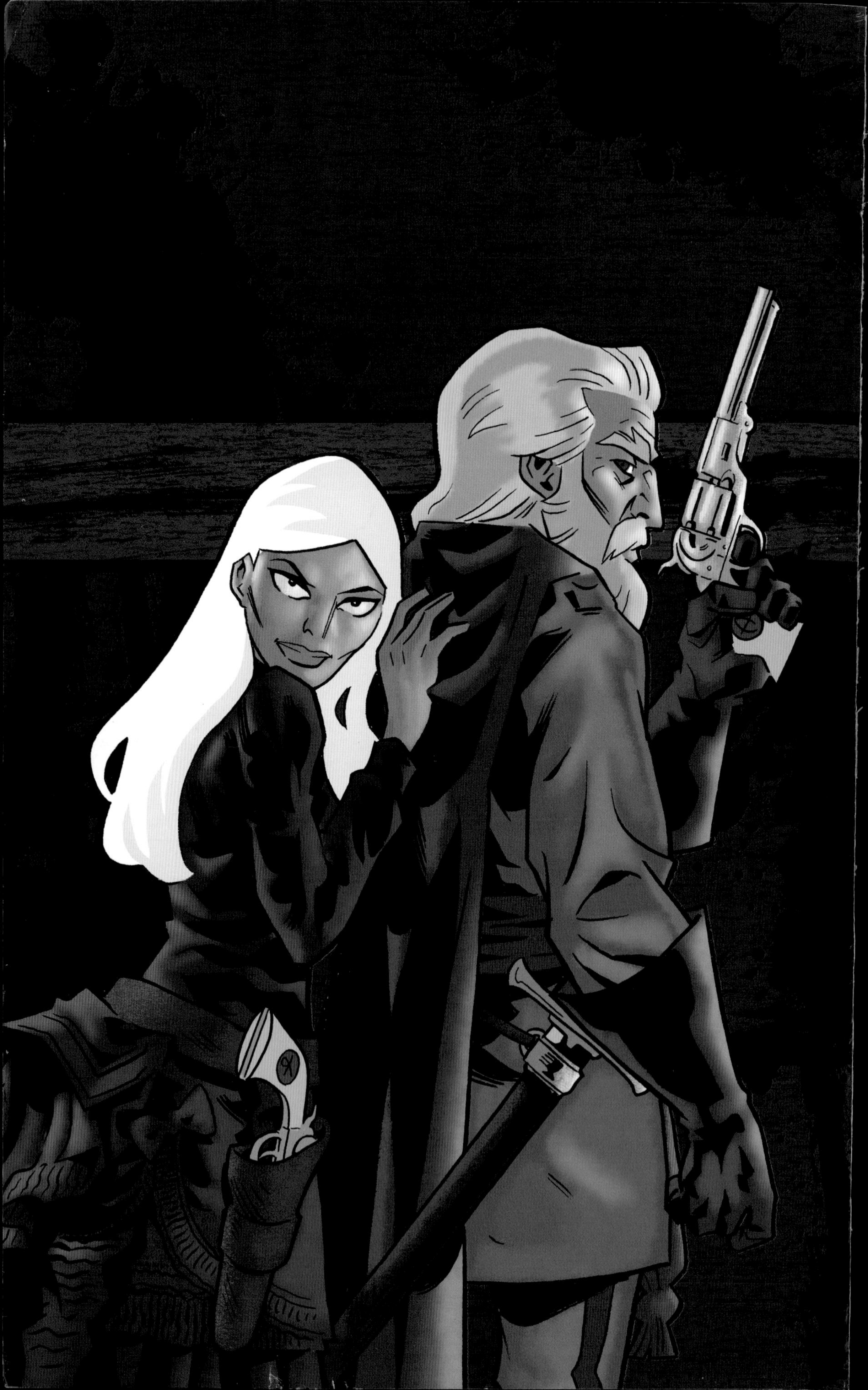

THE SIXTH GUN™

BOOK 6: GHOST DANCE

WRITTEN BY
CULLEN BUNN

ILLUSTRATED BY
BRIAN HURTT

COLORED BY
BILL CRABTREE

DOUGLAS E. SHERWOOD

CHAP... ...BY
ED BRISSON

EDITED BY
CHARLIE CHU

DESIGNED BY
KEITH WOOD

AN ONI PRESS PUBLICATION

THE SIXTH GUN™

BY CULLEN BUNN & BRIAN HURTT

PUBLISHED BY ONI PRESS, INC.

JOE NOZEMACK *publisher*

JAMES LUCAS JONES *editor in chief*

KEITH WOOD *art director*

JOHN SCHORK *director of publicity*

CHEYENNE ALLOTT *director of sales*

JILL BEATON *editor*

CHARLIE CHU *editor*

TROY LOOK *digital prepress lead*

JASON STOREY *graphic designer*

ROBIN HERRERA *administrative assistant*

THE SIXTH GUN: GHOST DANCE, FEBRUARY 2014. Published
by Oni Press, Inc. 1305 SE Martin Luther King Jr. Blvd., Suite A,
Portland, OR 97214. THE SIXTH GUN is ™ & © 2014 Cullen Bunn
& Brian Hurtt. Oni Press logo and icon are ™ & © 2014 Oni Press,
Inc. All rights reserved. Oni Press logo and icon artwork created by
Keith A. Wood. The events, institutions, and characters presented in
this book are fictional. Any resemblance to actual persons, living or
dead, is purely coincidental. No portion of this publication may be
reproduced, by any means, without the express written permission of
the copyright holders.

This volume collects issues #30-35 of the Oni Press series
The Sixth Gun.

ONI PRESS, INC.
1305 SE MARTIN LUTHER KING JR. BLVD.
SUITE A
PORTLAND, OR 97214
USA

onipress.com
facebook.com/onipress
twitter.com/onipress
onipress.tumblr.com

cullenbunn.com • @cullenbunn
brihurtt.com • @brihurtt
@crabtree_bill

First edition: February 2014

ISBN 978-1-62010-016-5
eISBN 978-1-62010-054-7

Library of Congress Control Number: 2013937934

10 9 8 7 6 5 4 3 2 1

Printed in China

BECKY MONTCRIEF - A brave young woman who holds the Sixth Gun, a weapon that can divine the future.

DRAKE SINCLAIR - A treasure hunter with a bleak past. He possesses four of the Six, and he believes he is destined to use the weapons to recreate reality.

GORD CANTRELL - Drake and Becky's ally. He knows some small measure of the dark arts, and he's uncovered a set of books that detail the terrible history of the Six.

KIRBY HALE - A charming rogue who used Becky's affections against her. He hopes to make amends.

MISSY HUME - Widow of the evil General Hume. She is dead set on claiming the Six for herself.

ASHER COBB - The Nine-foot Mystery Mummy with prophetic powers.

CHAPTER ONE

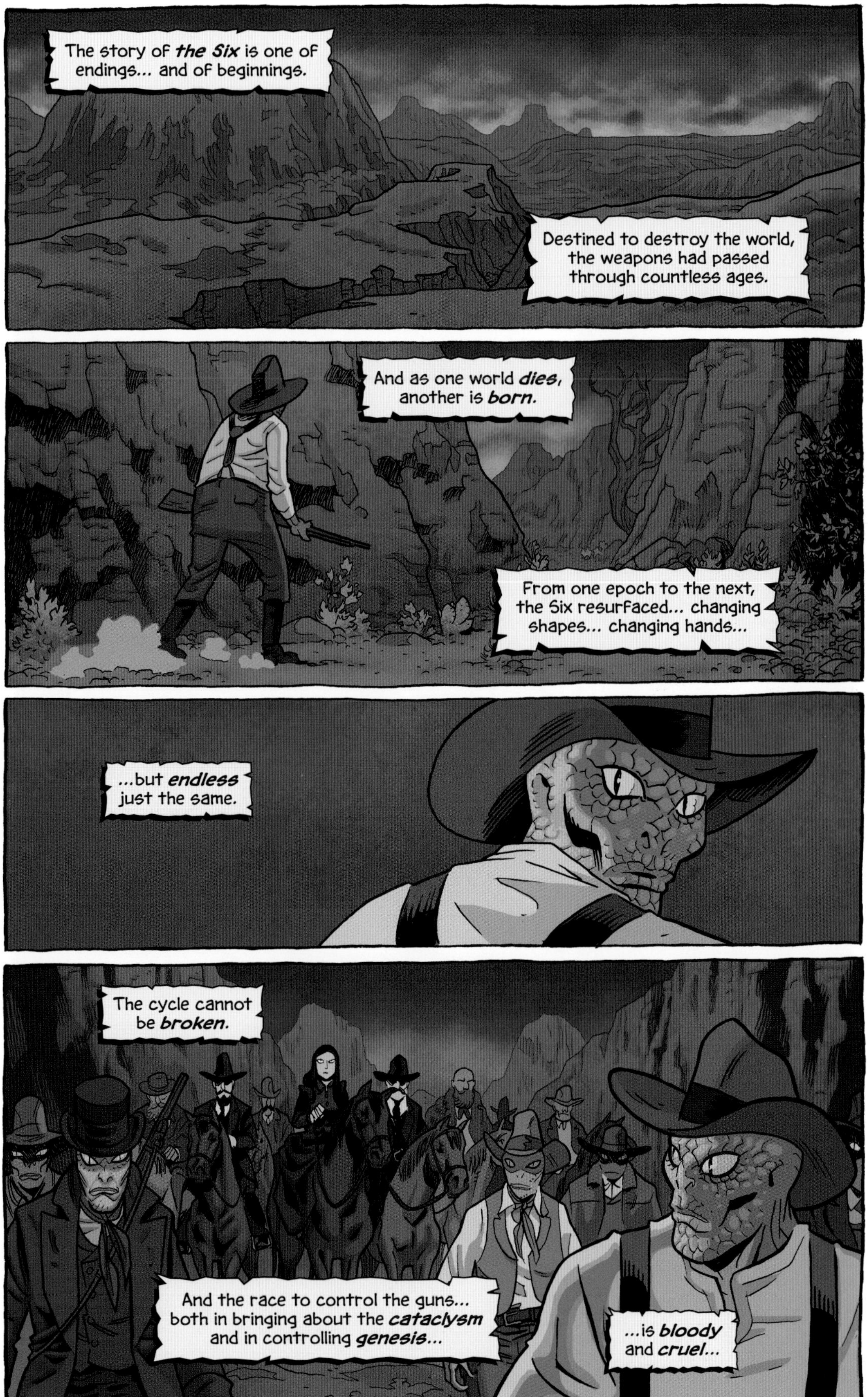
The story of the Six is one of endings... and of beginnings.
Destined to destroy the world, the weapons had passed through countless ages.
And as one world dies, another is born.
From one epoch to the next, the Six resurfaced... changing shapes... changing hands...
...but endless just the same.
The cycle cannot be broken.
And the race to control the guns... both in bringing about the cataclysm and in controlling genesis...
...is bloody and cruel...

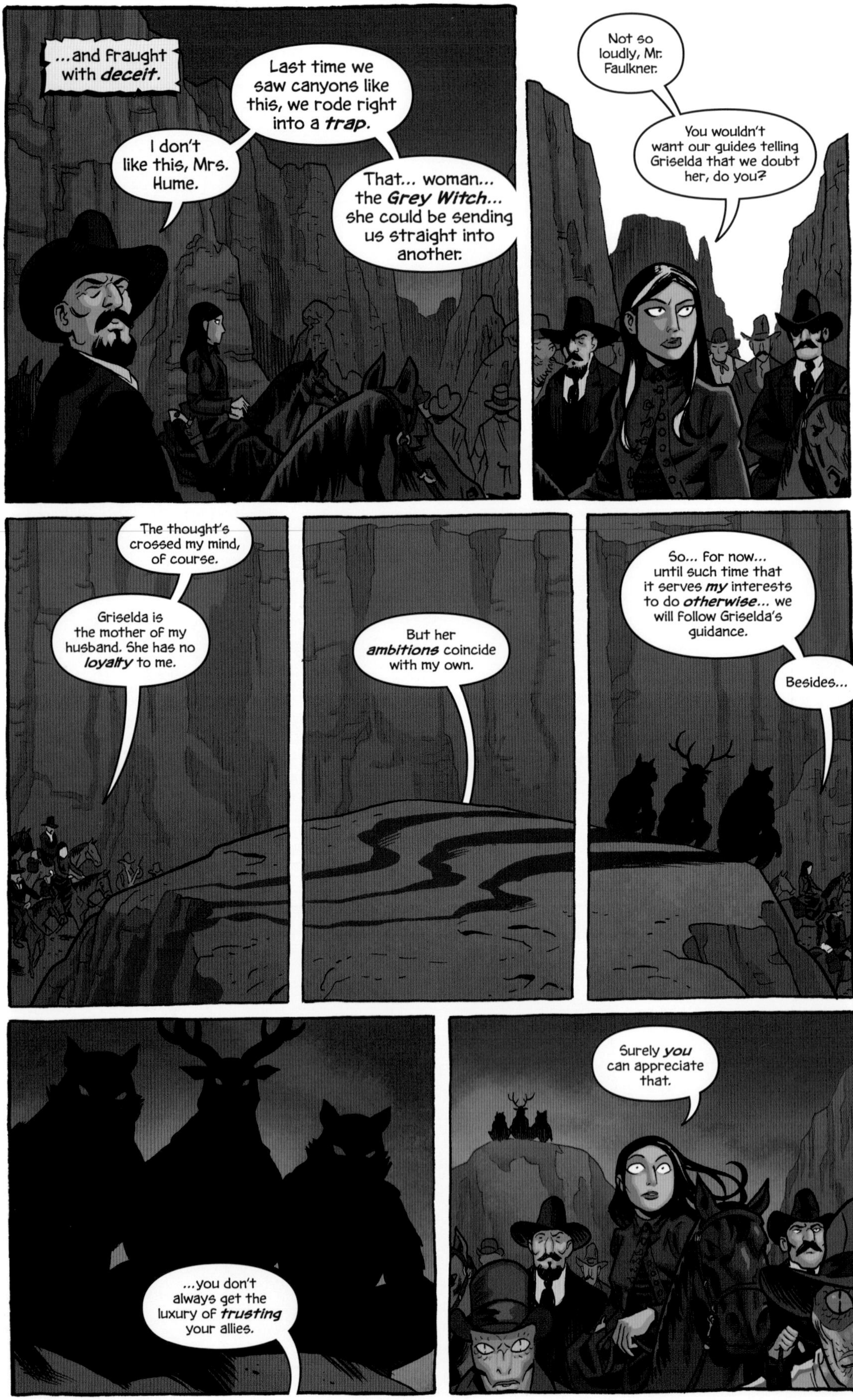
...and fraught with *deceit*.
I don't like this, Mrs. Hume.
Last time we saw canyons like this, we rode right into a *trap*.
That... woman... the *Grey Witch*... she could be sending us straight into another.
Not so loudly, Mr. Faulkner.
You wouldn't want our guides telling Griselda that we doubt her, do you?
The thought's crossed my mind, of course.
Griselda is the mother of my husband. She has no *loyalty* to me.
But her *ambitions* coincide with my own.
So... for now... until such time that it serves *my* interests to do *otherwise*... we will follow Griselda's guidance.
Besides...
...you don't always get the luxury of *trusting* your allies.
Surely *you* can appreciate that.

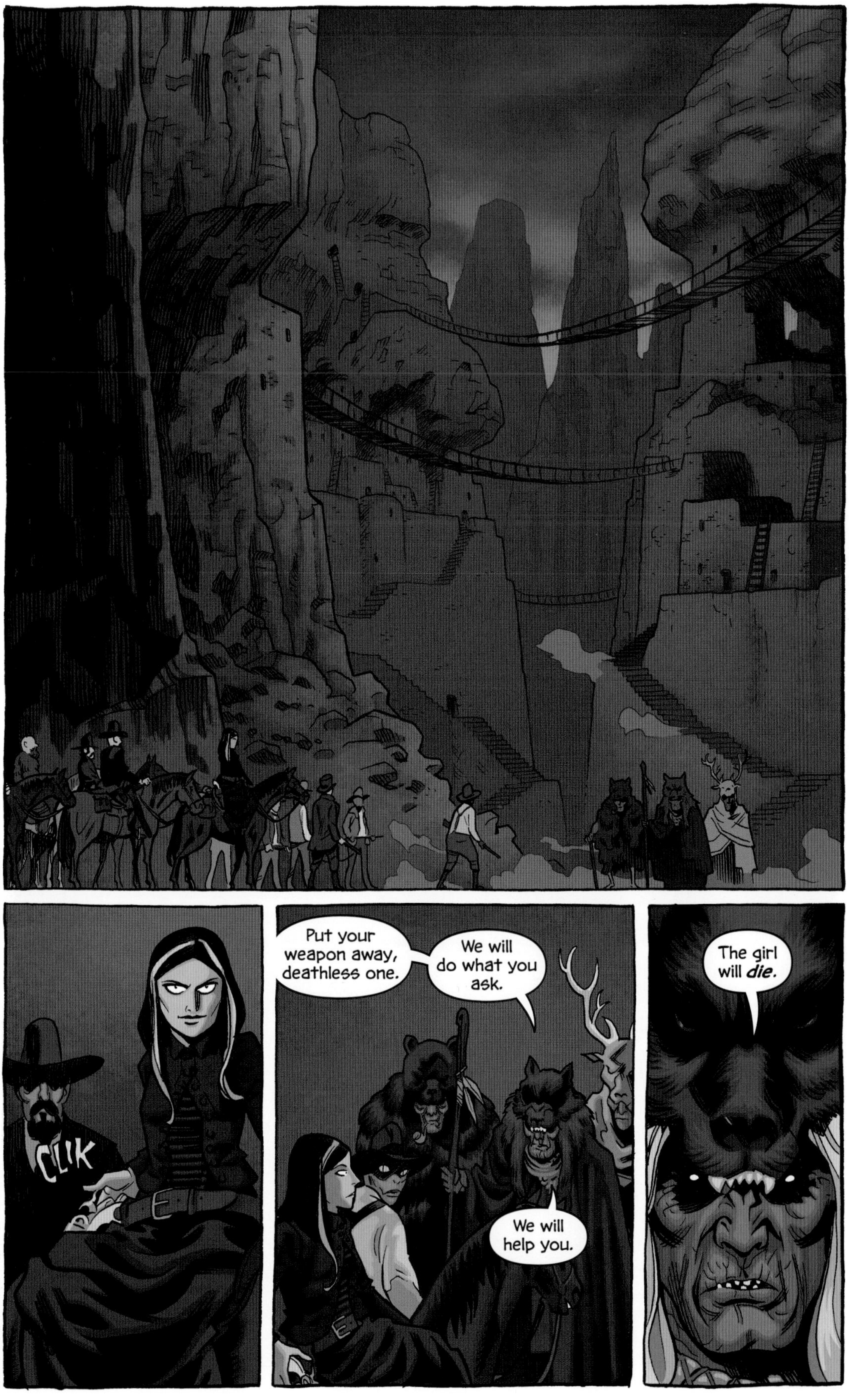
CLIK
Put your weapon away, deathless one.
We will do what you ask.
We will help you.
The girl will *die.*

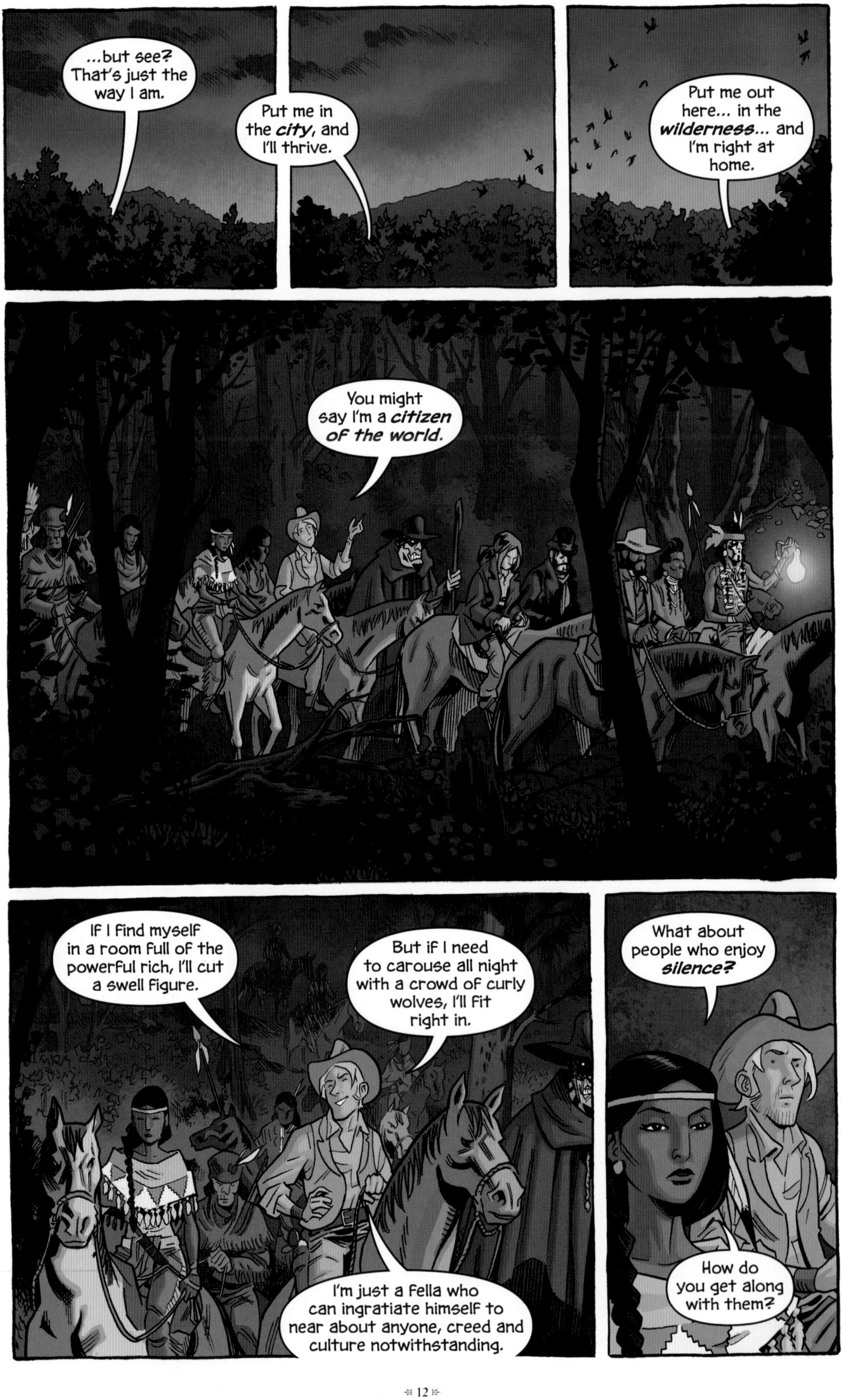
...but see? That's just the way I am.
Put me in the *city*, and I'll thrive.
Put me out here... in the *wilderness*... and I'm right at home.
You might say I'm a *citizen of the world.*
If I find myself in a room full of the powerful rich, I'll cut a swell figure.
But if I need to carouse all night with a crowd of curly wolves, I'll fit right in.
I'm just a fella who can ingratiate himself to near about anyone, creed and culture notwithstanding.
What about people who enjoy *silence?*
How do you get along with them?

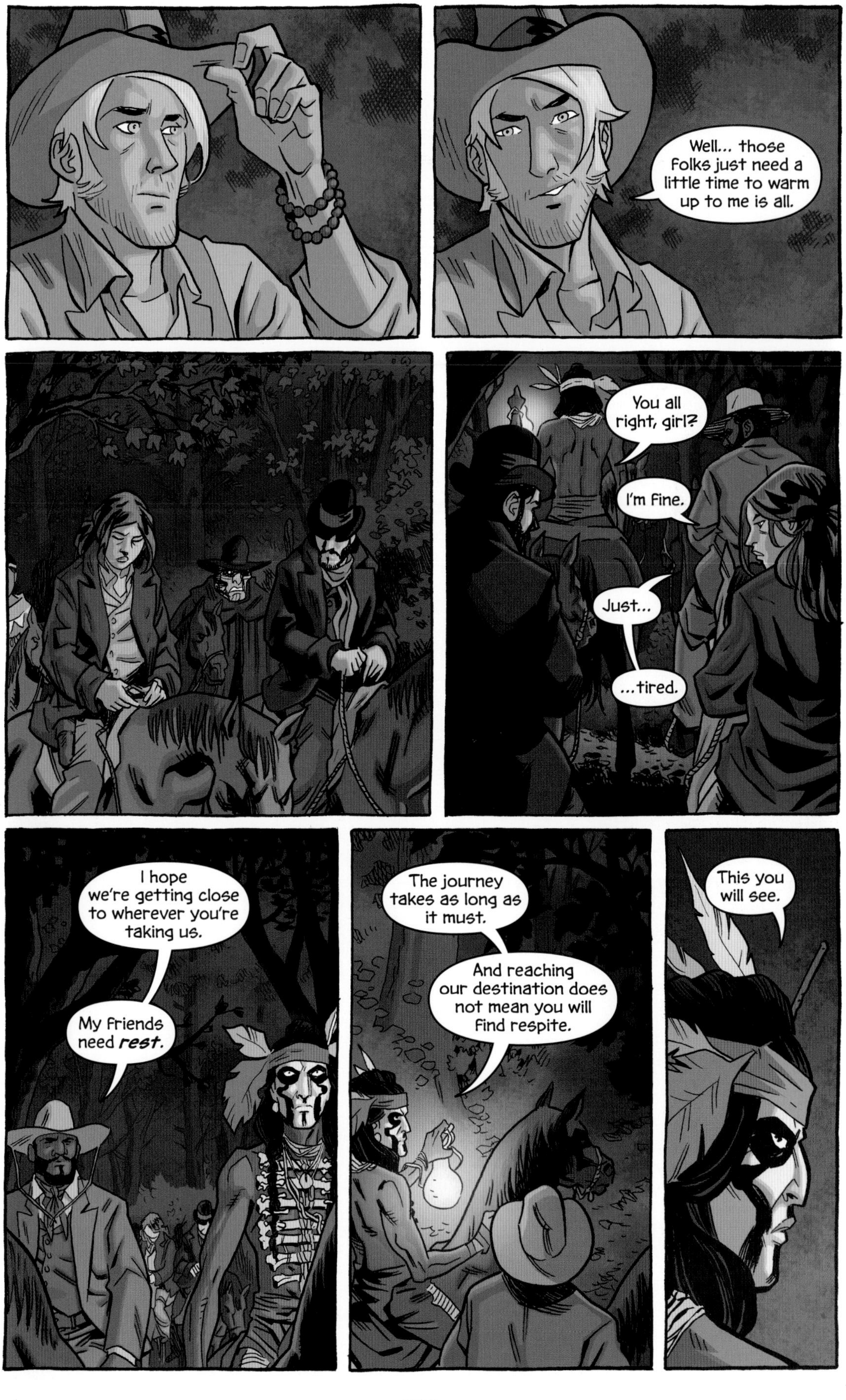
Well... those folks just need a little time to warm up to me is all.
You all right, girl?
I'm fine.
Just...
...tired.
I hope we're getting close to wherever you're taking us.
My friends need *rest*.
The journey takes as long as it must.
And reaching our destination does not mean you will find respite.
This you will see.

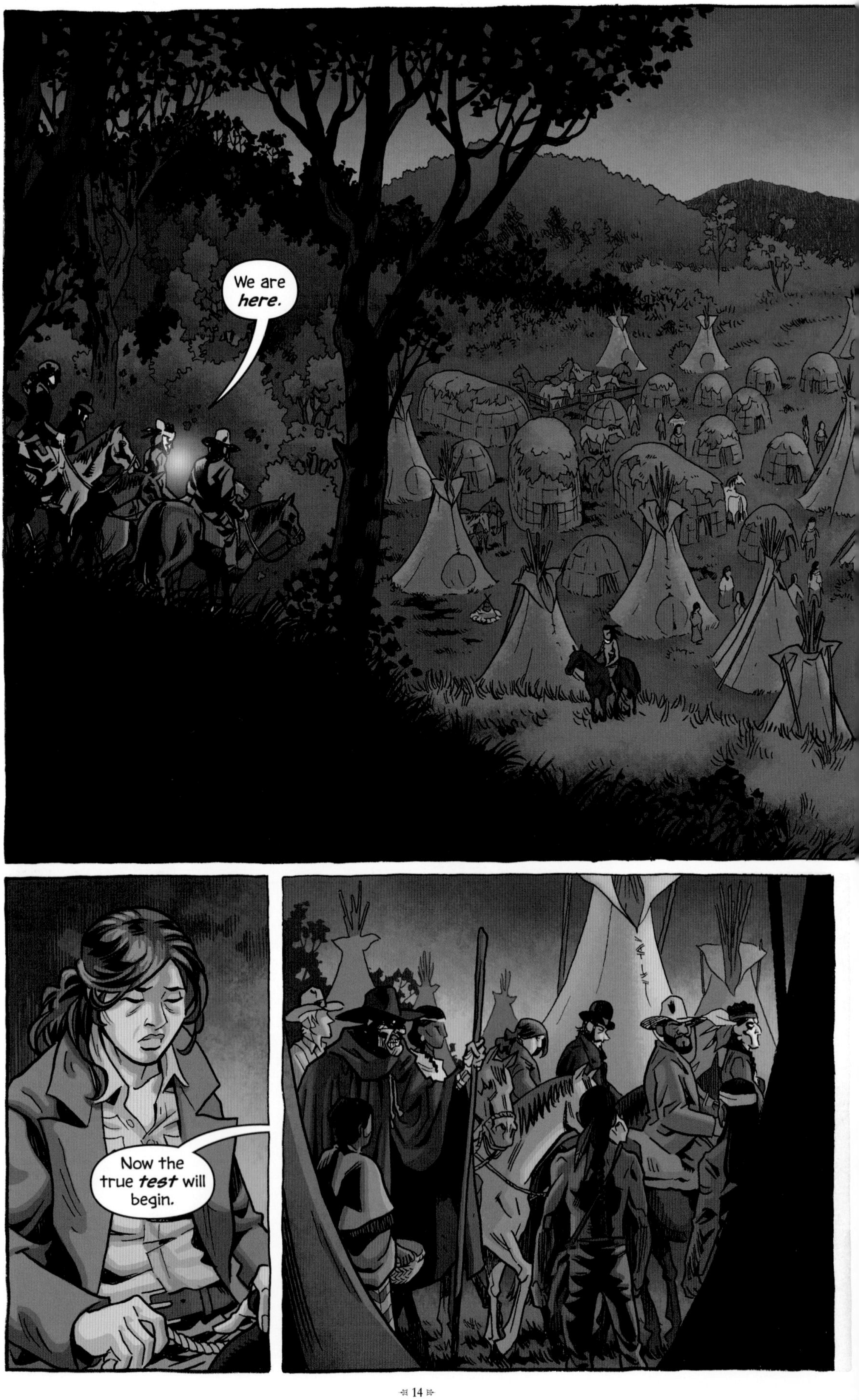
We are *here.*
Now the true *test* will begin.

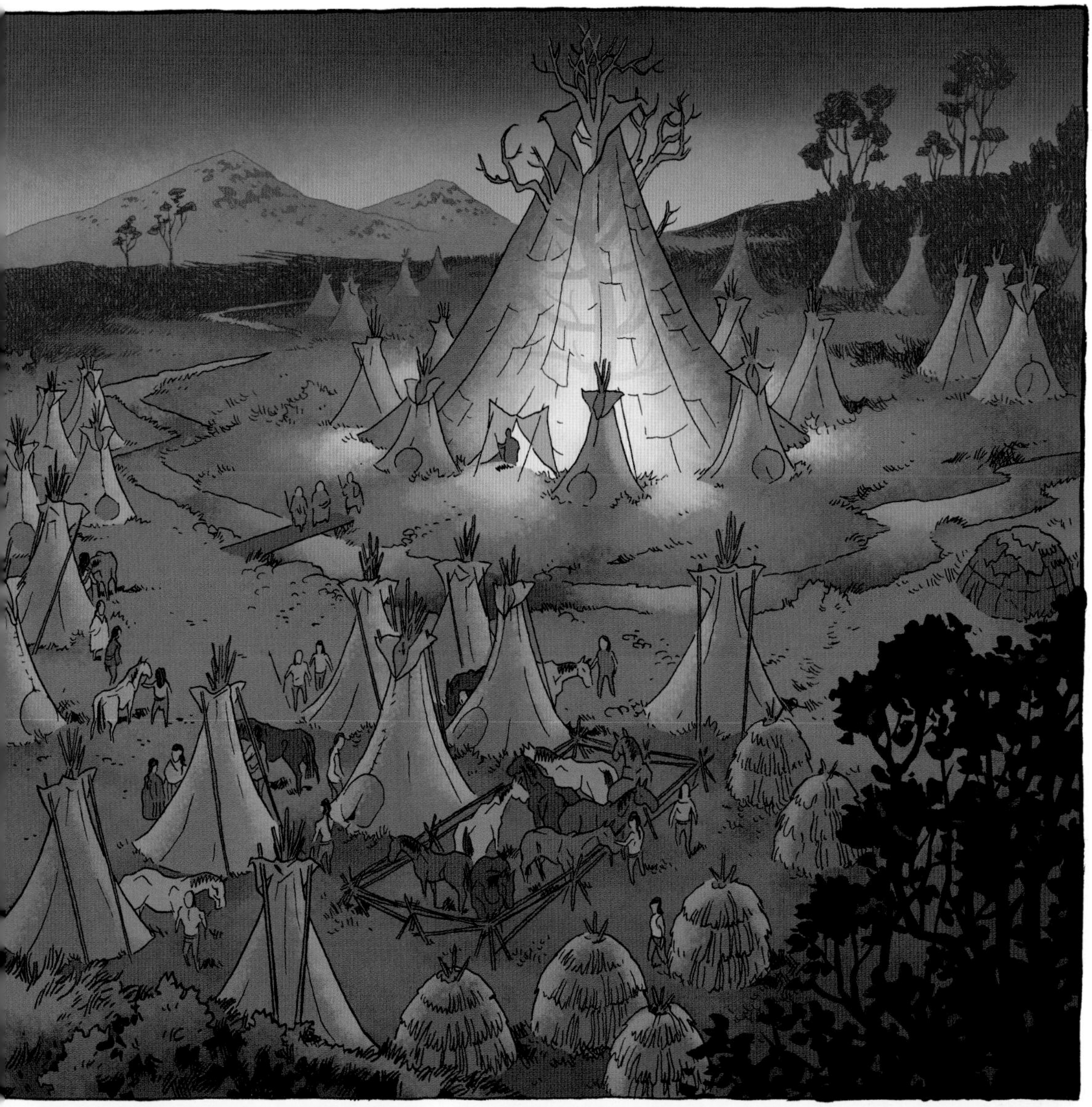

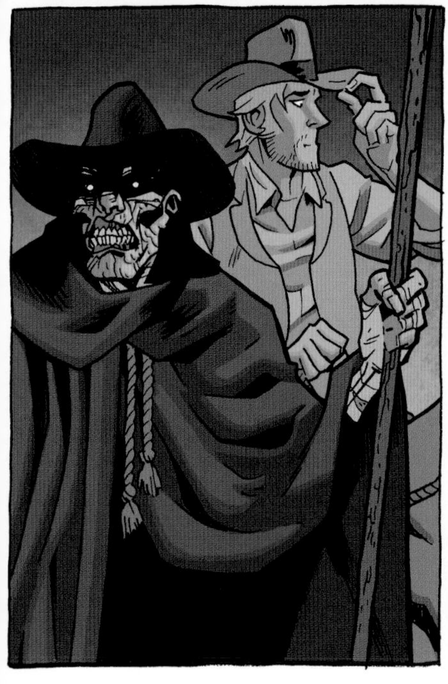

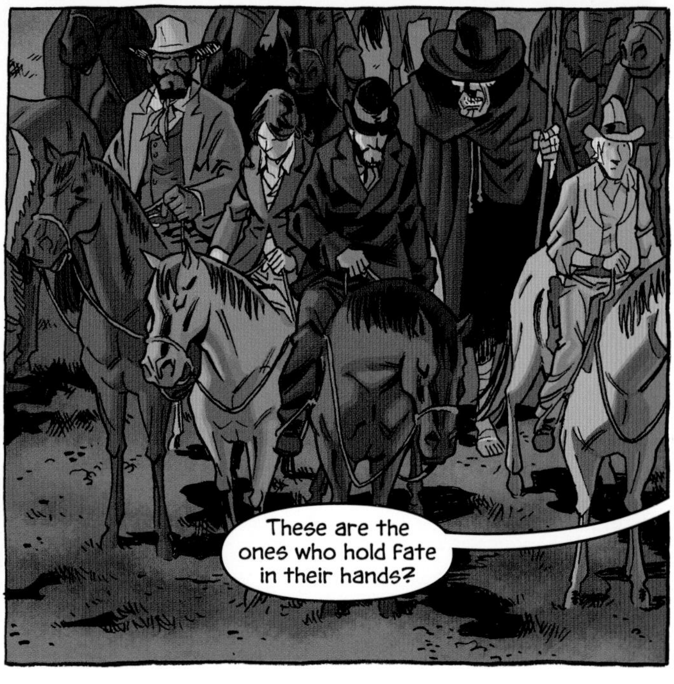
These are the ones who hold fate in their hands?

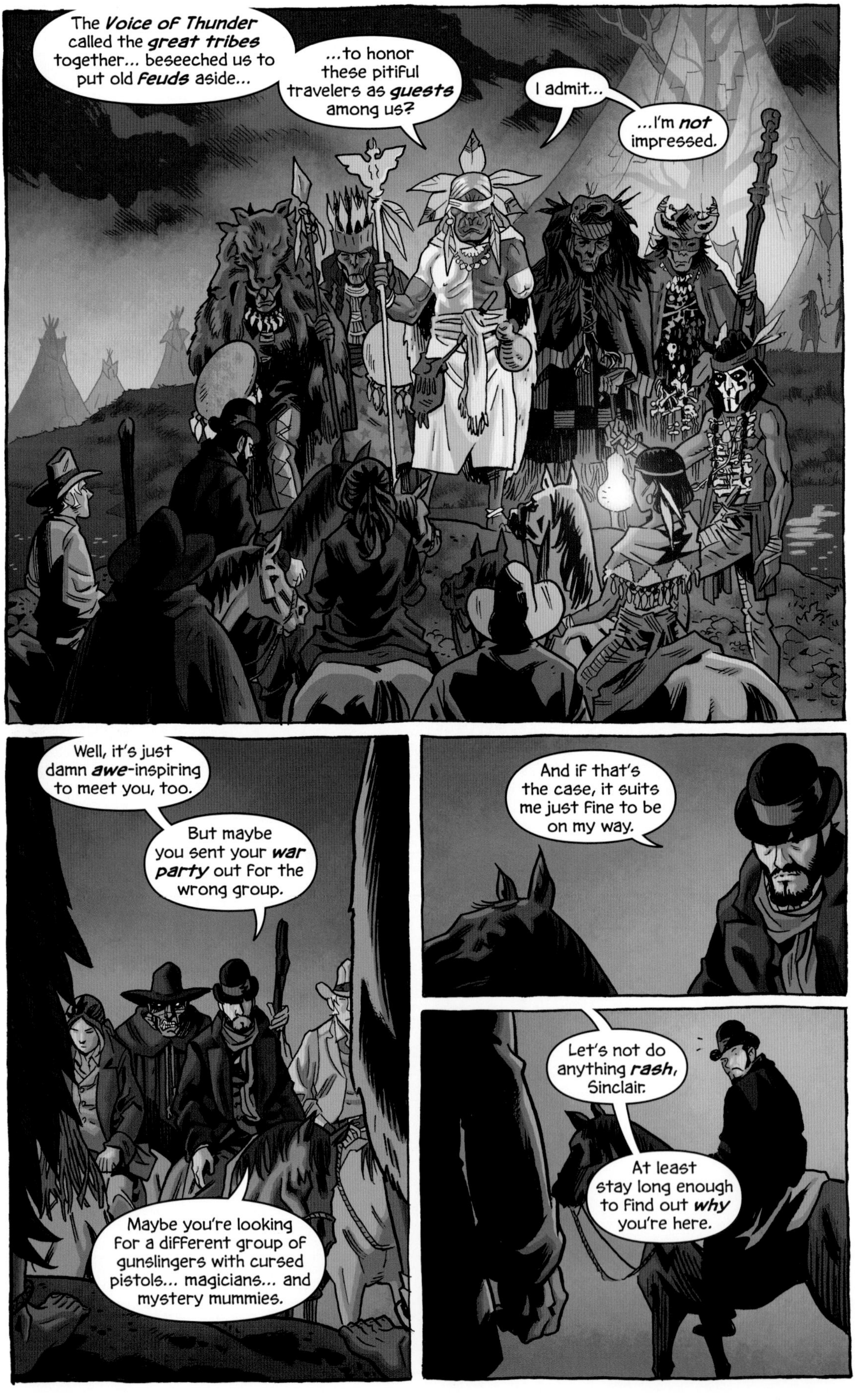
The Voice of Thunder called the great tribes together... beseeched us to put old feuds aside...
...to honor these pitiful travelers as guests among us?
I admit...
...I'm not impressed.
Well, it's just damn awe-inspiring to meet you, too.
But maybe you sent your war party out for the wrong group.
Maybe you're looking for a different group of gunslingers with cursed pistols... magicians... and mystery mummies.
And if that's the case, it suits me just fine to be on my way.
Let's not do anything rash, Sinclair.
At least stay long enough to find out why you're here.

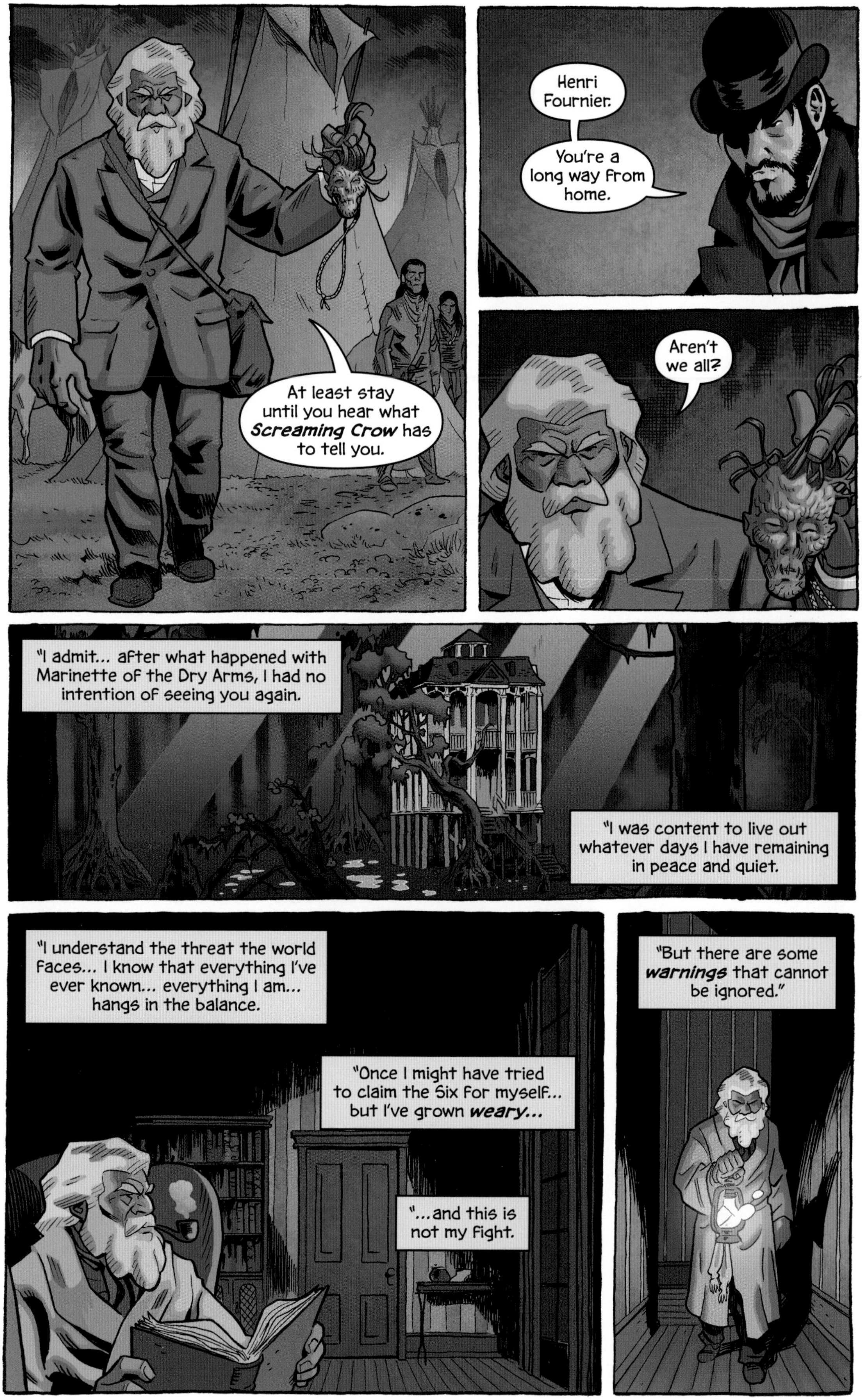
Henri Fournier.
You're a long way from home.
At least stay until you hear what Screaming Crow has to tell you.
Aren't we all?
"I admit... after what happened with Marinette of the Dry Arms, I had no intention of seeing you again.
"I was content to live out whatever days I have remaining in peace and quiet.
"I understand the threat the world faces... I know that everything I've ever known... everything I am... hangs in the balance.
"Once I might have tried to claim the Six for myself... but I've grown weary...
"...and this is not my fight.
"But there are some warnings that cannot be ignored."

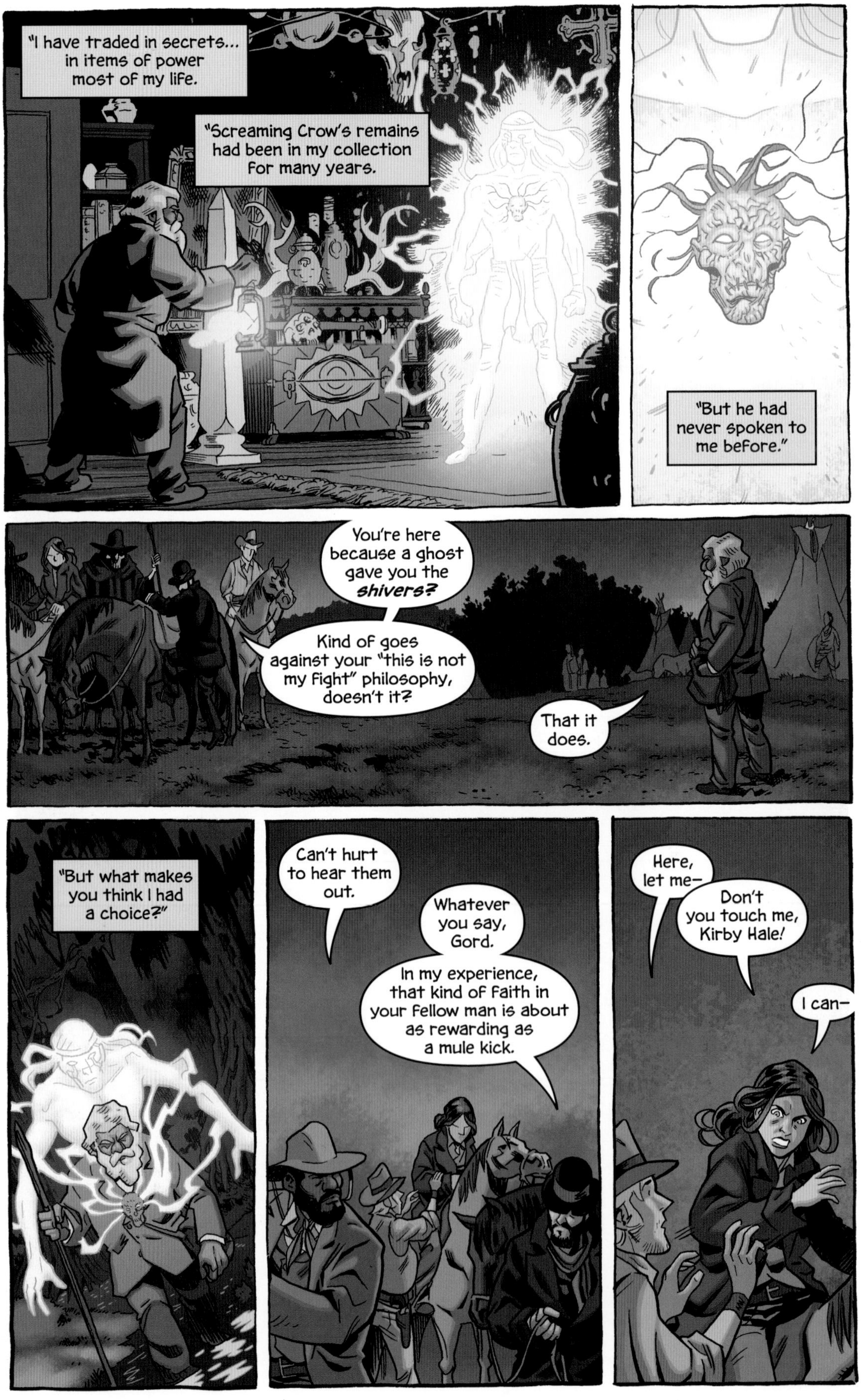
"I have traded in secrets... in items of power most of my life.
"Screaming Crow's remains had been in my collection for many years.
"But he had never spoken to me before."
You're here because a ghost gave you the *shivers?*
Kind of goes against your "this is not my fight" philosophy, doesn't it?
That it does.
"But what makes you think I had a choice?"
Can't hurt to hear them out.
Whatever you say, Gord.
In my experience, that kind of faith in your fellow man is about as rewarding as a mule kick.
Here, let me—
Don't you touch me, Kirby Hale!
I can—

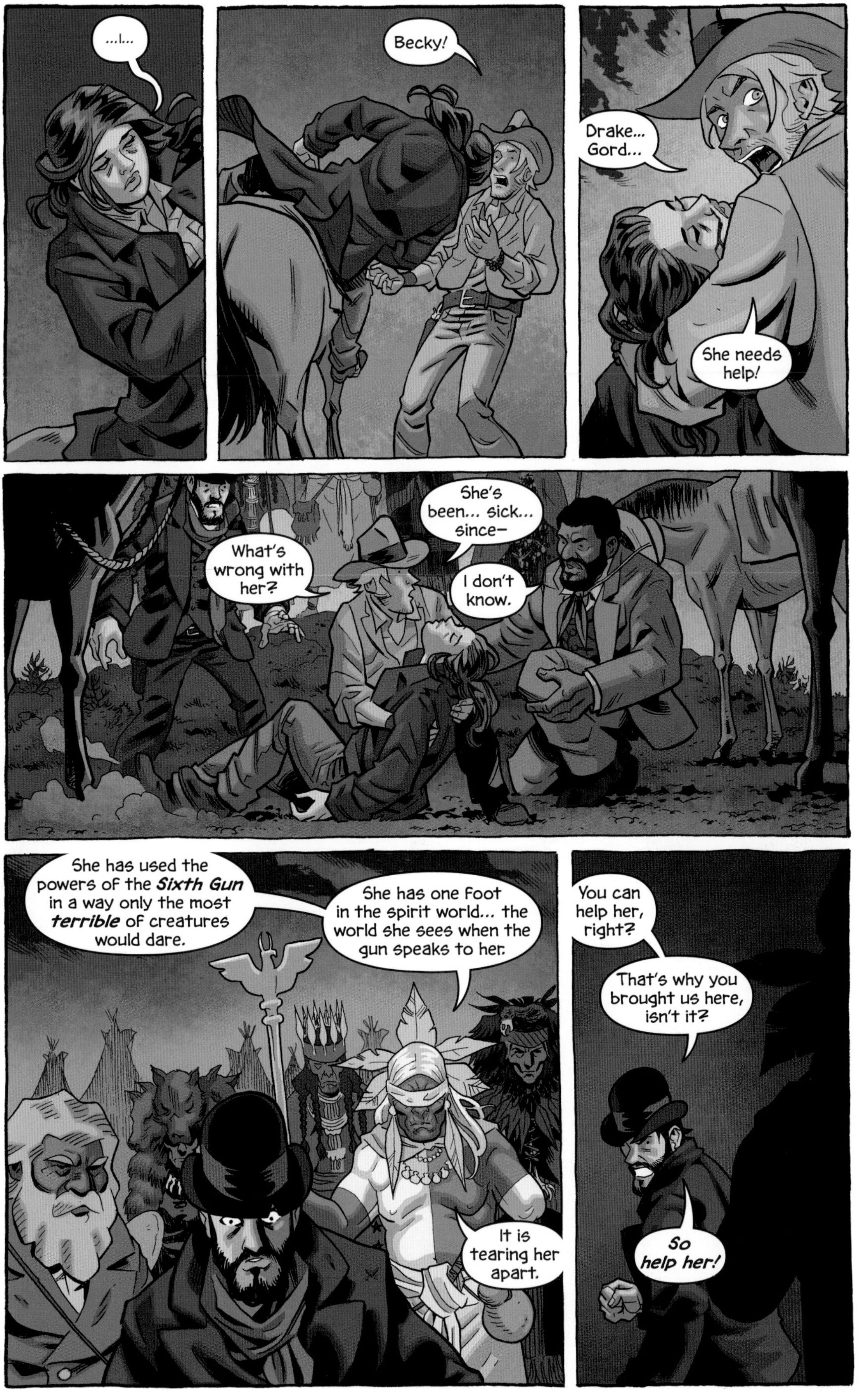
...I...
Becky!
Drake... Gord...
She needs help!
What's wrong with her?
She's been... sick... since—
I don't know.
She has used the powers of the *Sixth Gun* in a way only the most *terrible* of creatures would dare.
She has one foot in the spirit world... the world she sees when the gun speaks to her.
It is tearing her apart.
You can help her, right?
That's why you brought us here, isn't it?
So help her!

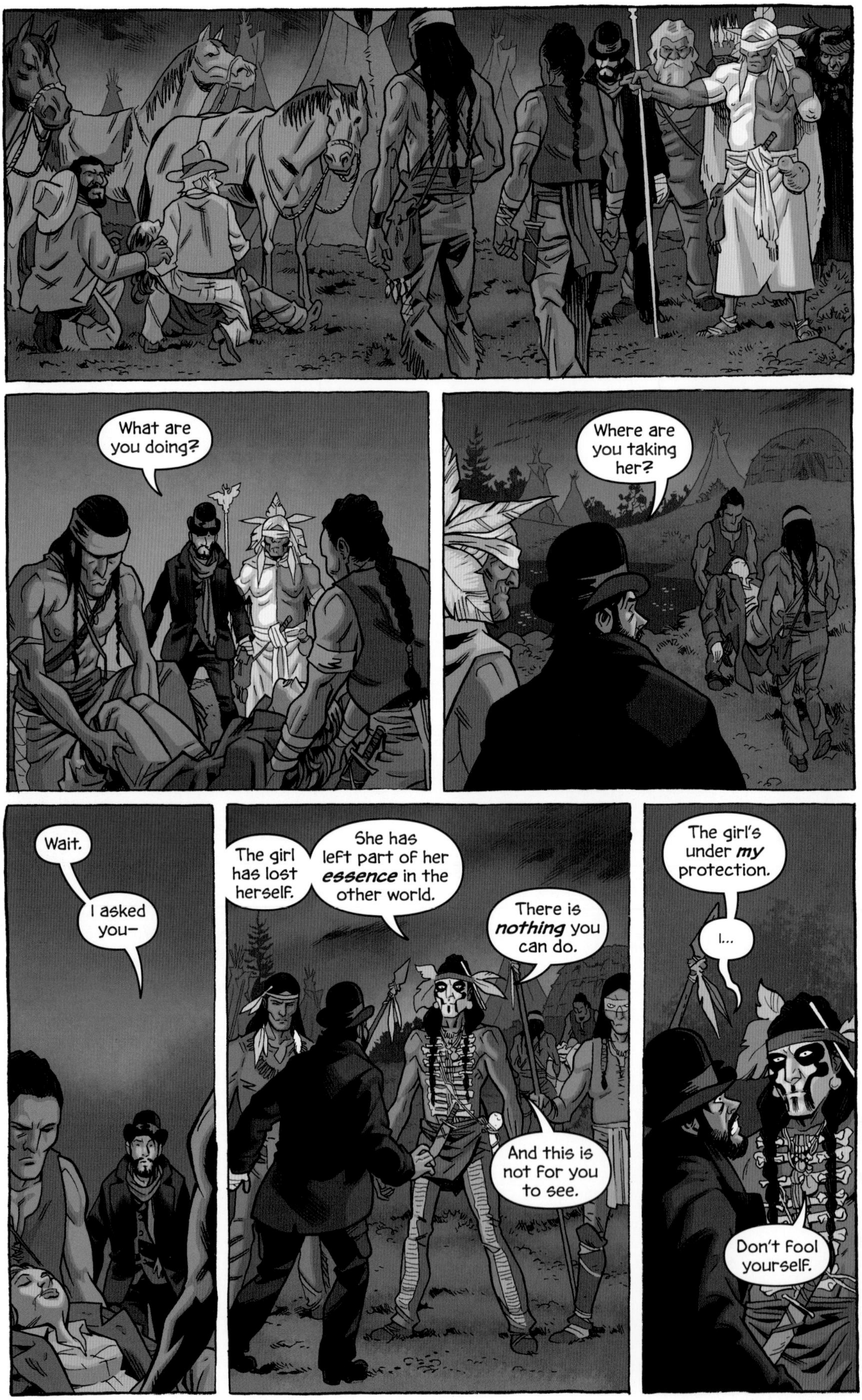
What are you doing?
Where are you taking her?
Wait.
I asked you–
The girl has lost herself.
She has left part of her *essence* in the other world.
There is *nothing* you can do.
And this is not for you to see.
The girl's under *my* protection.
I...
Don't fool yourself.

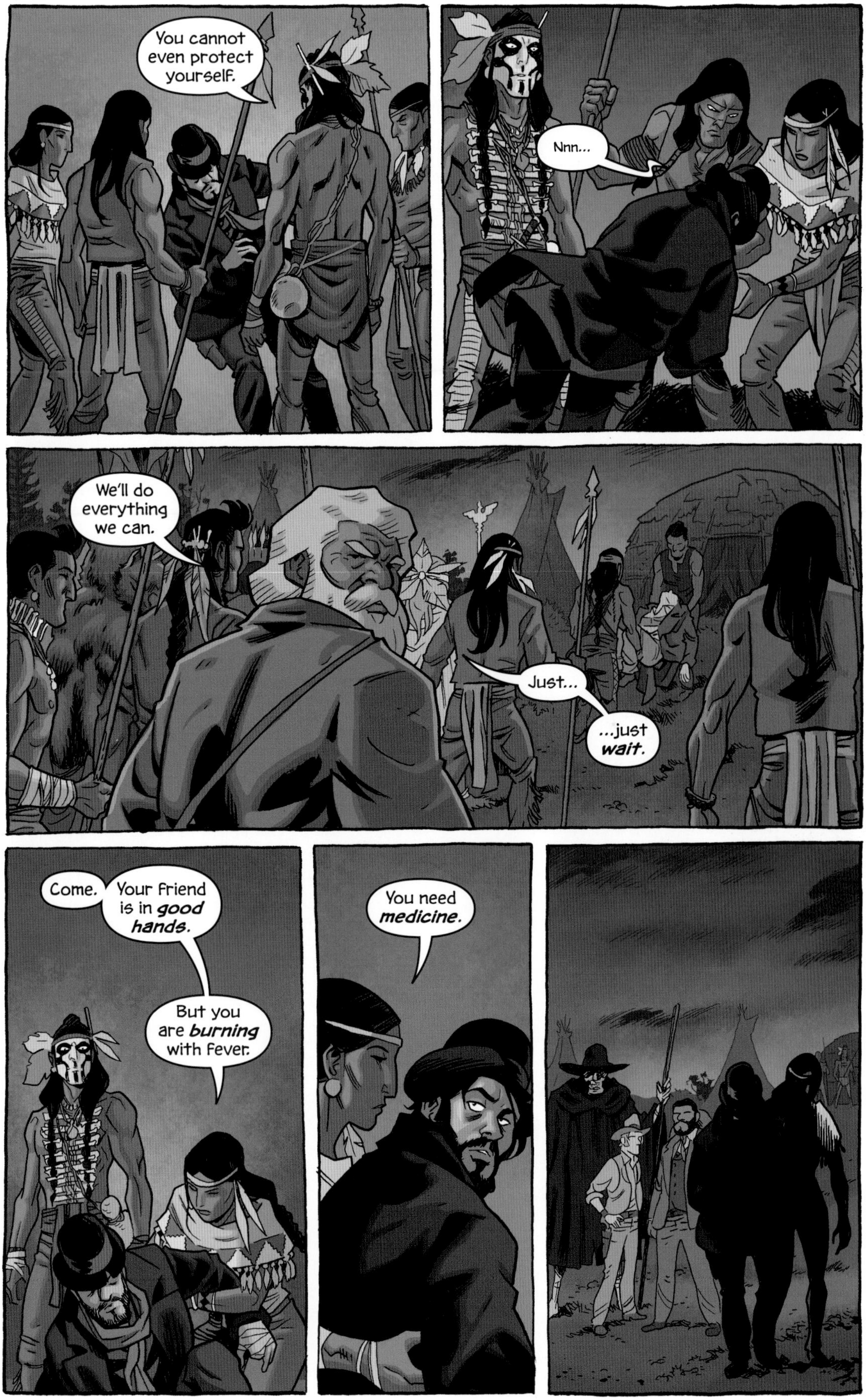

You cannot even protect yourself.
Nnn...
We'll do everything we can.
Just...
...just *wait*.
Come.
Your friend is in *good hands*.
But you are *burning* with fever.
You need *medicine*.

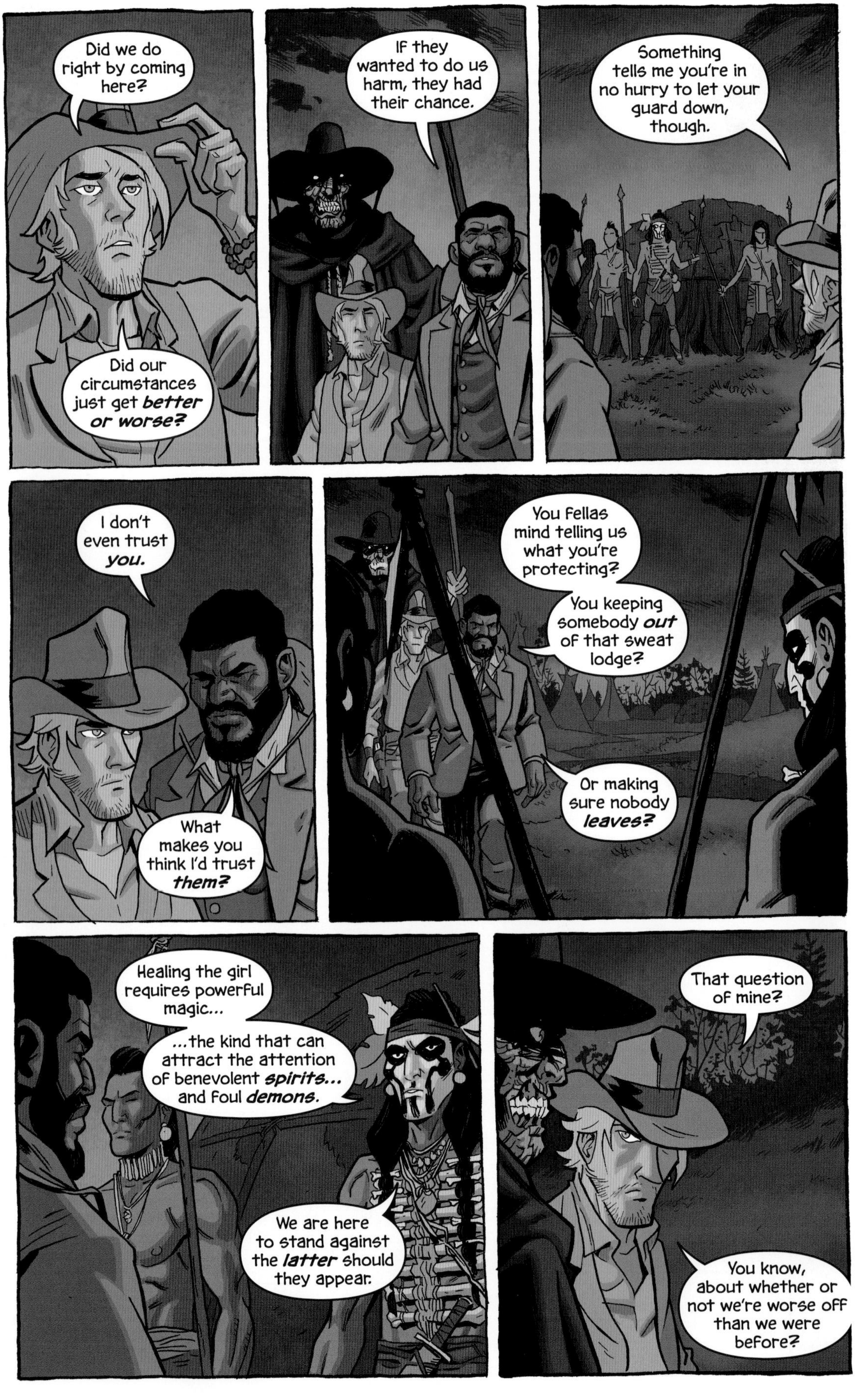
Did we do right by coming here?
Did our circumstances just get *better or worse?*
If they wanted to do us harm, they had their chance.
Something tells me you're in no hurry to let your guard down, though.
I don't even trust *you.*
What makes you think I'd trust *them?*
You fellas mind telling us what you're protecting?
You keeping somebody *out* of that sweat lodge?
Or making sure nobody *leaves?*
Healing the girl requires powerful magic...
...the kind that can attract the attention of benevolent *spirits...* and foul *demons.*
We are here to stand against the *latter* should they appear.
That question of mine?
You know, about whether or not we're worse off than we were before?

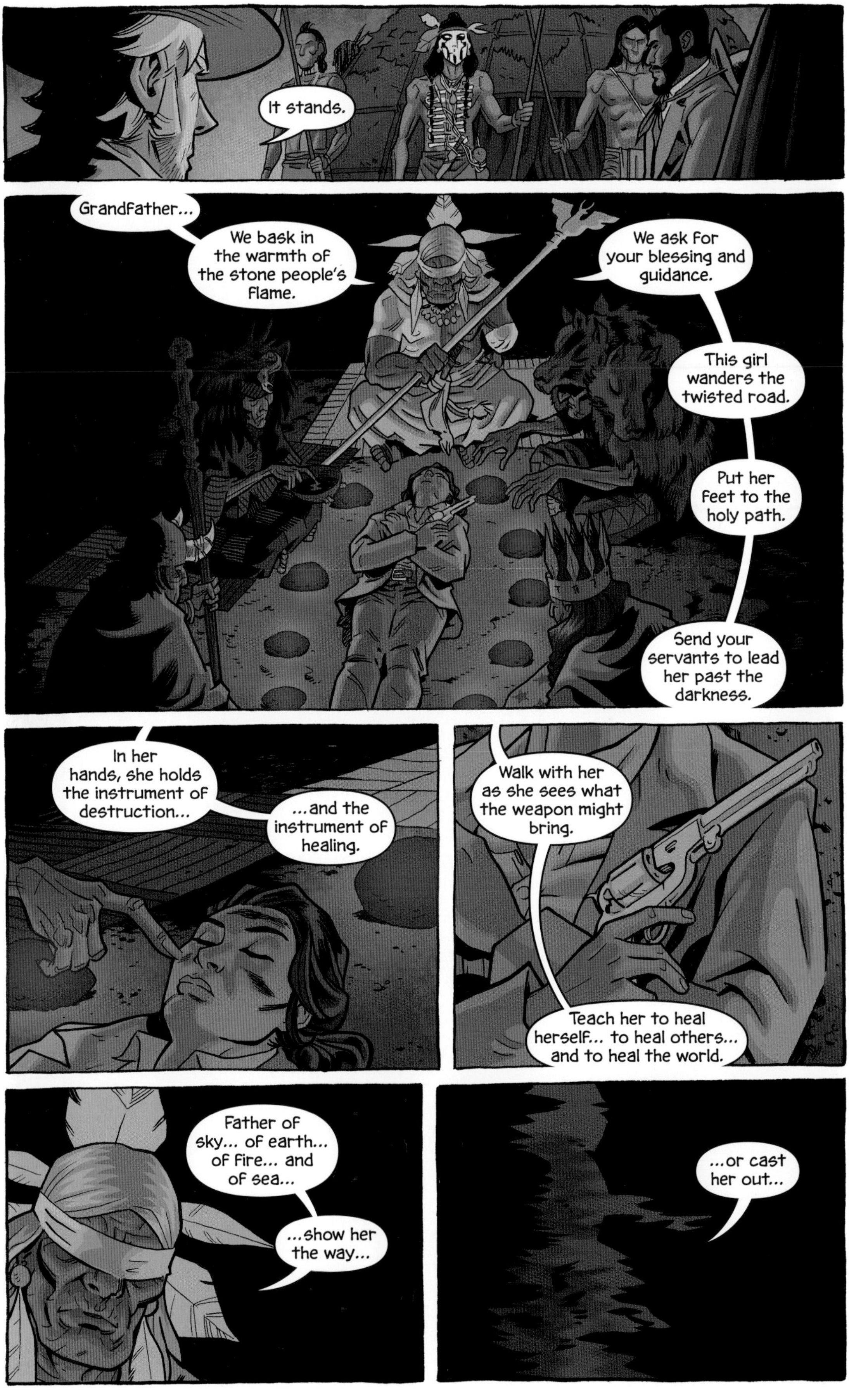
It stands.
Grandfather...
We bask in the warmth of the stone people's flame.
We ask for your blessing and guidance.
This girl wanders the twisted road.
Put her feet to the holy path.
Send your servants to lead her past the darkness.
In her hands, she holds the instrument of destruction...
...and the instrument of healing.
Walk with her as she sees what the weapon might bring.
Teach her to heal herself... to heal others... and to heal the world.
Father of sky... of earth... of fire... and of sea...
...show her the way...
...or cast her out...

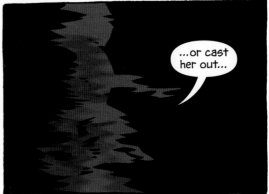

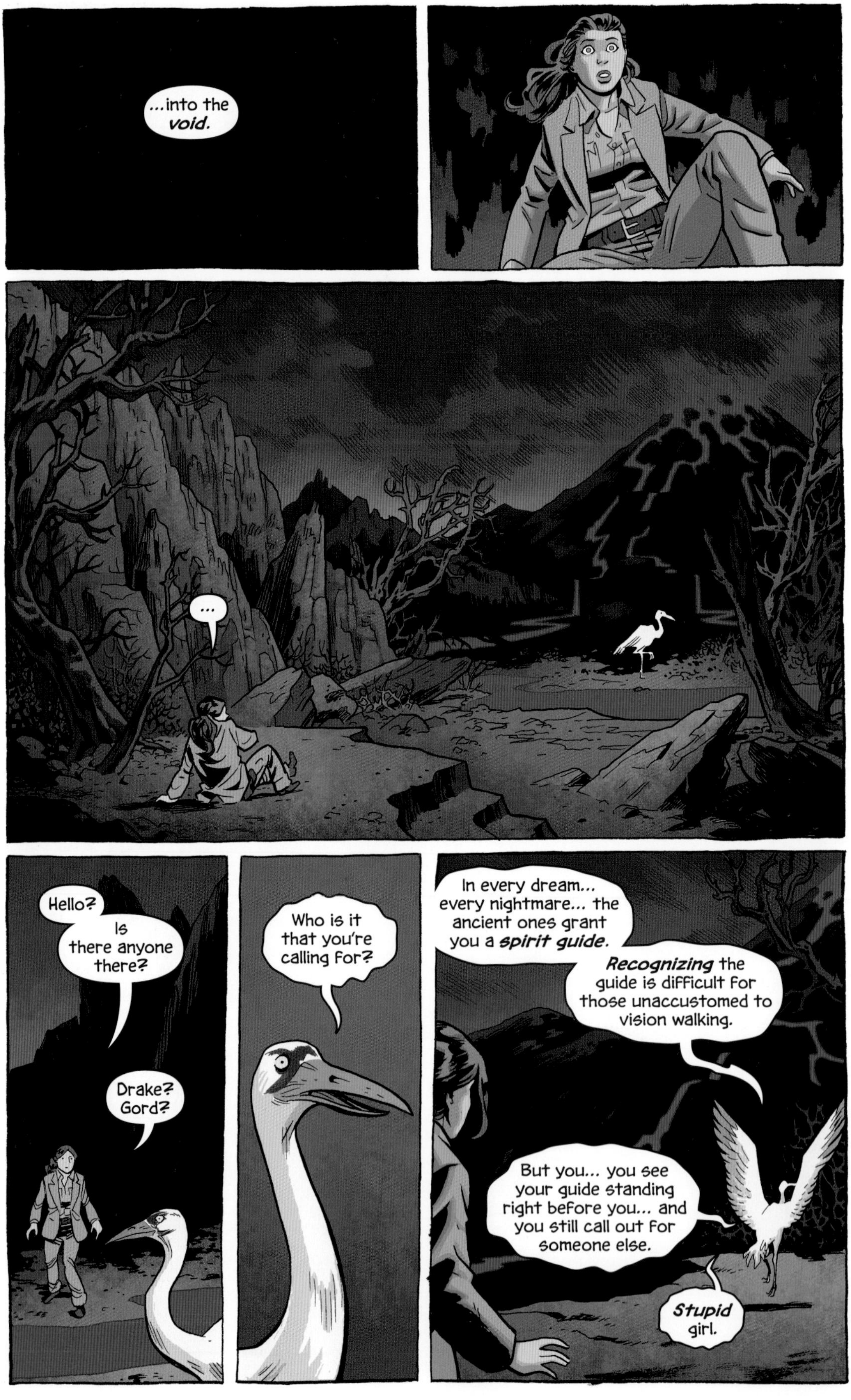
...into the *void.*
...
Hello?
Is there anyone there?
Drake? Gord?
Who is it that you're calling for?
In every dream... every nightmare... the ancient ones grant you a *spirit guide*.
Recognizing the guide is difficult for those unaccustomed to vision walking.
But you... you see your guide standing right before you... and you still call out for someone else.
Stupid girl.

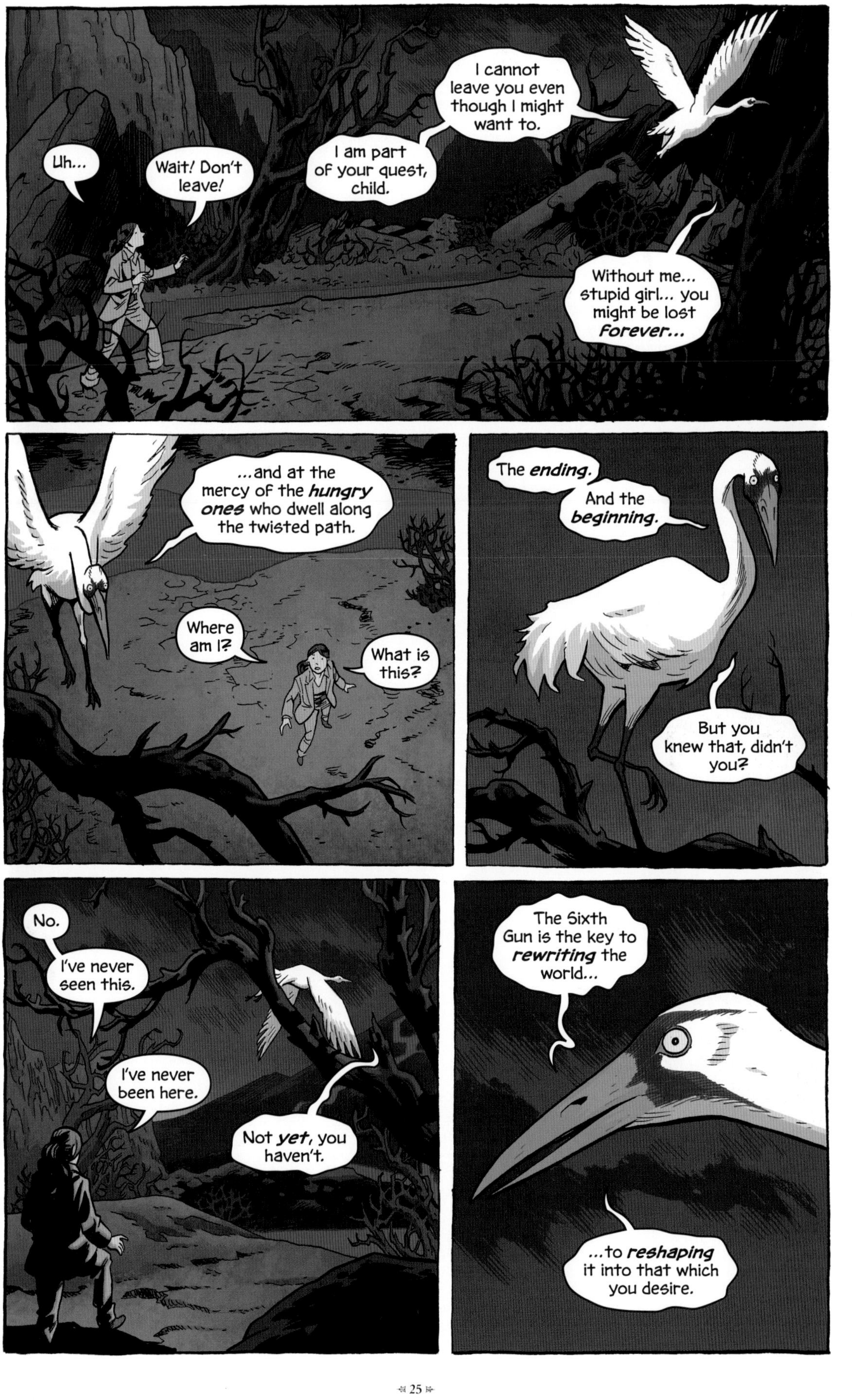
Uh...
Wait! Don't leave!
I am part of your quest, child.
I cannot leave you even though I might want to.
Without me... stupid girl... you might be lost *forever...*
...and at the mercy of the ***hungry ones*** who dwell along the twisted path.
Where am I?
What is this?
The *ending.*
And the *beginning.*
But you knew that, didn't you?
No.
I've never seen this.
I've never been here.
Not *yet,* you haven't.
The Sixth Gun is the key to *rewriting* the world...
...to *reshaping* it into that which you desire.

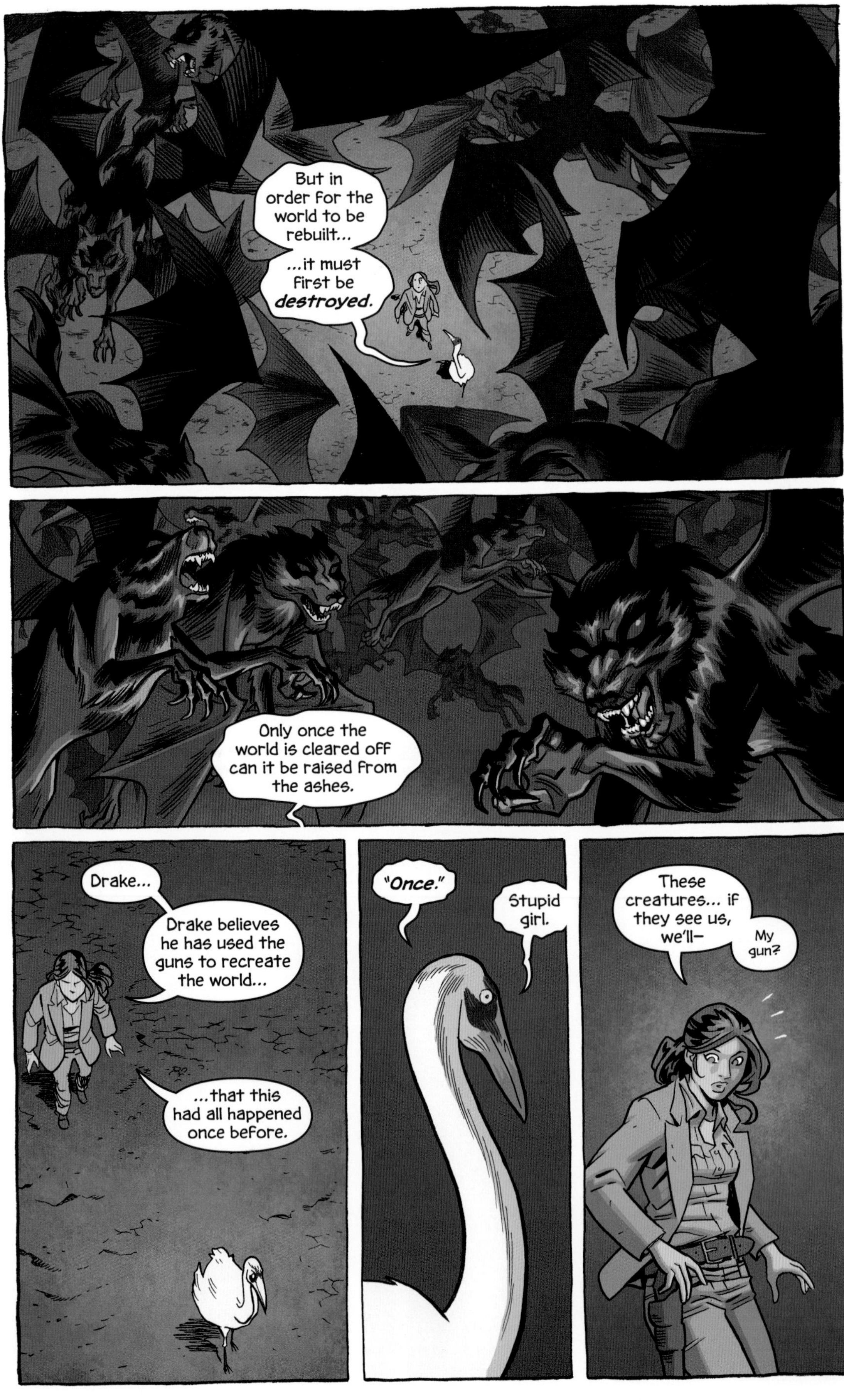

But in order for the world to be rebuilt...
...it must first be *destroyed*.
Only once the world is cleared off can it be raised from the ashes.
Drake...
Drake believes he has used the guns to recreate the world...
...that this had all happened once before.
"Once."
Stupid girl.
These creatures... if they see us, we'll—
My gun?

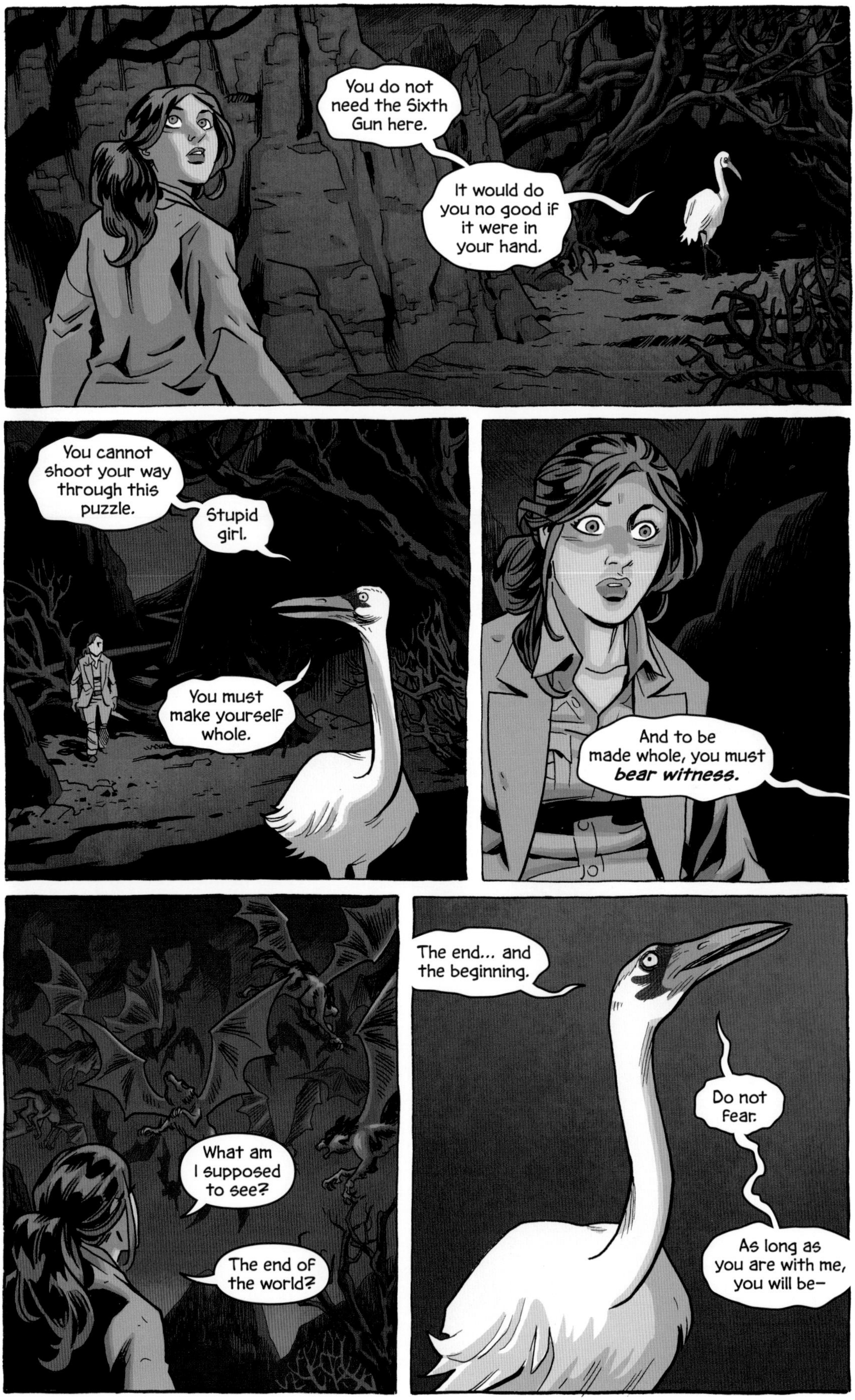
You do not need the Sixth Gun here.
It would do you no good if it were in your hand.
You cannot shoot your way through this puzzle.
Stupid girl.
You must make yourself whole.
And to be made whole, you must ***bear witness.***
What am I supposed to see?
The end of the world?
The end... and the beginning.
Do not fear.
As long as you are with me, you will be—

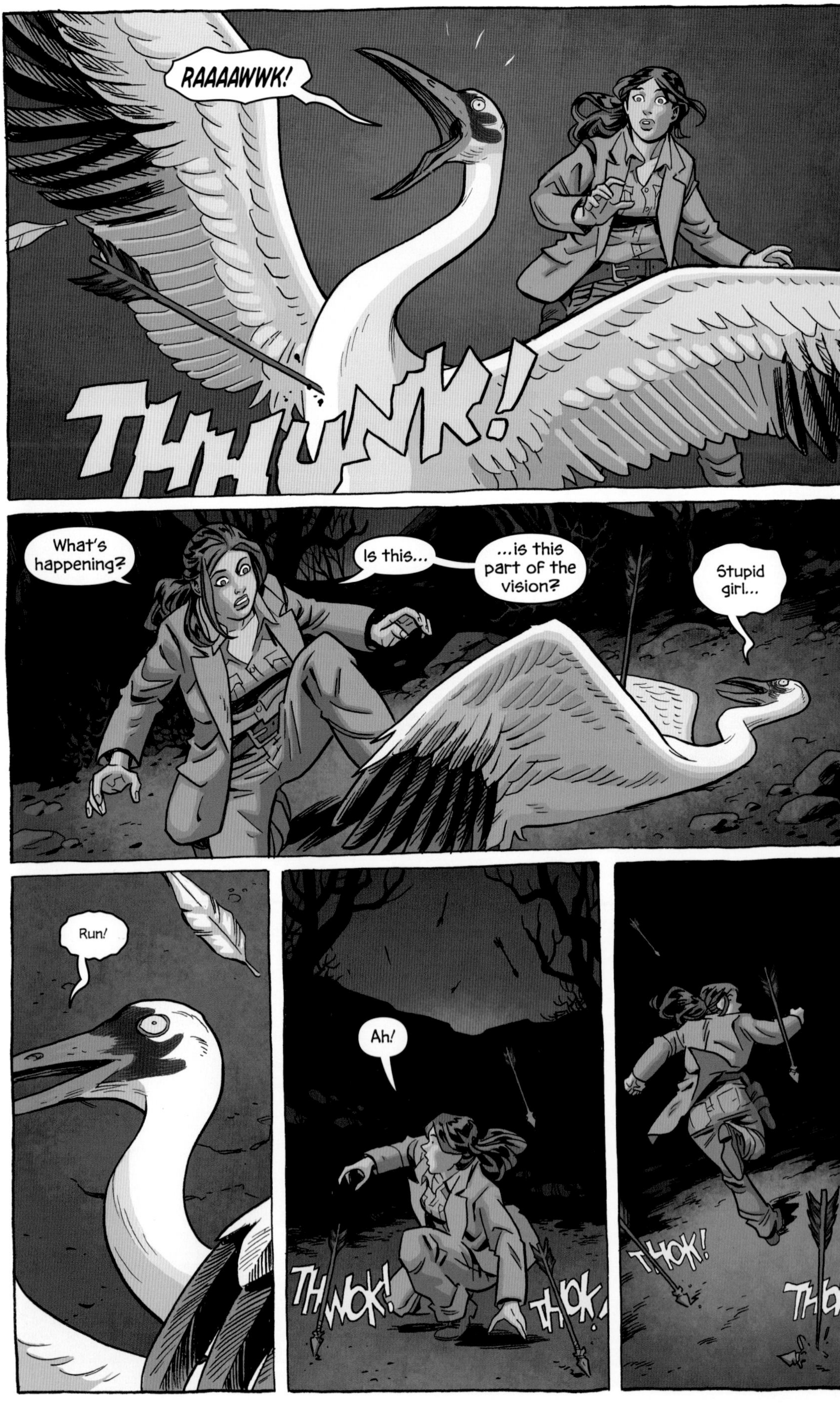
RAAAAWWK!
THHUNK!
What's happening?
Is this...
...is this part of the vision?
Stupid girl...
Run!
Ah!
THWOK!
THOK!
THOK!
THOK!

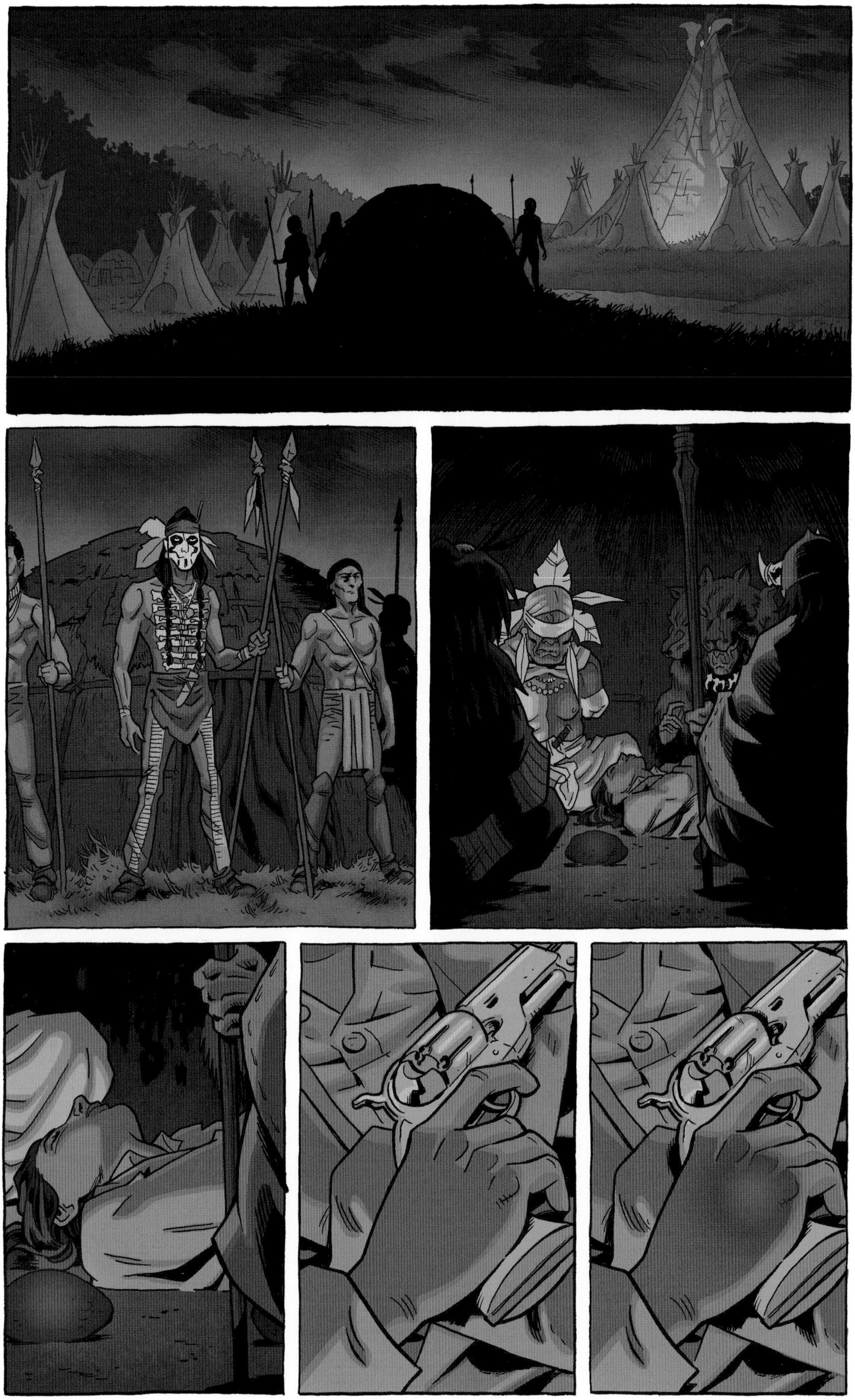

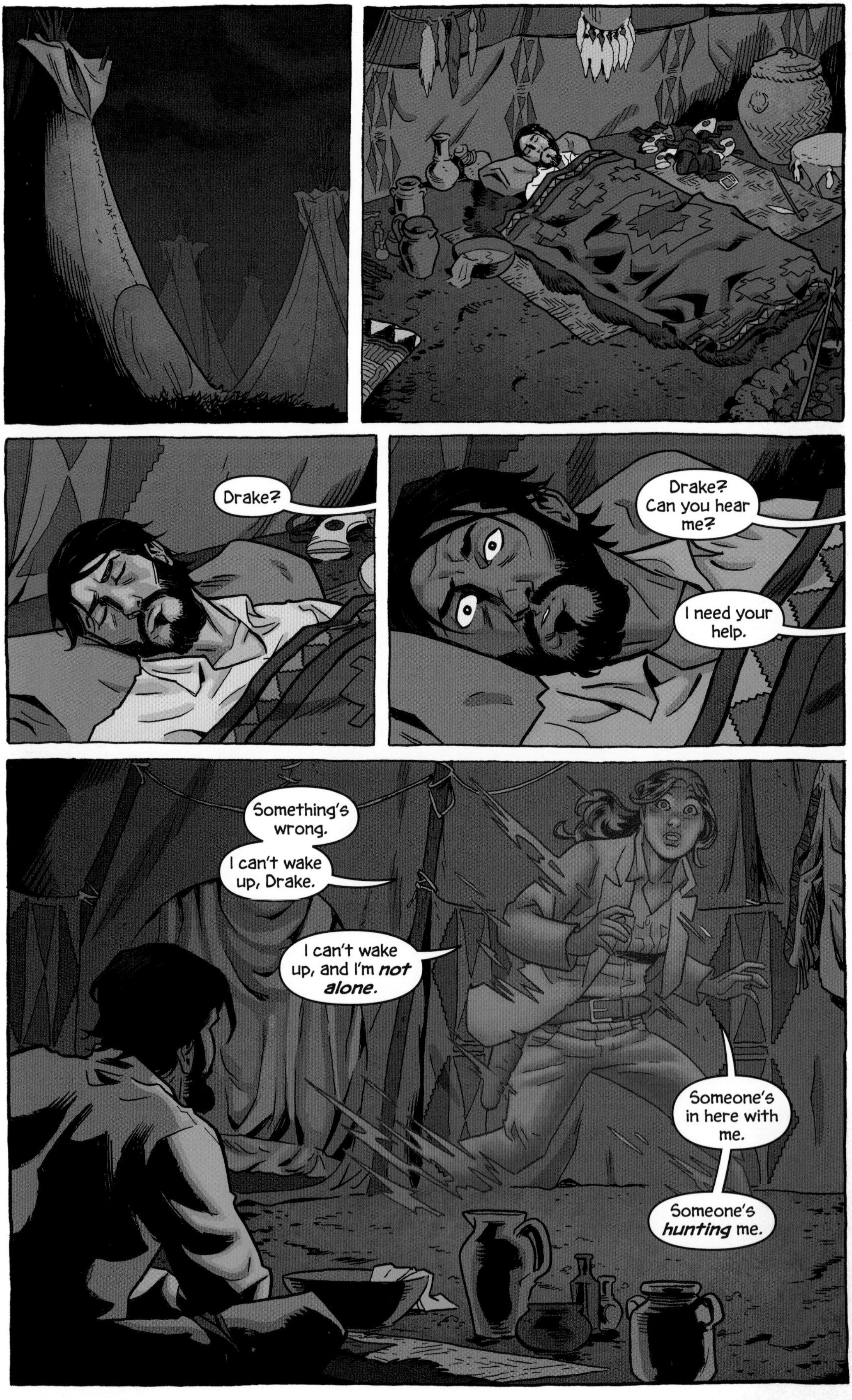
Drake?
Drake? Can you hear me?
I need your help.
Something's wrong.
I can't wake up, Drake.
I can't wake up, and I'm *not alone.*
Someone's in here with me.
Someone's *hunting* me.

CHAPTER TWO

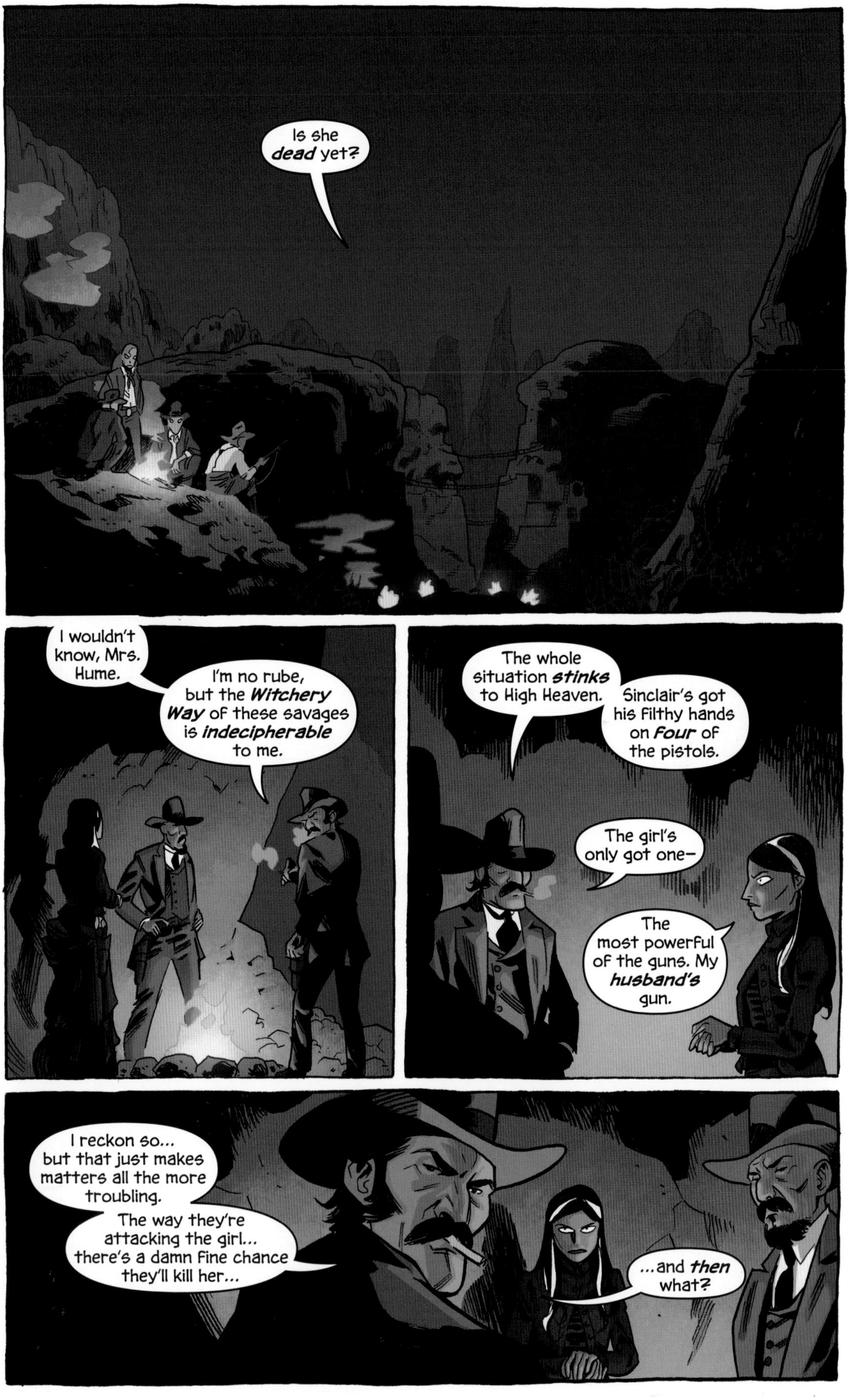
Is she *dead* yet?
I wouldn't know, Mrs. Hume.
I'm no rube, but the *Witchery Way* of these savages is *indecipherable* to me.
The whole situation *stinks* to High Heaven.
Sinclair's got his filthy hands on *four* of the pistols.
The girl's only got one—
The most powerful of the guns. My *husband's* gun.
I reckon so... but that just makes matters all the more troubling.
The way they're attacking the girl... there's a damn fine chance they'll kill her...
...and *then* what?

I can appreciate your position, Mrs. Hume. You can't be hurt physically, but your pride's free-roaming game.

Somebody made sport of me the way that girl did you, I'd want them dead, too.

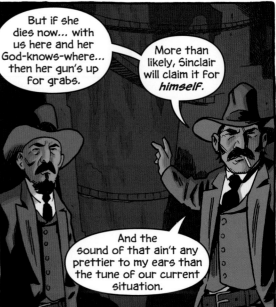

But if she dies now... with us here and her God-knows-where... then her gun's up for grabs.

More than likely, Sinclair will claim it for *himself*.

And the sound of that ain't any prettier to my ears than the tune of our current situation.

You're right, Mr. Faulkner. Of course you are.

But insomuch as I'd savor a torment and a hellish death for Becky Montcrief, I've not lost sight of our objectives.

When Griselda sent us out here, I spoke with her about the very question you've raised.

And do you know what she said?

THE GIRL'S MORE IMPORTANT THAN YOU REALIZE. KILLING HER FIRST COULD SERVE US WELL.

ONCE SHE'S DEAD, DRAKE SINCLAIR WILL COME STRAIGHT AT US.

HE'LL EITHER COME SEEKING REVENGE... OR HE'LL COME IN HOPES OF STEALING YOUR WEAPON FOR HIMSELF.

EITHER WAY, HE'LL COME.

AND THEN WE'VE *WON*.

And that's it? You didn't press her for any additional details?

Mr. Faulkner... one does not "press" the Grey Witch.

Besides... as you said... Becky Montcrief insulted me.

So, there was really only one question on my mind...

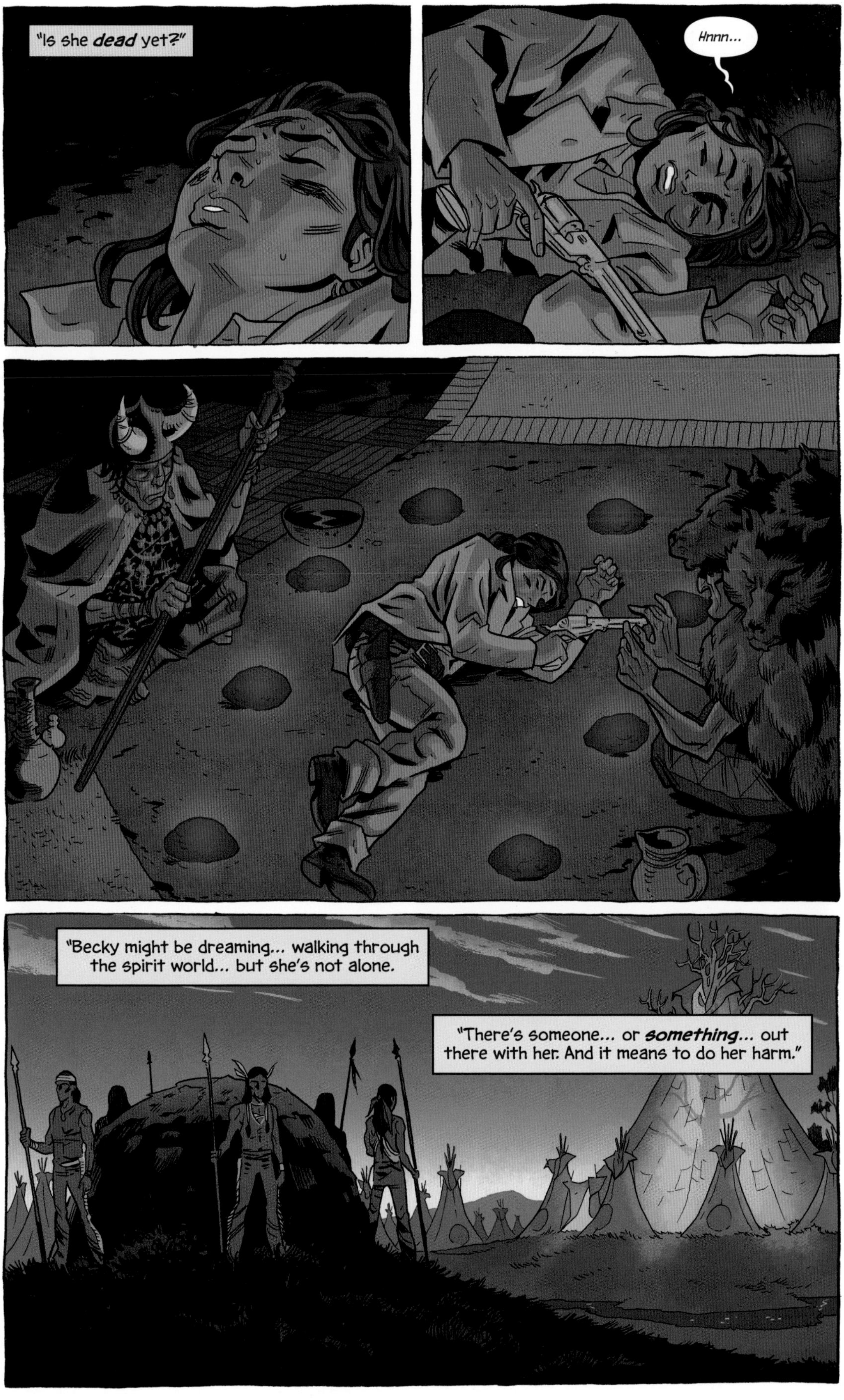
"Is she *dead* yet?"
Hnnn...
"Becky might be dreaming... walking through the spirit world... but she's not alone.
"There's someone... or *something*... out there with her. And it means to do her harm."

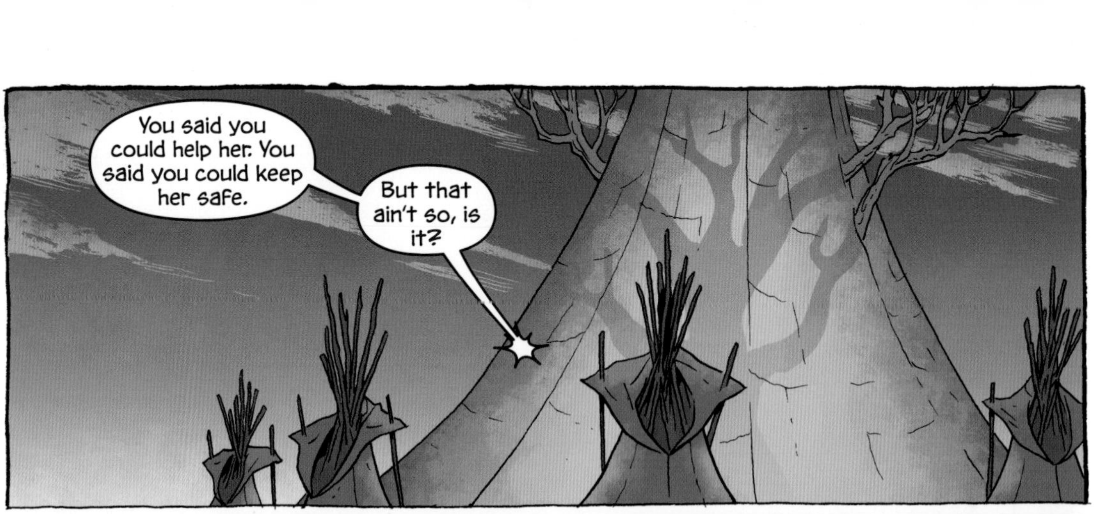
You said you could help her. You said you could keep her safe.
But that ain't so, is it?

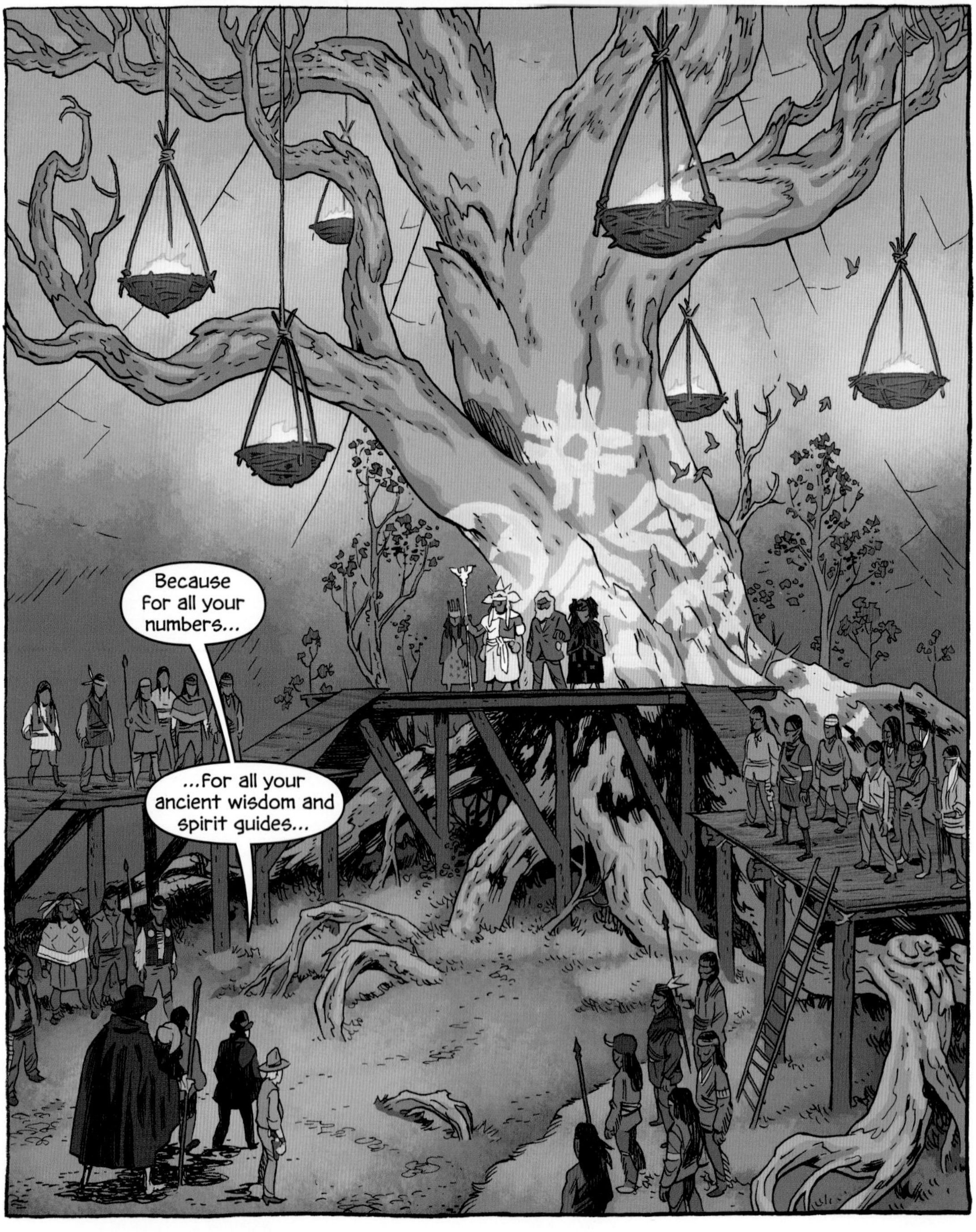
Because for all your numbers...
...For all your ancient wisdom and spirit guides...

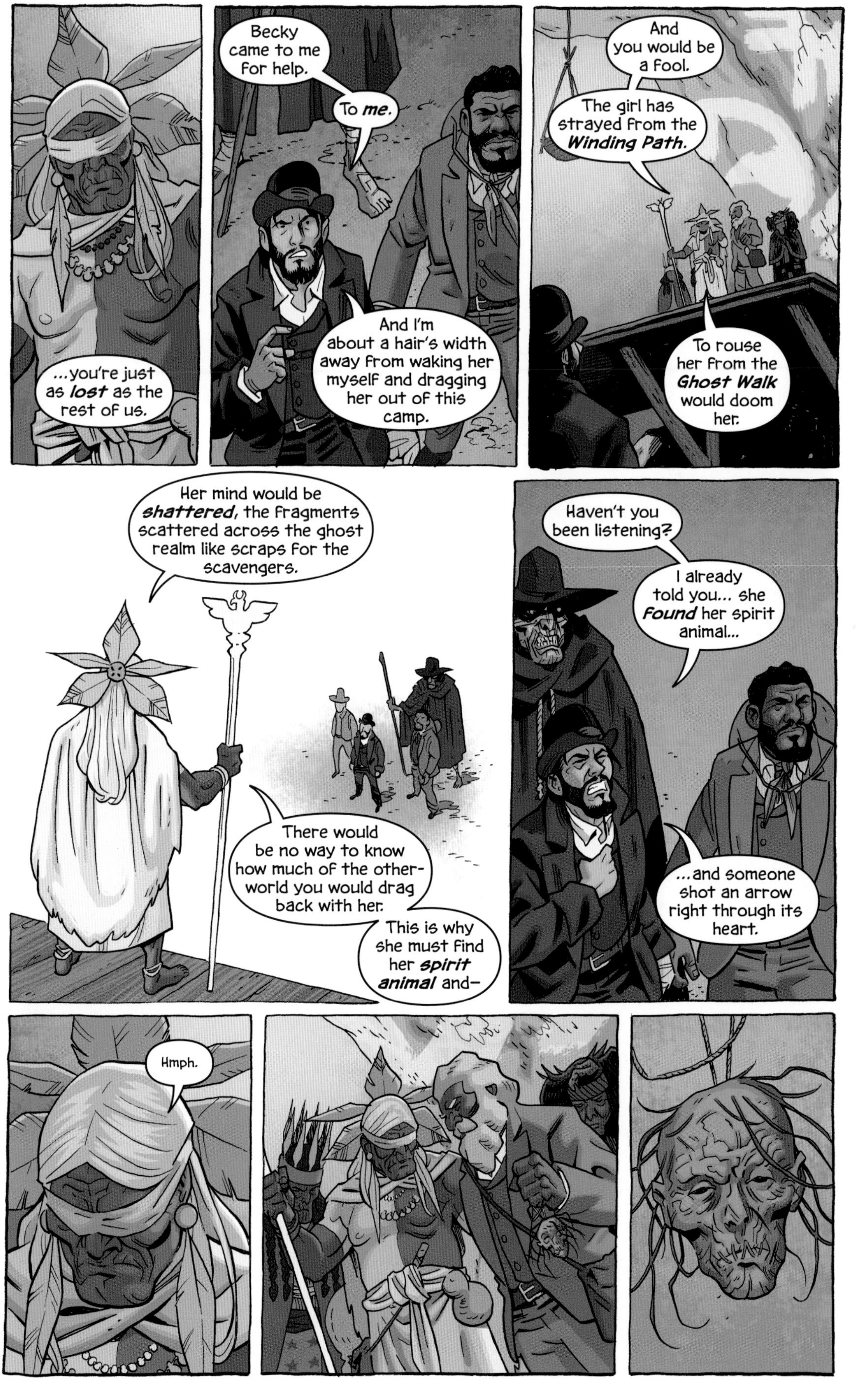

...you're just as lost as the rest of us.
Becky came to me for help.
To me.
And I'm about a hair's width away from waking her myself and dragging her out of this camp.
And you would be a fool.
The girl has strayed from the Winding Path.
To rouse her from the Ghost Walk would doom her.
Her mind would be shattered, the fragments scattered across the ghost realm like scraps for the scavengers.
There would be no way to know how much of the other-world you would drag back with her.
This is why she must find her spirit animal and–
Haven't you been listening?
I already told you... she found her spirit animal...
...and someone shot an arrow right through its heart.
Hmph.

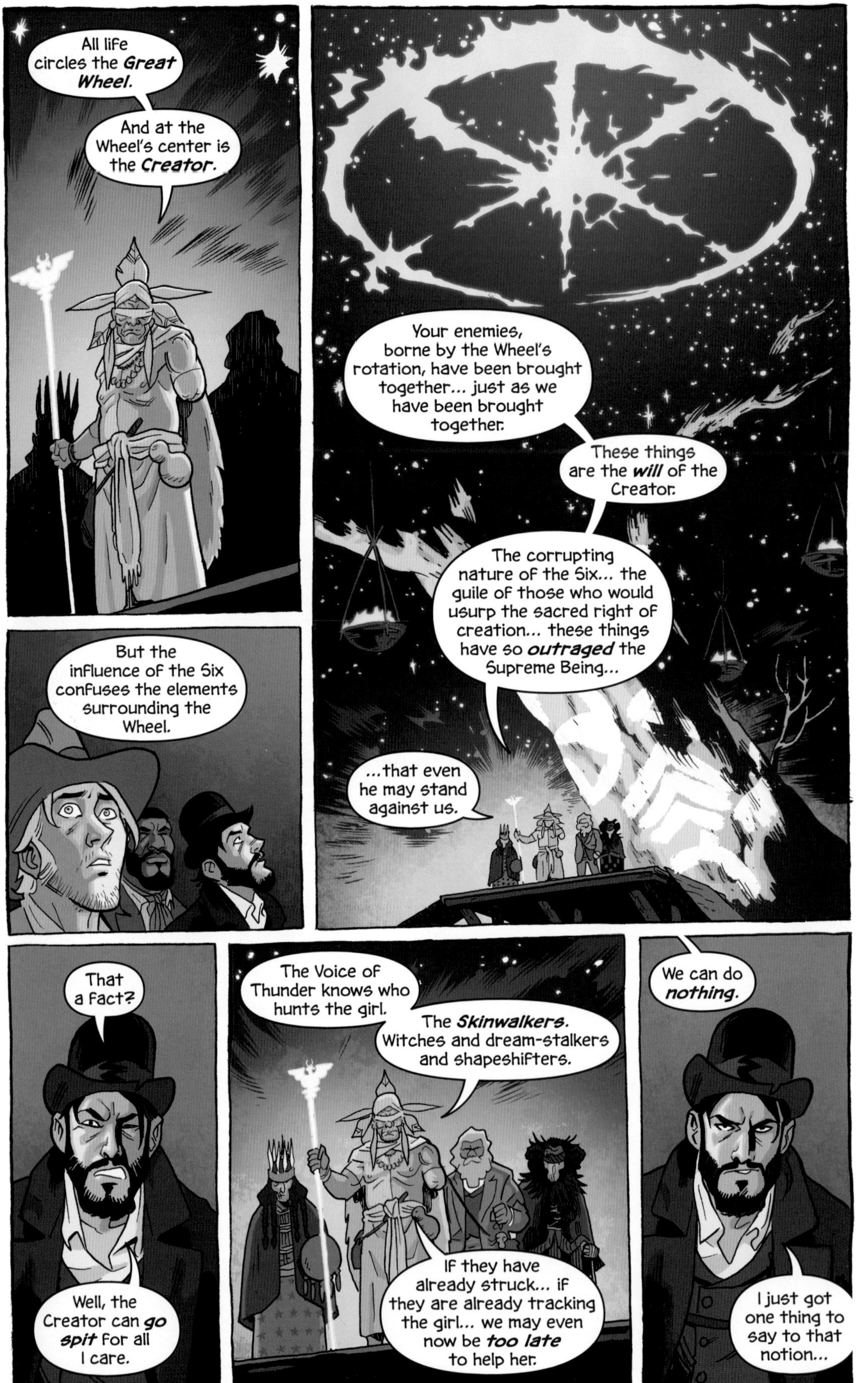
All life circles the *Great Wheel.*
And at the Wheel's center is the *Creator.*
Your enemies, borne by the Wheel's rotation, have been brought together... just as we have been brought together.
These things are the *will* of the Creator.
The corrupting nature of the Six... the guile of those who would usurp the sacred right of creation... these things have so *outraged* the Supreme Being...
But the influence of the Six confuses the elements surrounding the Wheel.
...that even he may stand against us.
That a fact?
Well, the Creator can *go spit* for all I care.
The Voice of Thunder knows who hunts the girl.
The *Skinwalkers.* Witches and dream-stalkers and shapeshifters.
If they have already struck... if they are already tracking the girl... we may even now be *too late* to help her.
We can do *nothing.*
I just got one thing to say to that notion...

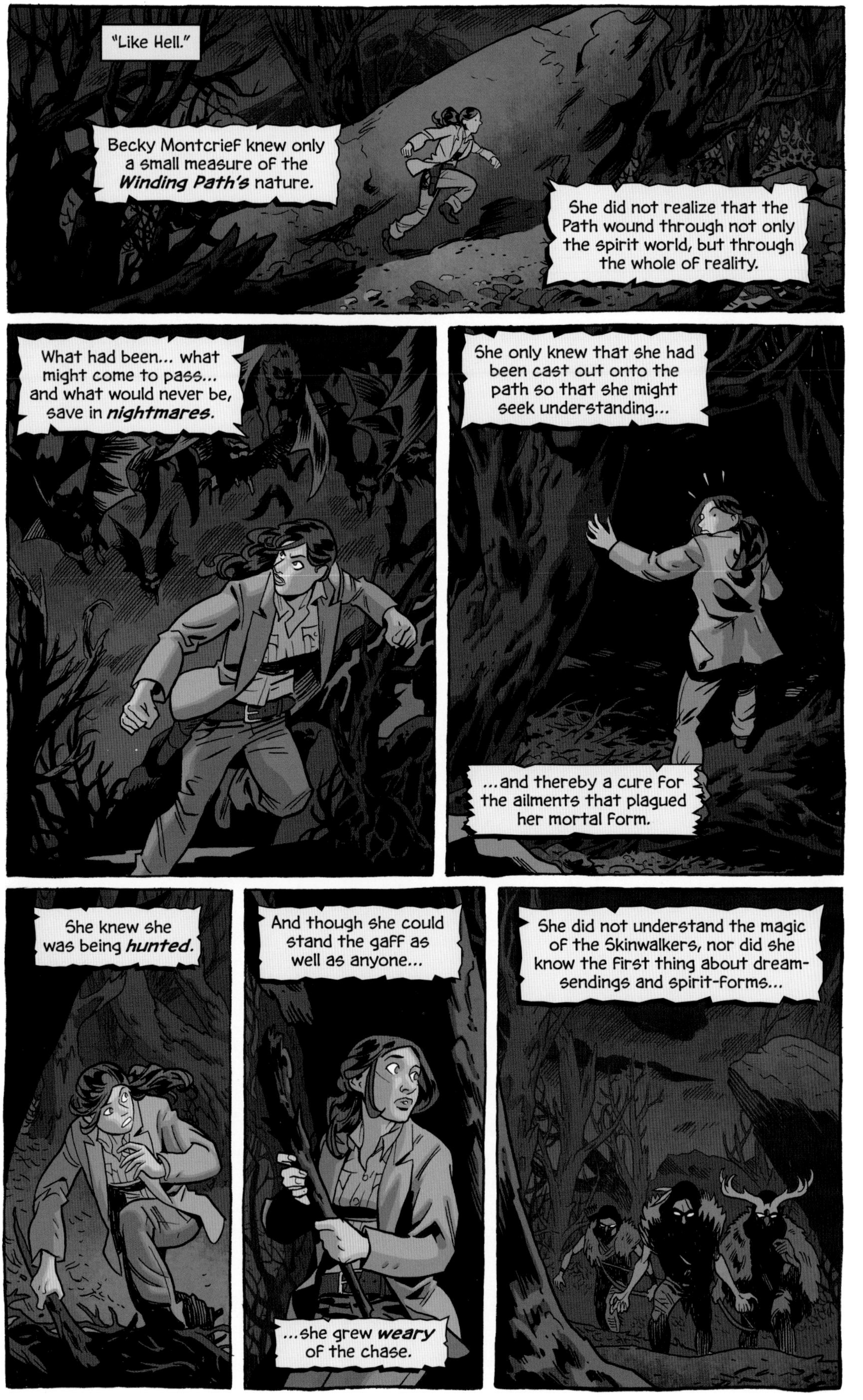
"Like Hell."
Becky Montcrief knew only a small measure of the *Winding Path's* nature.
She did not realize that the Path wound through not only the spirit world, but through the whole of reality.
What had been... what might come to pass... and what would never be, save in *nightmares*.
She only knew that she had been cast out onto the path so that she might seek understanding...
...and thereby a cure for the ailments that plagued her mortal form.
She knew she was being *hunted*.
And though she could stand the gaff as well as anyone...
...she grew *weary* of the chase.
She did not understand the magic of the Skinwalkers, nor did she know the first thing about dream-sendings and spirit-forms...

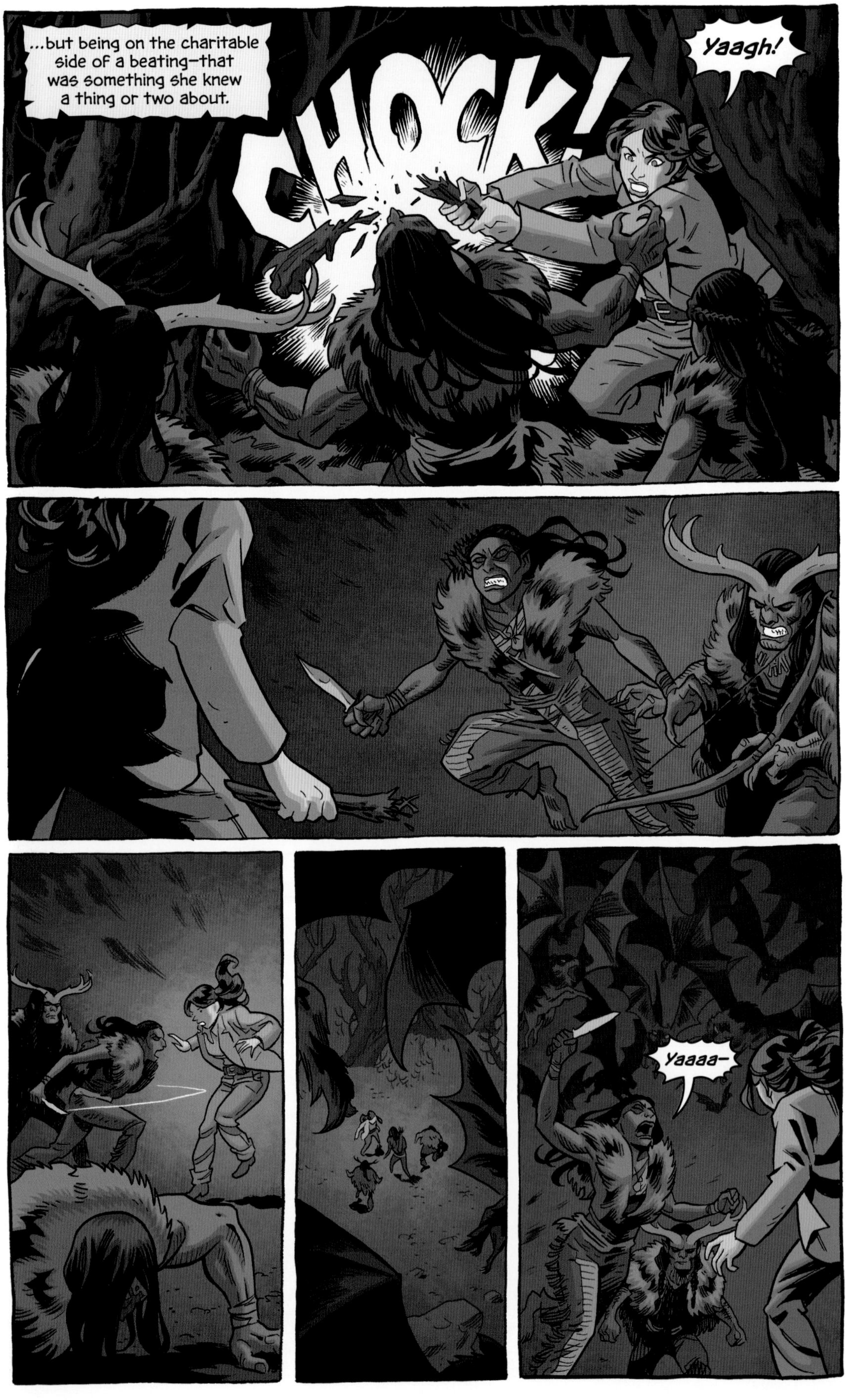
...but being on the charitable side of a beating—that was something she knew a thing or two about.
CHOCK!
Yaagh!
Yaaaa-

YEEEEAAARRGH!!!

YEEEAAARRK...

Runnf!

THWOK!

She had been warned not to stray too far from the Path lest she draw the attention of the *hungry ones* dwelling in the shadows...

...but chased by killers and abandoned by her spirit animal... she saw no other choice.

Uhh—

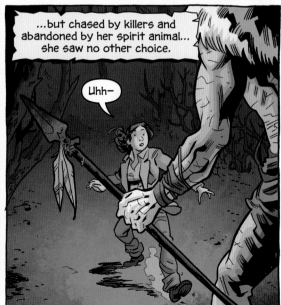

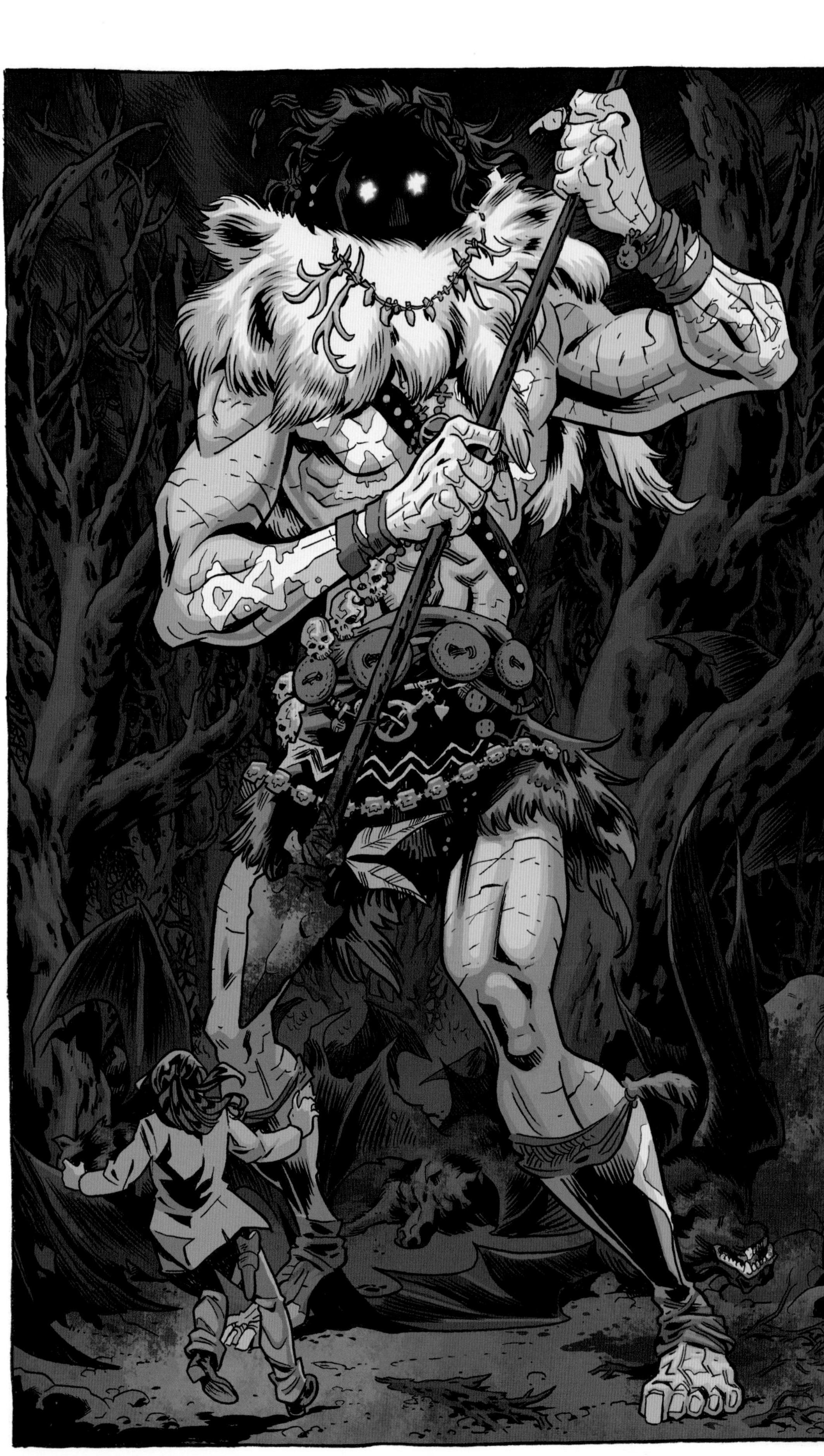

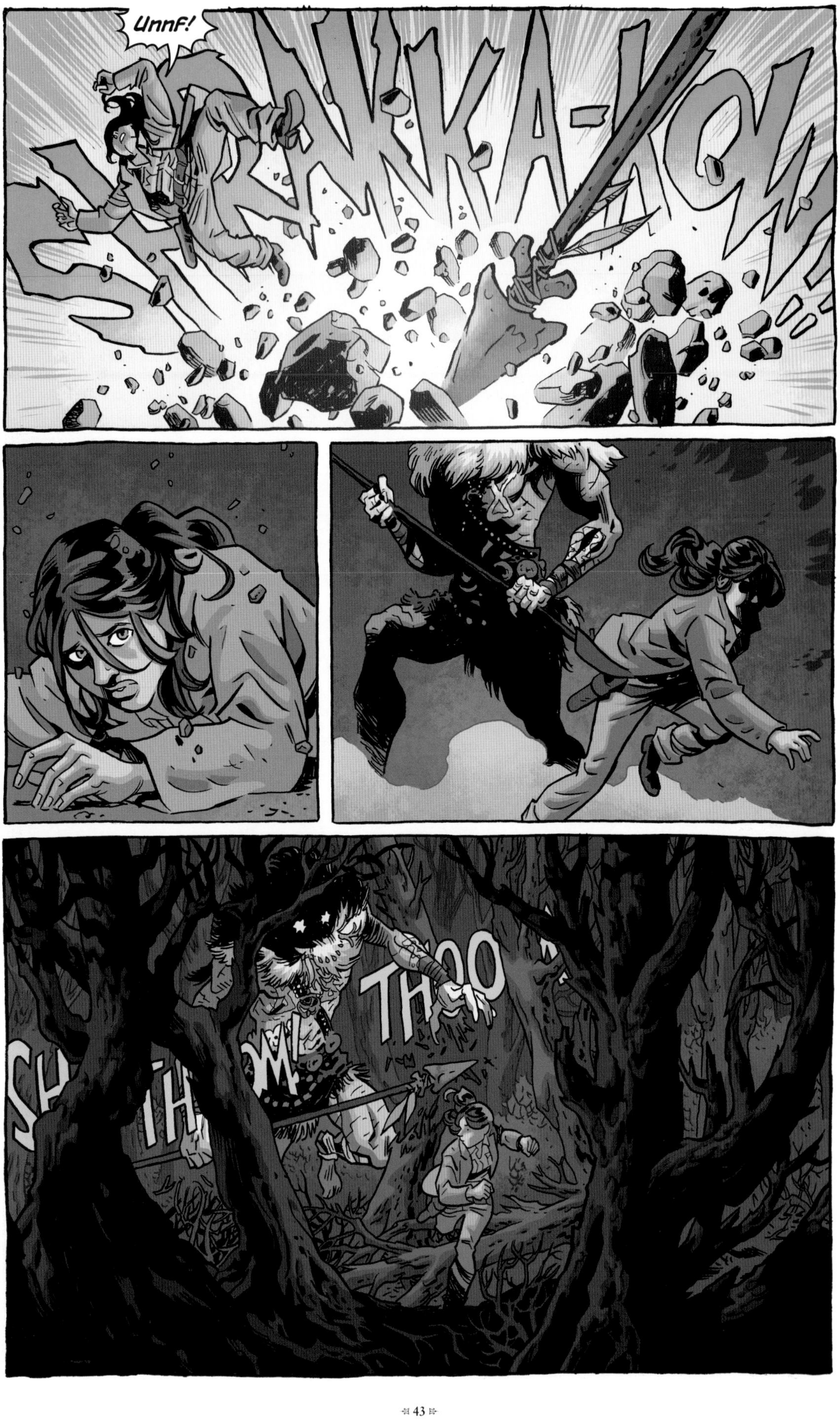
Unnf!

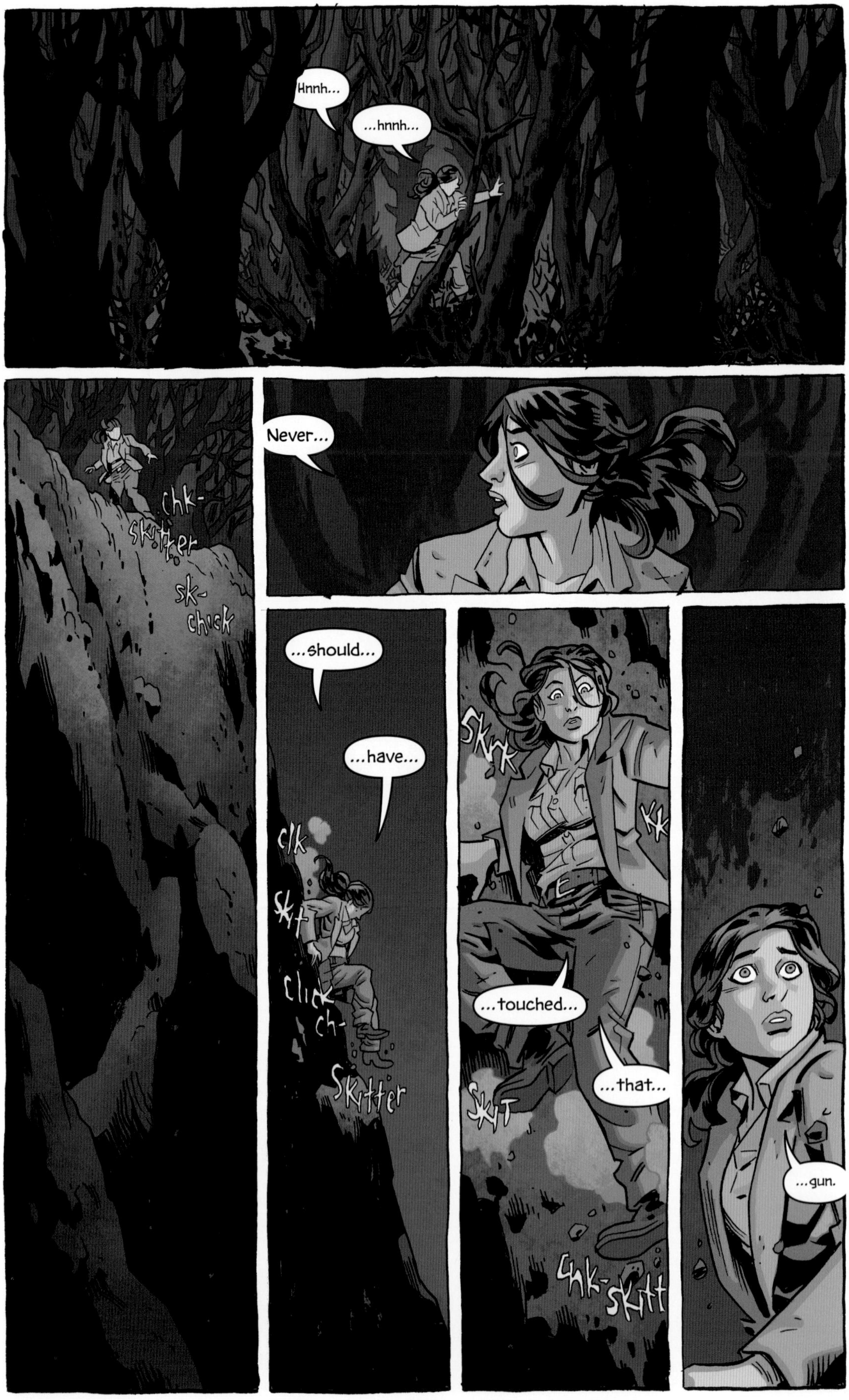
Hnnh...
...hnnh...
Chk-
skitter
sk-
chuck
Never...
...should...
...have...
clk
skit
click
ch-
skitter
Skrk
KK
...touched...
...that...
SKIT
Chk-skitt
...gun.

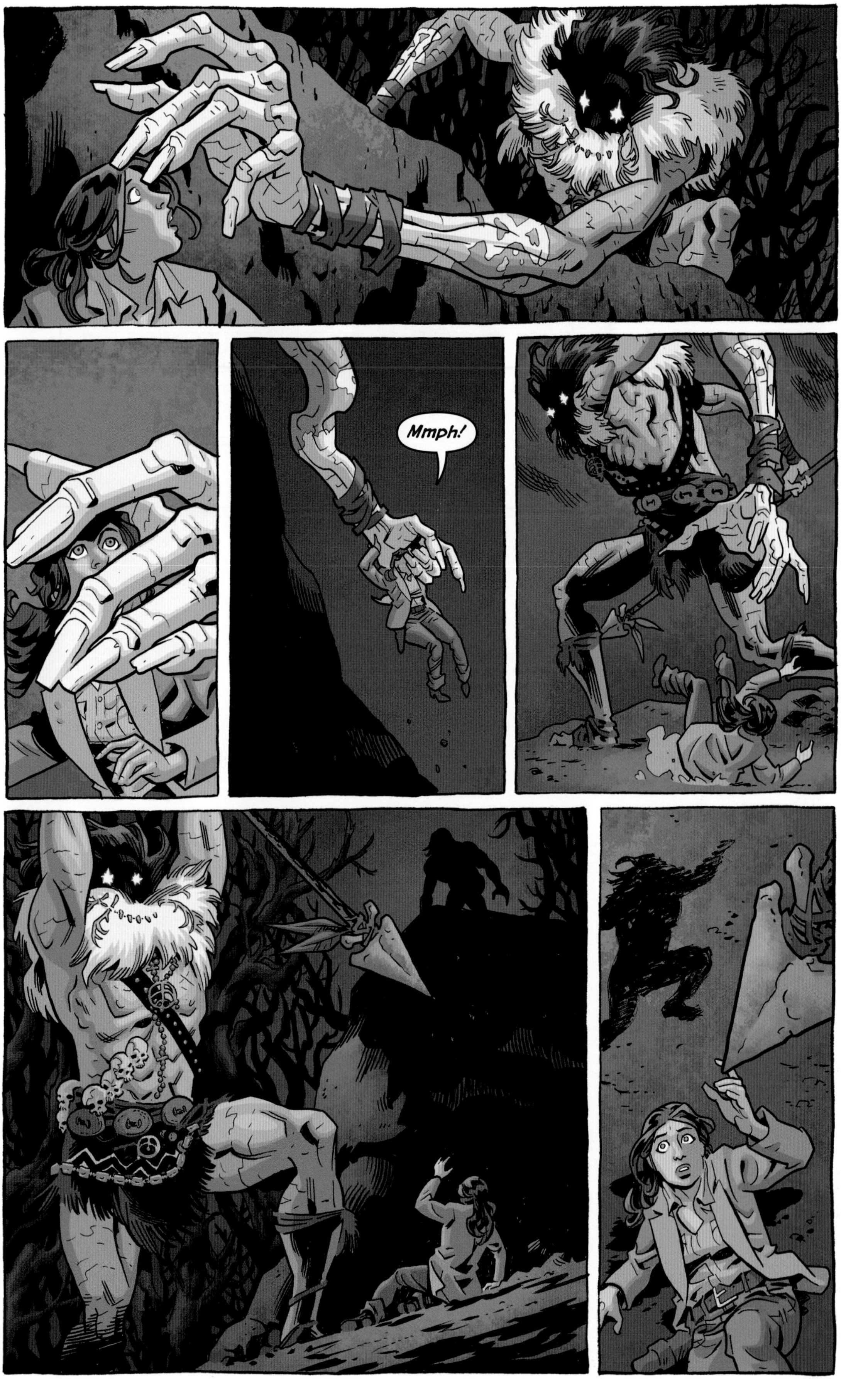
Mmph!

Rrrraggh!

Rrrr—

Grrrrrr...

The Six have known many different forms.

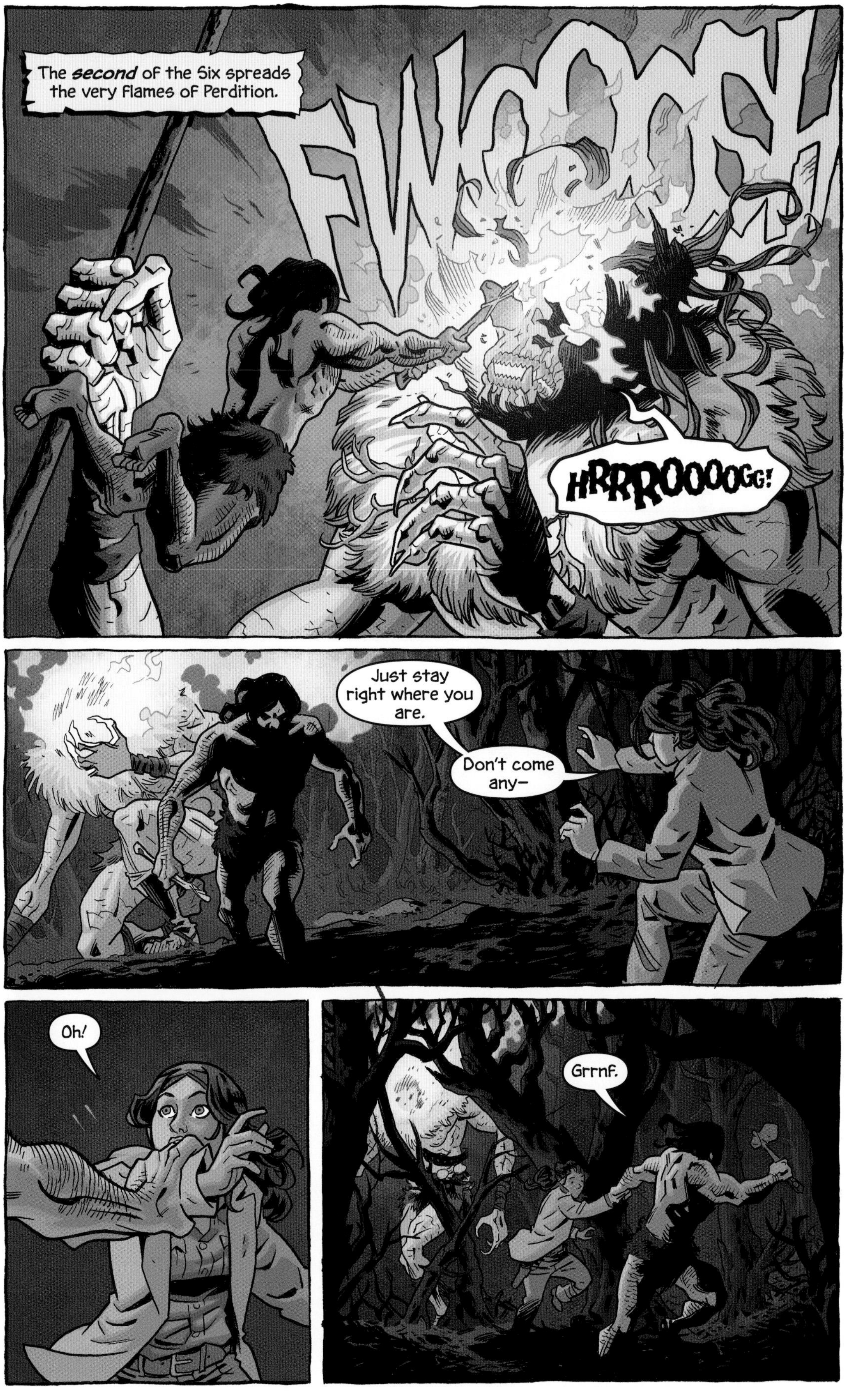
The *second* of the Six spreads the very flames of Perdition.
HRRROOOOGG!
Just stay right where you are.
Don't come any–
Oh!
Grrnf.

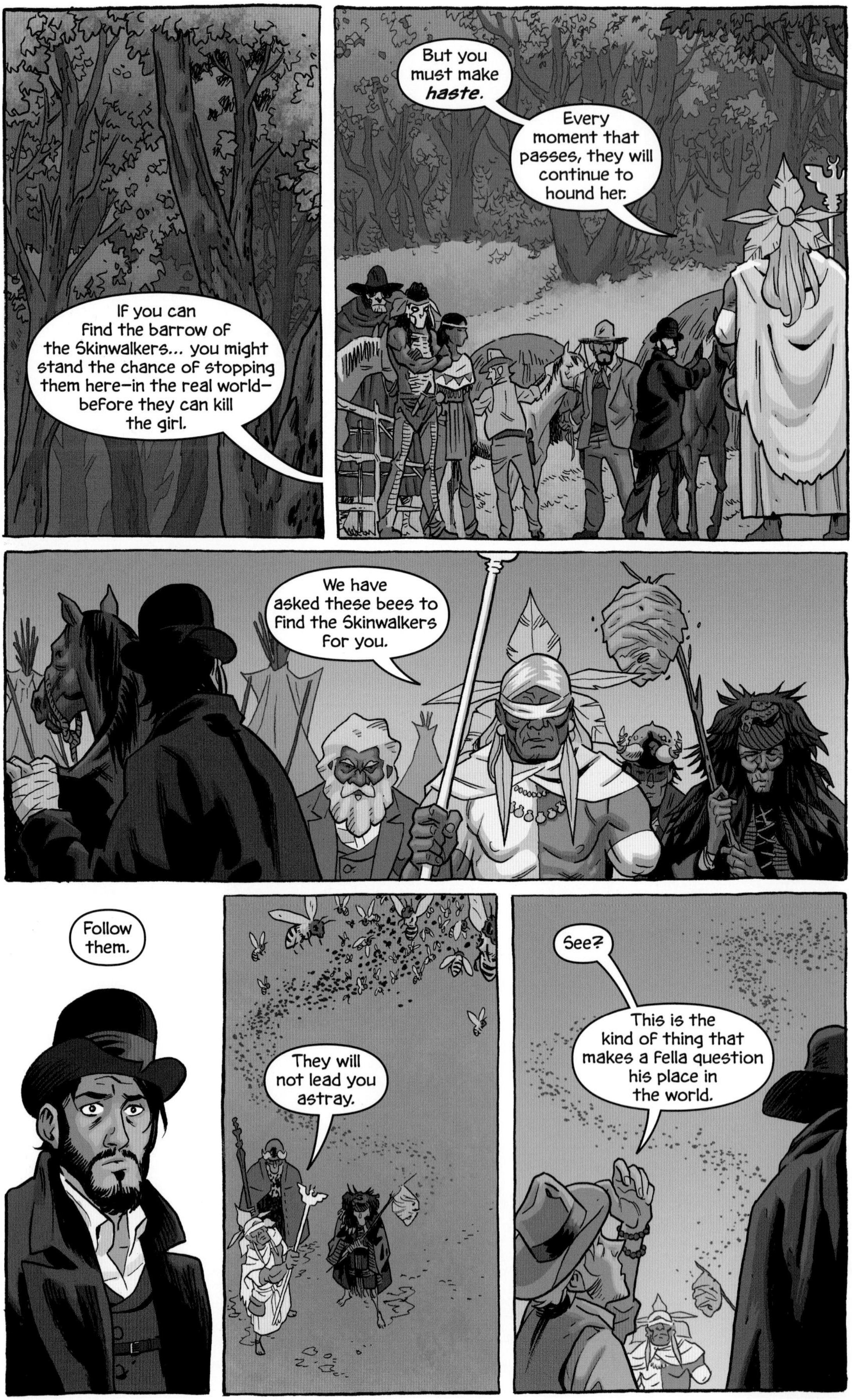
If you can find the barrow of the Skinwalkers... you might stand the chance of stopping them here—in the real world—before they can kill the girl.
But you must make *haste*.
Every moment that passes, they will continue to hound her.
We have asked these bees to find the Skinwalkers for you.
Follow them.
They will not lead you astray.
See?
This is the kind of thing that makes a fella question his place in the world.

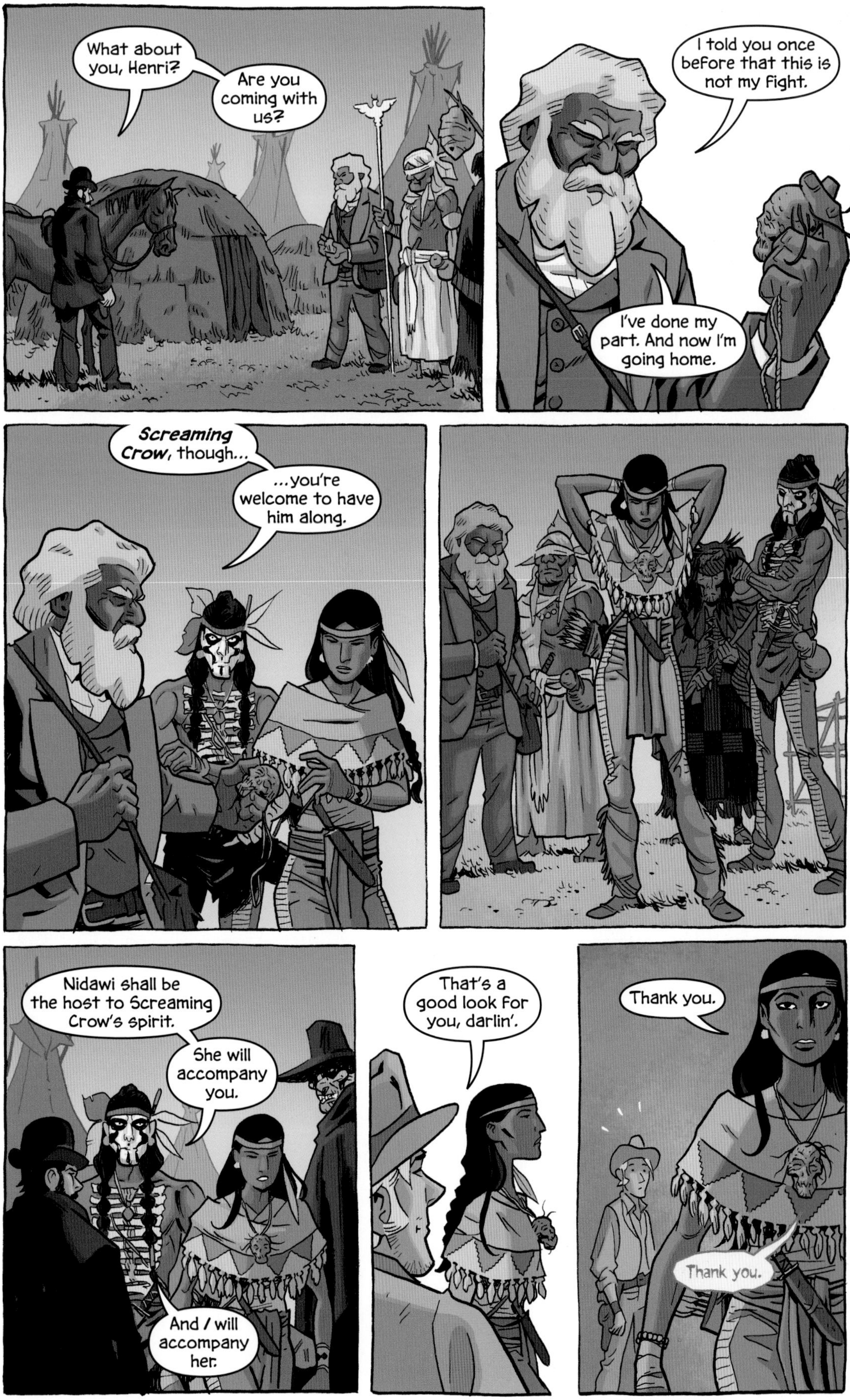
What about you, Henri?
Are you coming with us?
I told you once before that this is not my fight.
I've done my part. And now I'm going home.
Screaming Crow, though...
...you're welcome to have him along.
Nidawi shall be the host to Screaming Crow's spirit.
She will accompany you.
And *I* will accompany her.
That's a good look for you, darlin'.
Thank you.
Thank you.

Drake.

Can I have a word?

You're **not** coming with us.

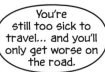

You're still too sick to travel... and you'll only get worse on the road.

You wouldn't do us a bit of good once we find these Skinwalkers if you did come with us.

Besides... someone needs to stay here... to watch over Becky.

I thought on that.

And if Becky doesn't live to see the other side of this, I think I'd rather it be **you** who was here.

Why me?

If she dies... someone has to take possession of the **Sixth Gun.**

And... I don't want it to be me.

That's **good.**

Hold onto that feeling, Drake.

Because anyone who would want to take that gun for them- selves **shouldn't** be trusted with it.

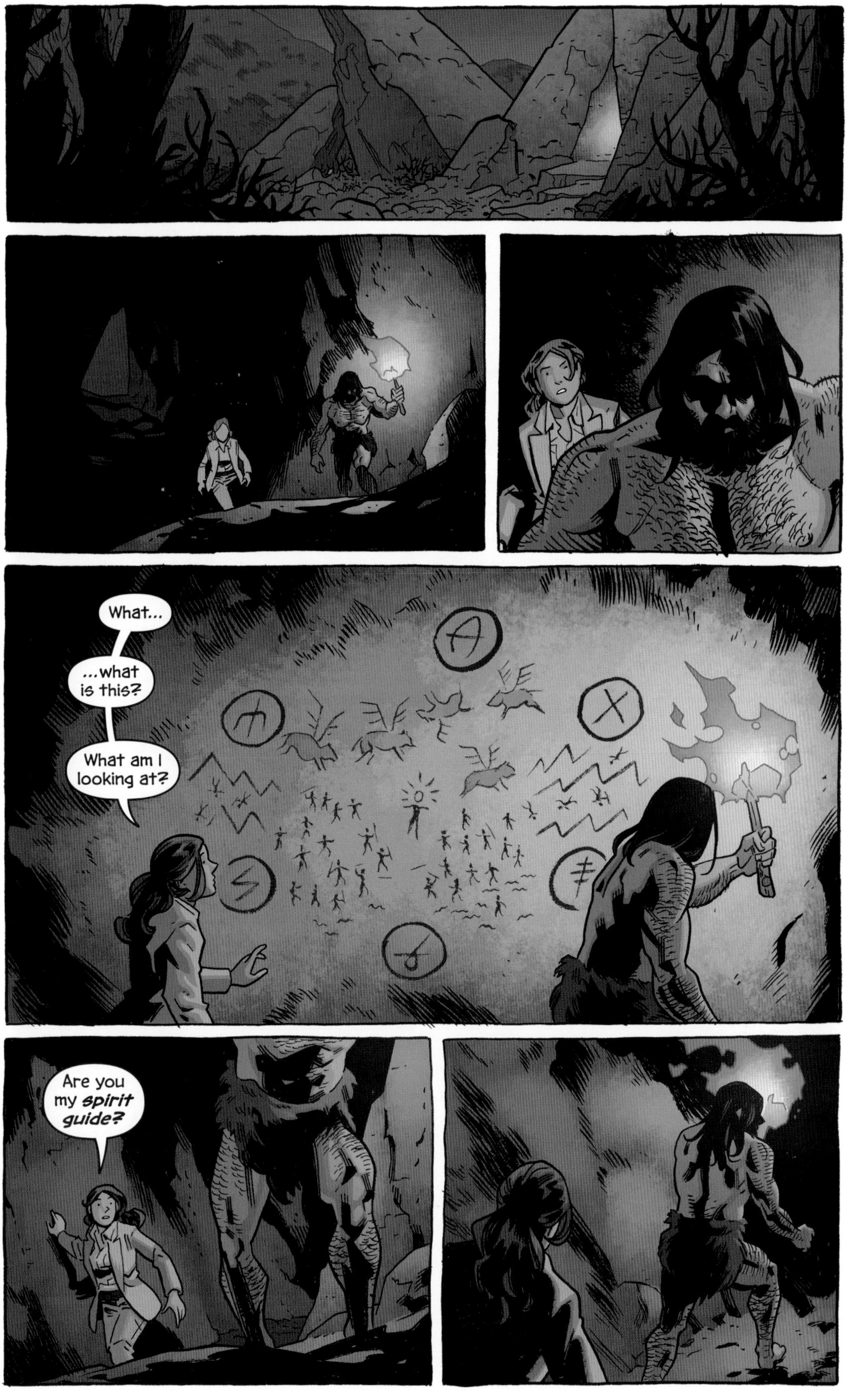
What...
...what is this?
What am I looking at?
Are you my *spirit guide?*

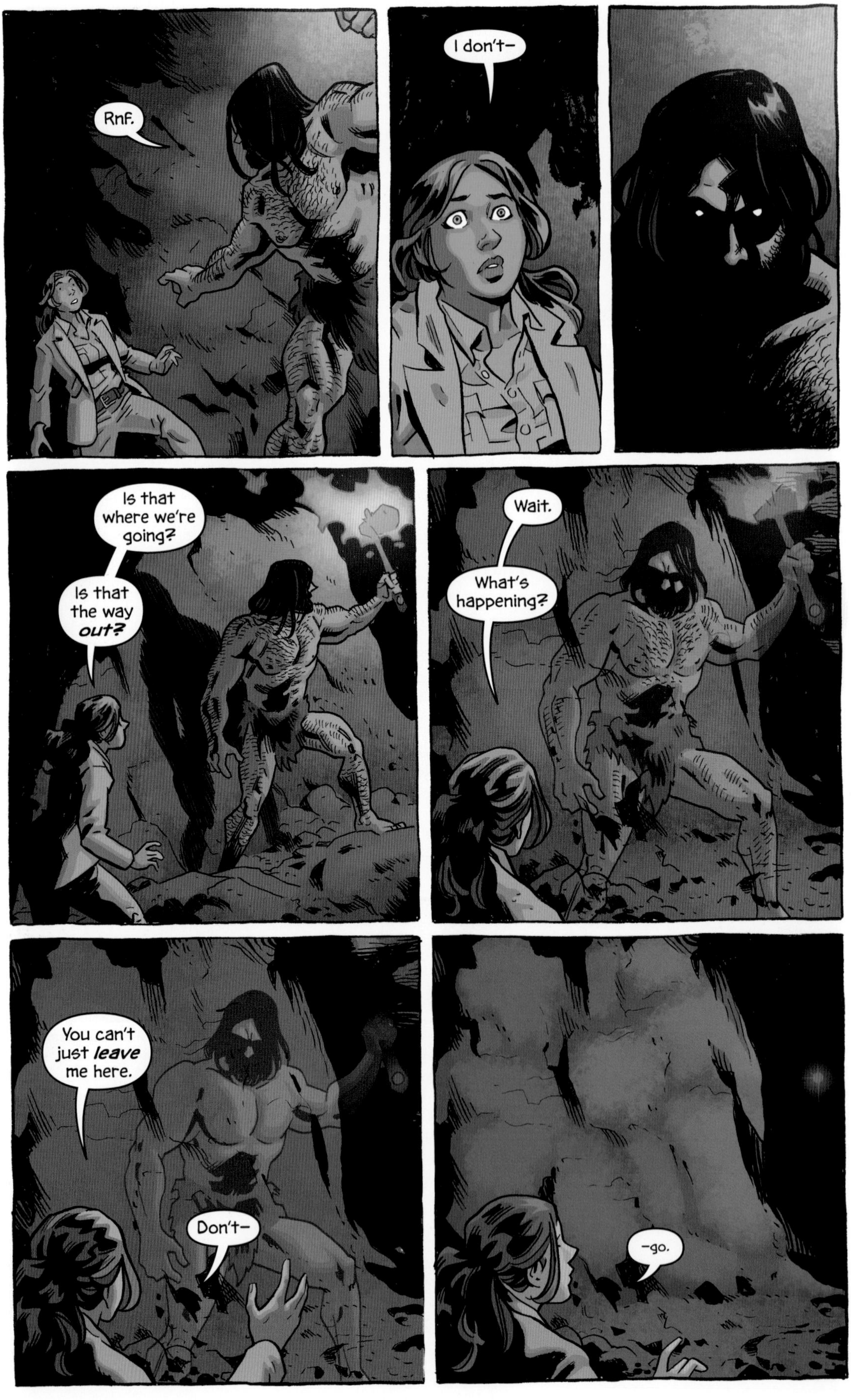
Rnf.
I don't–
Is that where we're going?
Is that the way *out?*
Wait.
What's happening?
You can't just *leave* me here.
Don't–
–go.

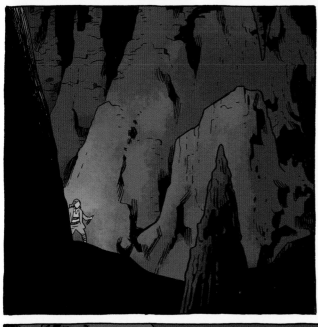

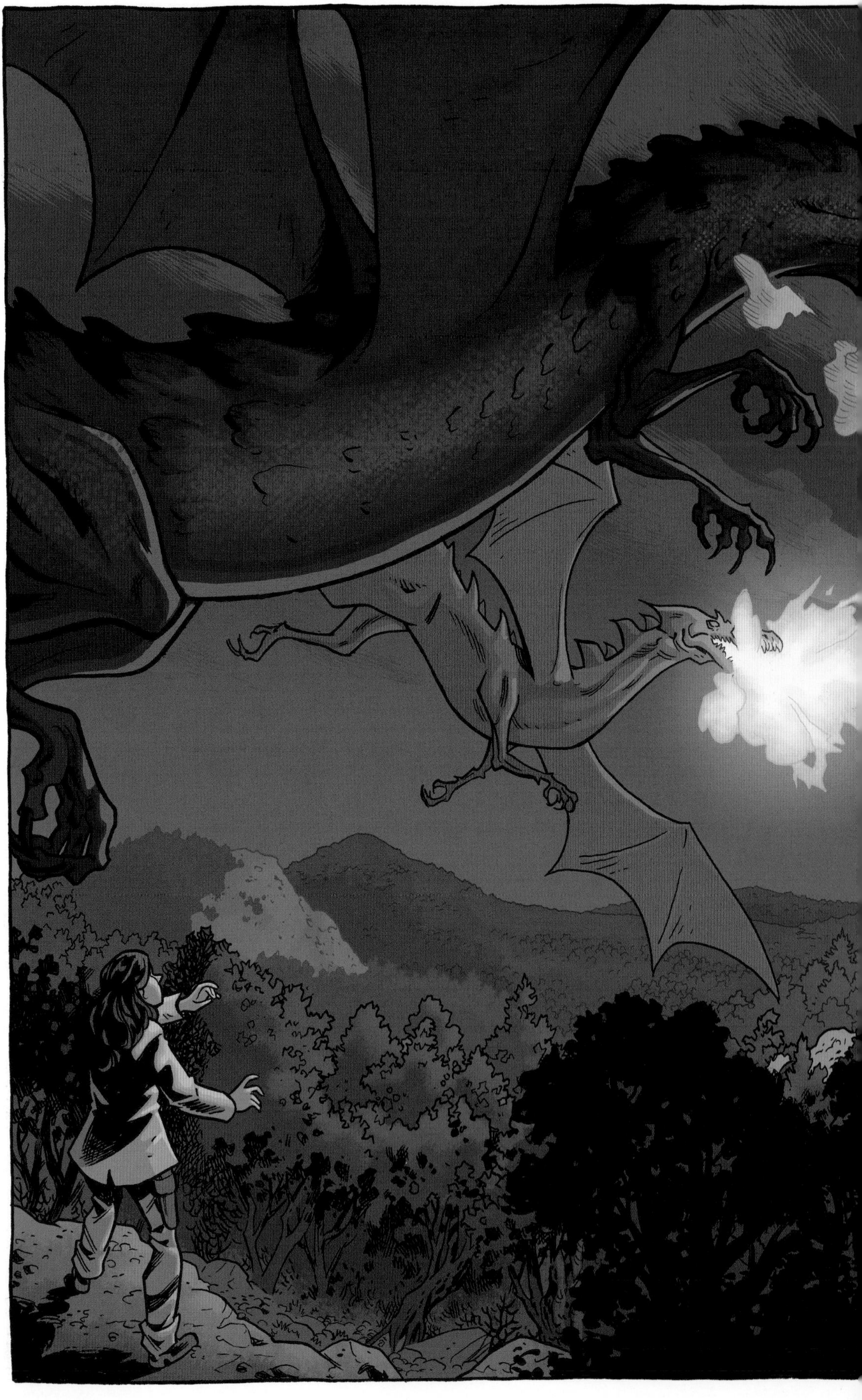

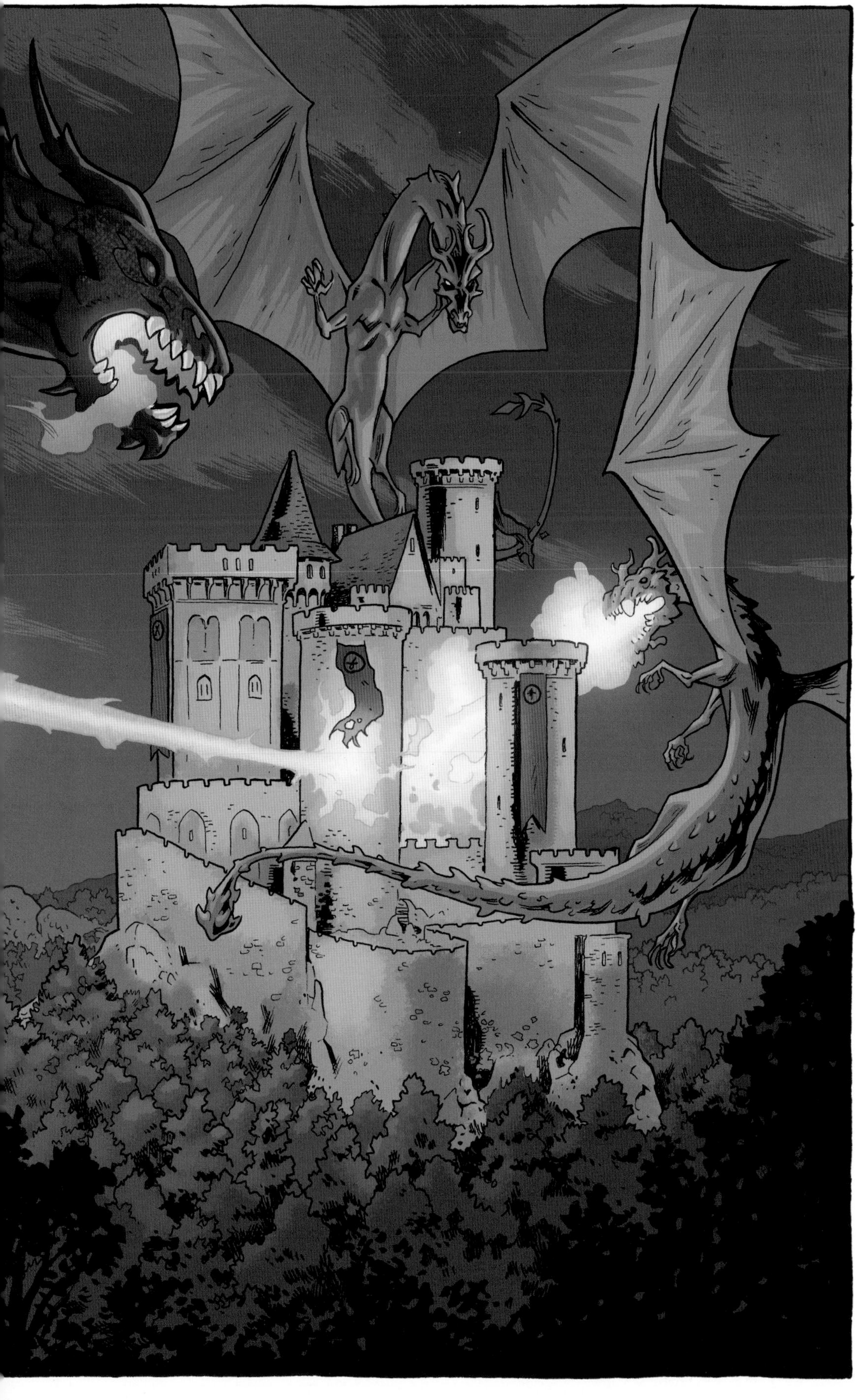

CHAPTER
THREE

Henri.

The man with the answers.

Just a *man* now.

I've told you everything I know.

I find that a trifle *unlikely*.

Suit yourself.

And now... what?

You're just going back to your swamp... to hole up and hope the world doesn't end?

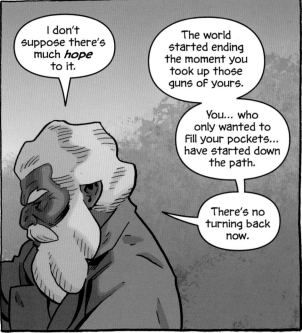

I don't suppose there's much *hope* to it.

The world started ending the moment you took up those guns of yours.

You... who only wanted to fill your pockets... have started down the path.

There's no turning back now.

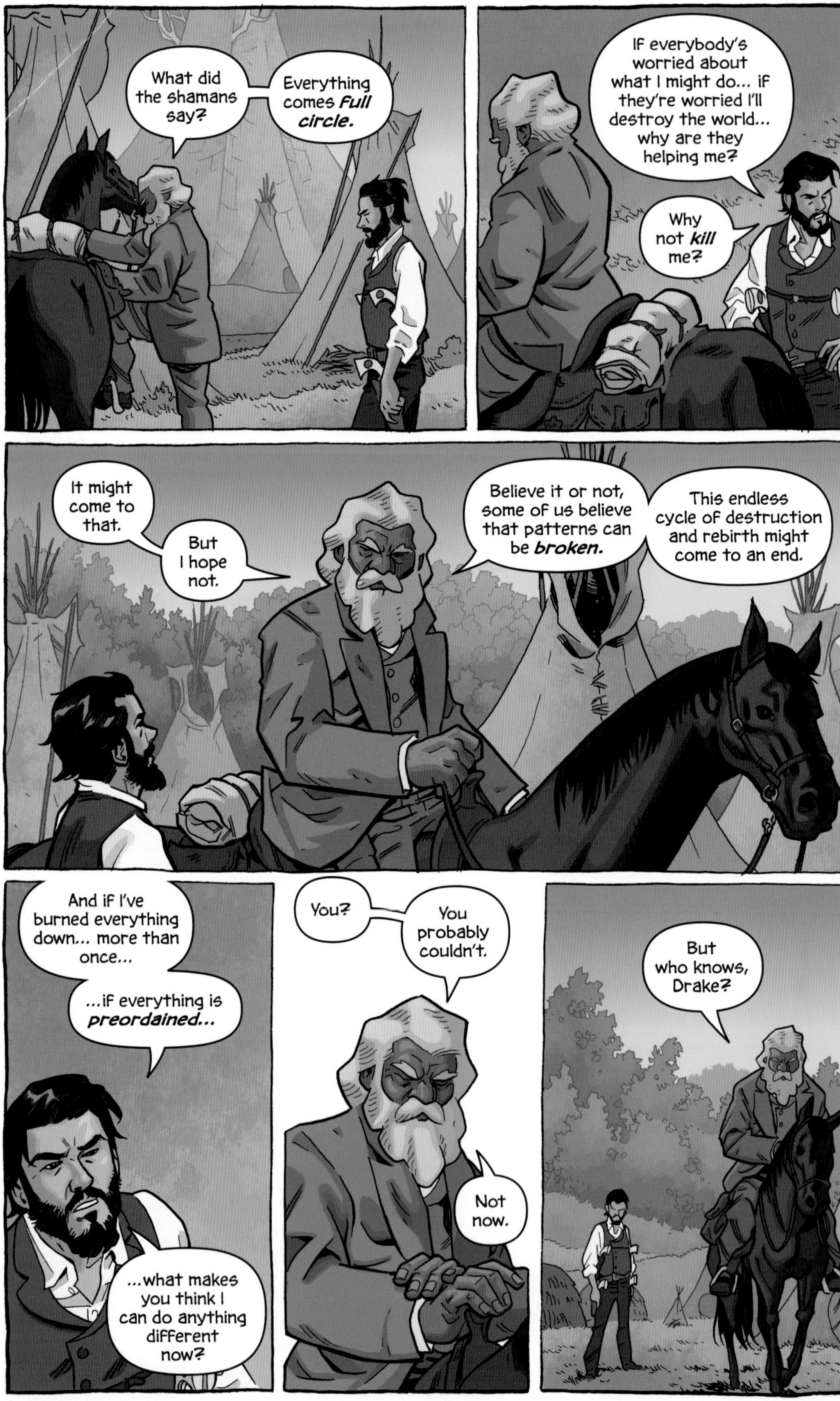
What did the shamans say?
Everything comes *full circle.*
If everybody's worried about what I might do... if they're worried I'll destroy the world... why are they helping me?
Why not *kill* me?
It might come to that.
But I hope not.
Believe it or not, some of us believe that patterns can be *broken.*
This endless cycle of destruction and rebirth might come to an end.
And if I've burned everything down... more than once...
...if everything is *preordained...*
...what makes you think I can do anything different now?
You?
You probably couldn't.
Not now.
But who knows, Drake?

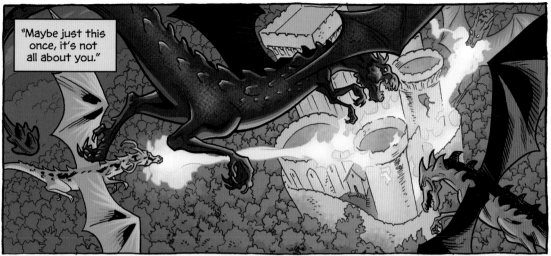

"Maybe just this once, it's not all about you."

There was a time when Becky Montcrief only dreamed of what waited outside the boundaries of the farm.

She knew there were sights to see and adventures to be had... but she never believed she was destined to see any of it.

Adventure, or so she believed, was meant for someone who didn't have *responsibilities*.

An ailing father to look after. A ranch to tend.

A life beyond the farm...

...that was the stuff of *daydreams*...

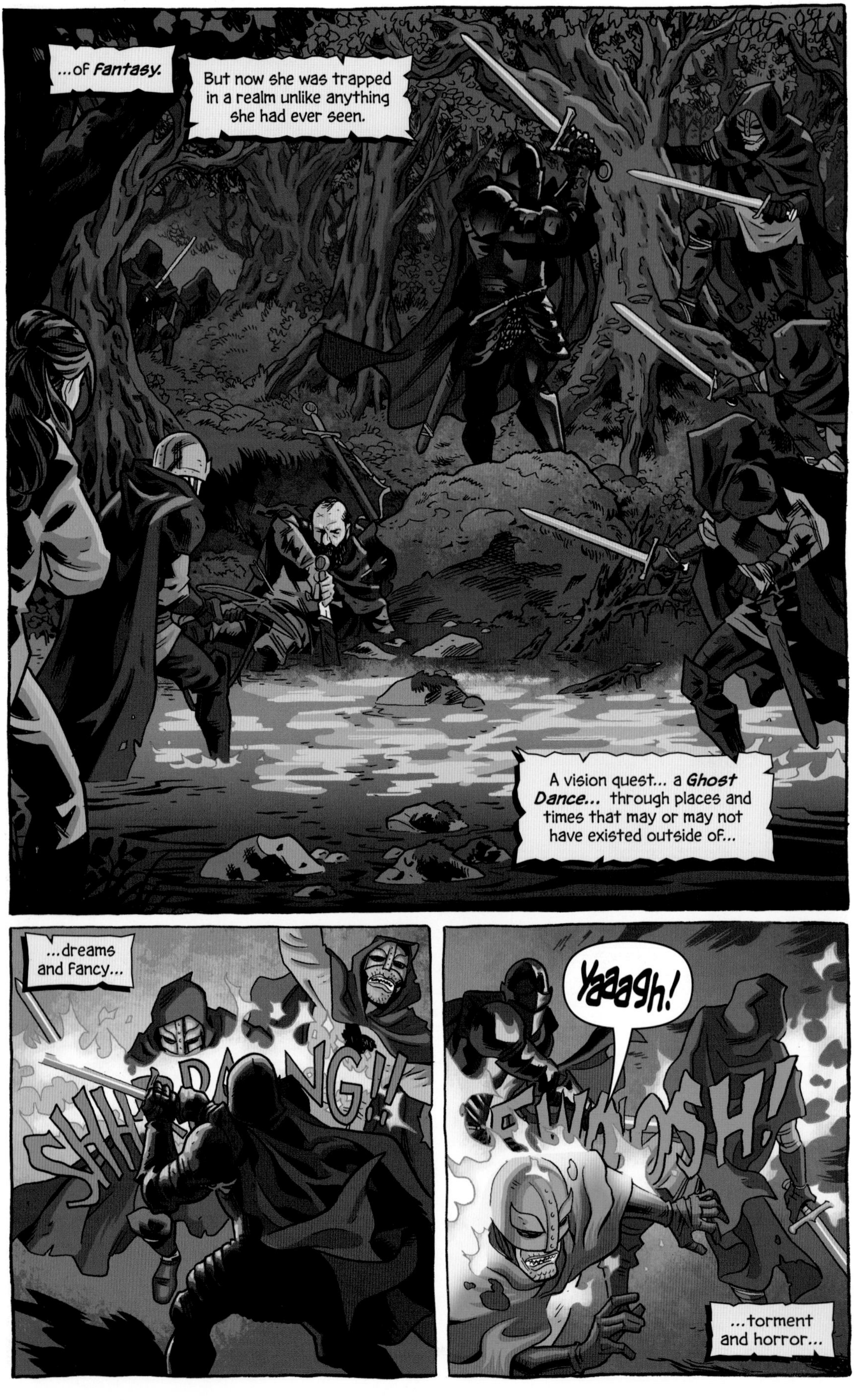
...of *Fantasy.*
But now she was trapped in a realm unlike anything she had ever seen.
A vision quest... a *Ghost Dance...* through places and times that may or may not have existed outside of...
...dreams and fancy...
Yaaagh!
...torment and horror...

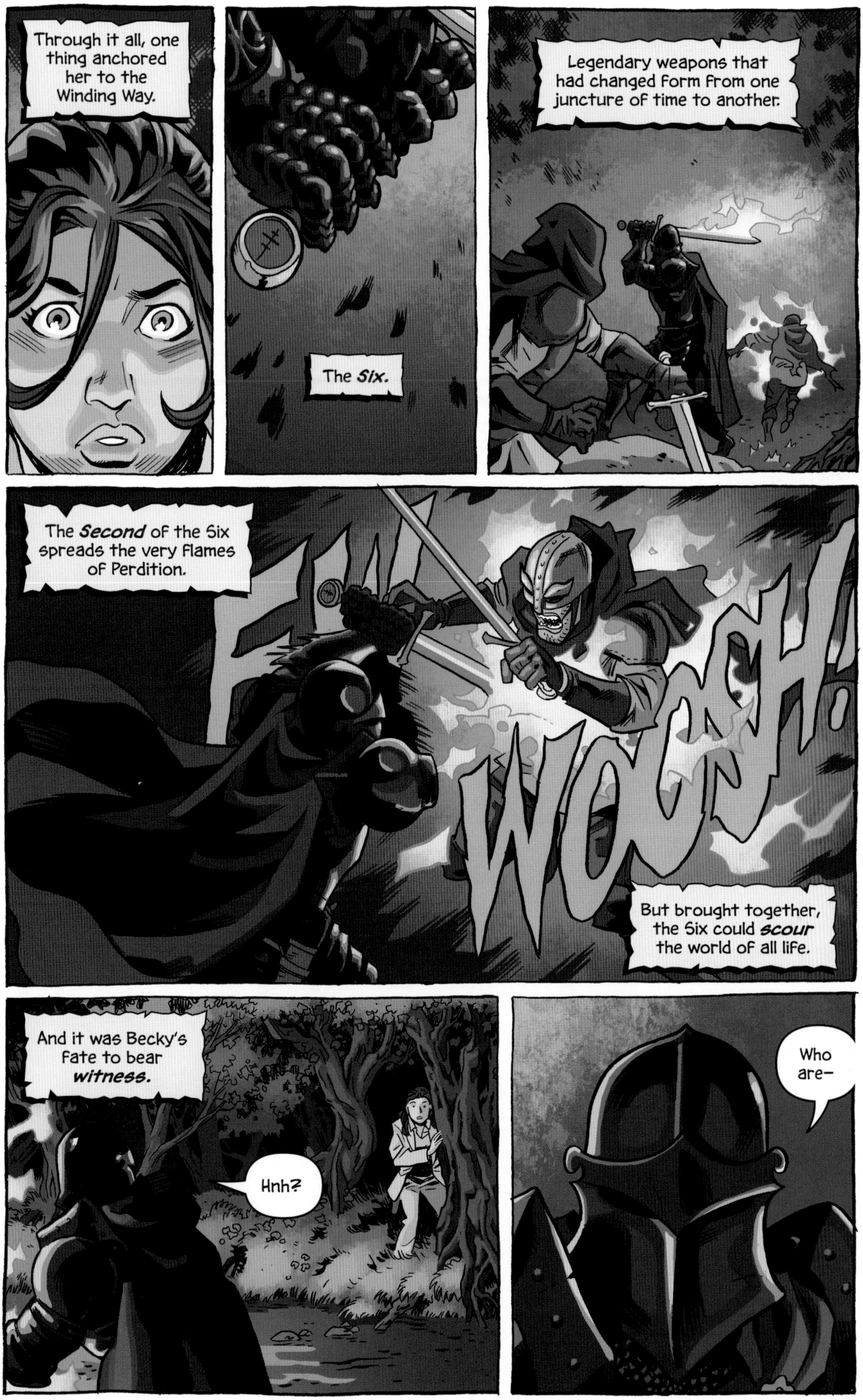
Through it all, one thing anchored her to the Winding Way.
The *Six.*
Legendary weapons that had changed form from one juncture of time to another.
The *Second* of the Six spreads the very flames of Perdition.
WOOSH!
But brought together, the Six could *scour* the world of all life.
And it was Becky's fate to bear *witness.*
Hnh?
Who are—

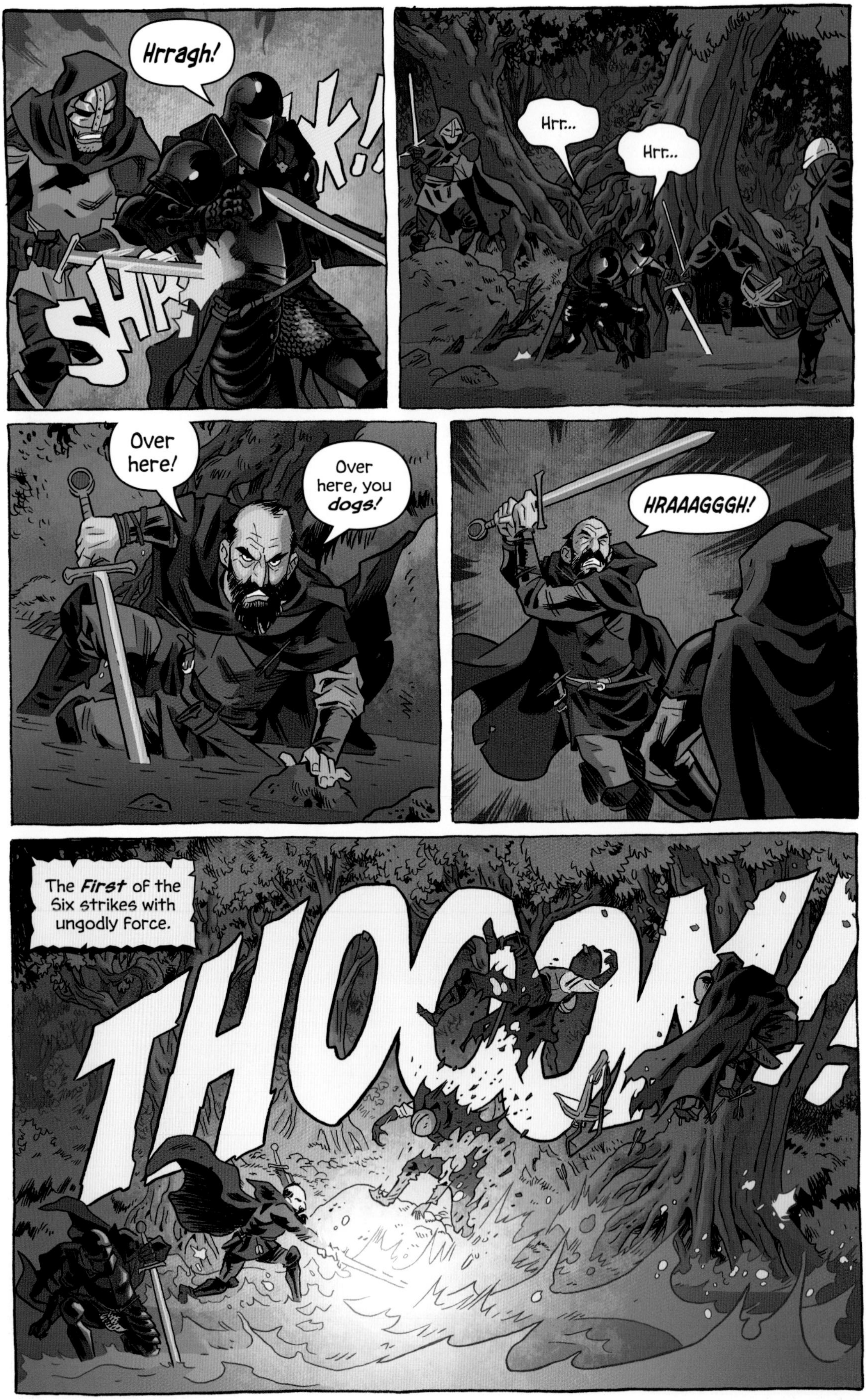
Hrragh!
Hrr...
Hrr...
Over here!
Over here, you dogs!
HRAAAGGGH!
The First of the Six strikes with ungodly force.

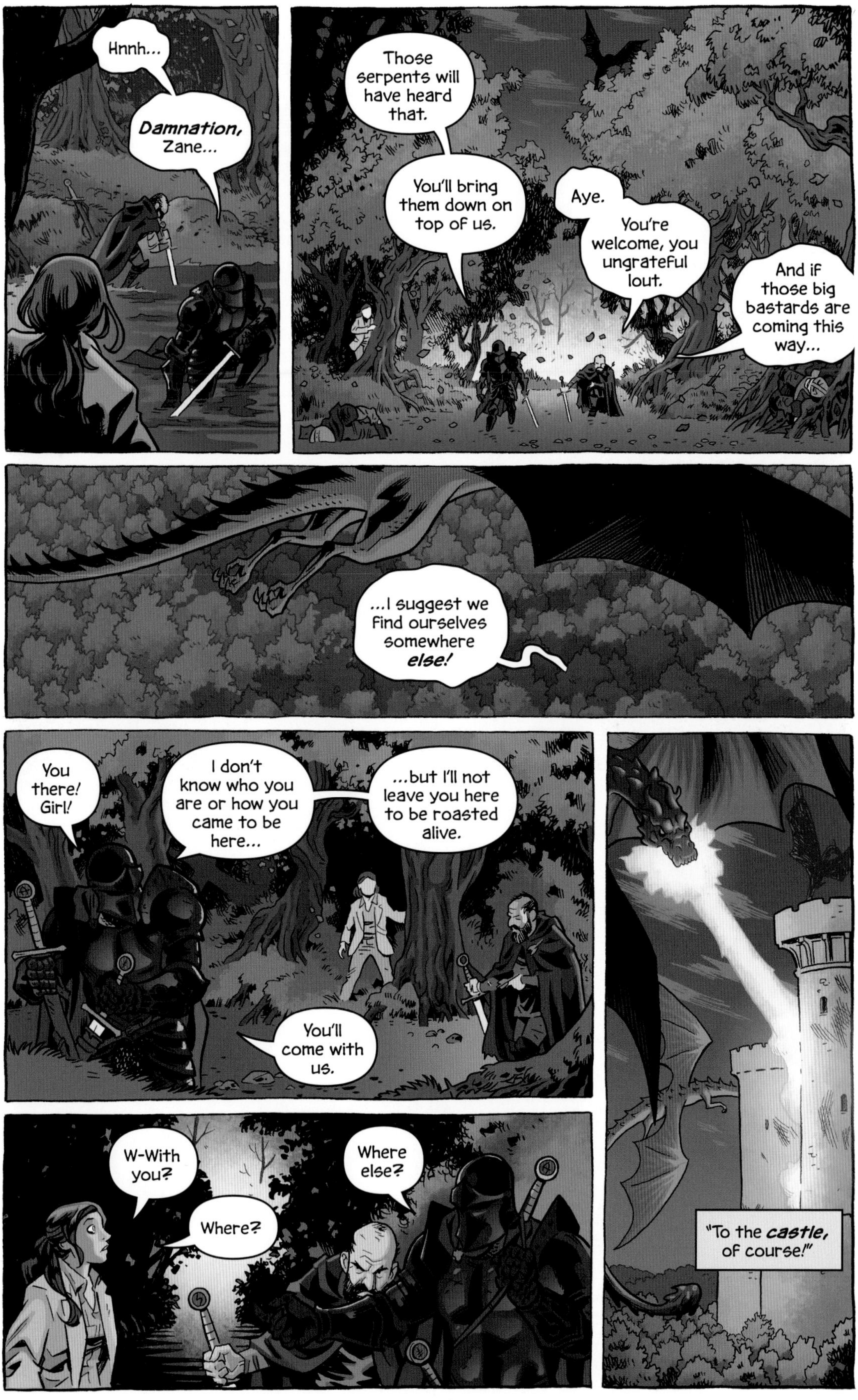
Hnnh...
Damnation, Zane...
Those serpents will have heard that.
You'll bring them down on top of us.
Aye.
You're welcome, you ungrateful lout.
And if those big bastards are coming this way...
...I suggest we find ourselves somewhere else!
You there! Girl!
I don't know who you are or how you came to be here...
...but I'll not leave you here to be roasted alive.
You'll come with us.
W-With you?
Where?
Where else?
"To the castle, of course!"

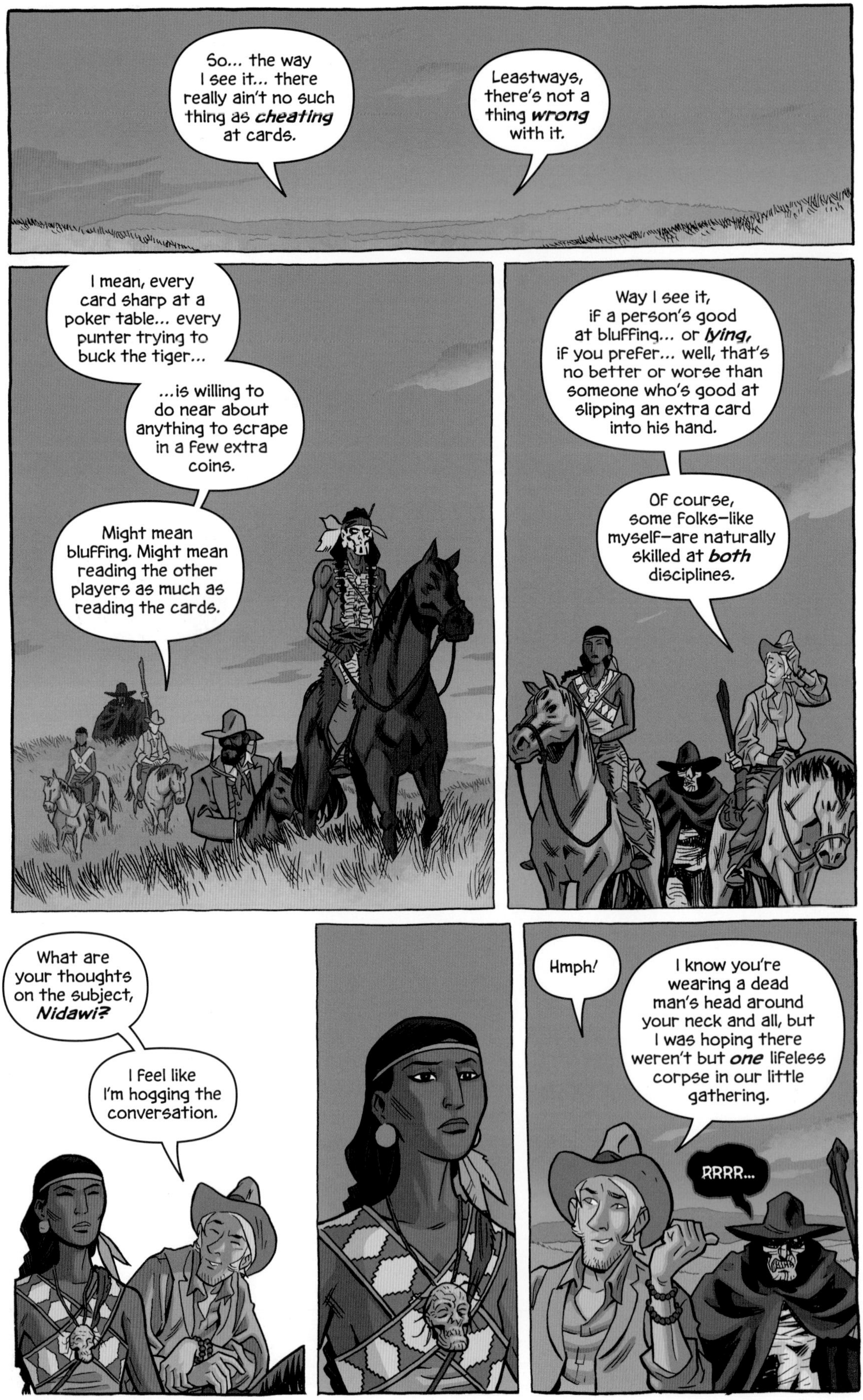
So... the way I see it... there really ain't no such thing as *cheating* at cards.
Leastways, there's not a thing *wrong* with it.
I mean, every card sharp at a poker table... every punter trying to buck the tiger...
...is willing to do near about anything to scrape in a few extra coins.
Might mean bluffing. Might mean reading the other players as much as reading the cards.
Way I see it, if a person's good at bluffing... or *lying,* if you prefer... well, that's no better or worse than someone who's good at slipping an extra card into his hand.
Of course, some folks—like myself—are naturally skilled at *both* disciplines.
What are your thoughts on the subject, *Nidawi?*
I feel like I'm hogging the conversation.
Hmph!
I know you're wearing a dead man's head around your neck and all, but I was hoping there weren't but *one* lifeless corpse in our little gathering.
RRRR...

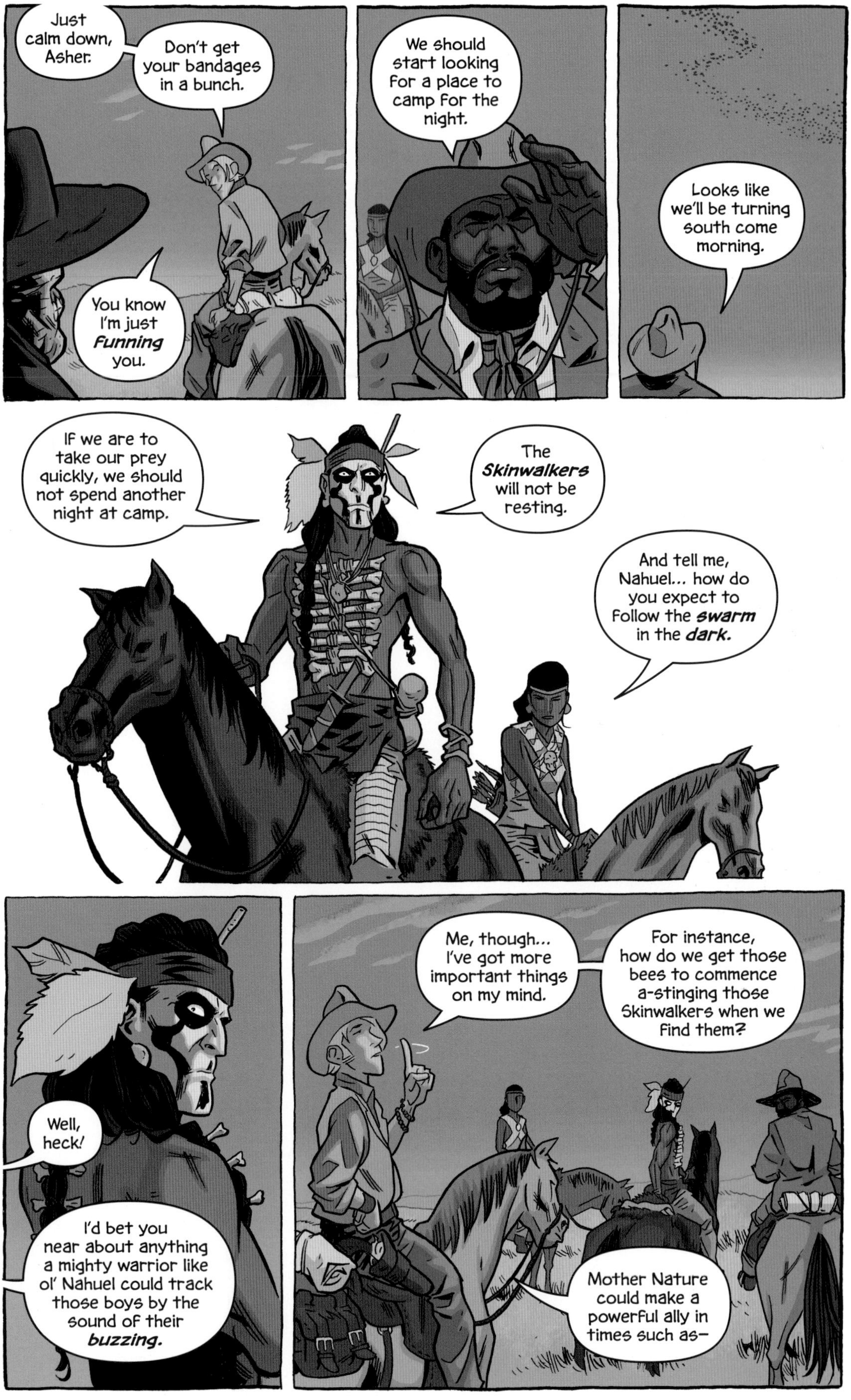
Just calm down, Asher.
Don't get your bandages in a bunch.
You know I'm just *funning* you.
We should start looking for a place to camp for the night.
Looks like we'll be turning south come morning.
If we are to take our prey quickly, we should not spend another night at camp.
The *Skinwalkers* will not be resting.
And tell me, Nahuel... how do you expect to follow the *swarm* in the *dark.*
Well, heck!
I'd bet you near about anything a mighty warrior like ol' Nahuel could track those boys by the sound of their *buzzing.*
Me, though... I've got more important things on my mind.
For instance, how do we get those bees to commence a-stinging those Skinwalkers when we find them?
Mother Nature could make a powerful ally in times such as–

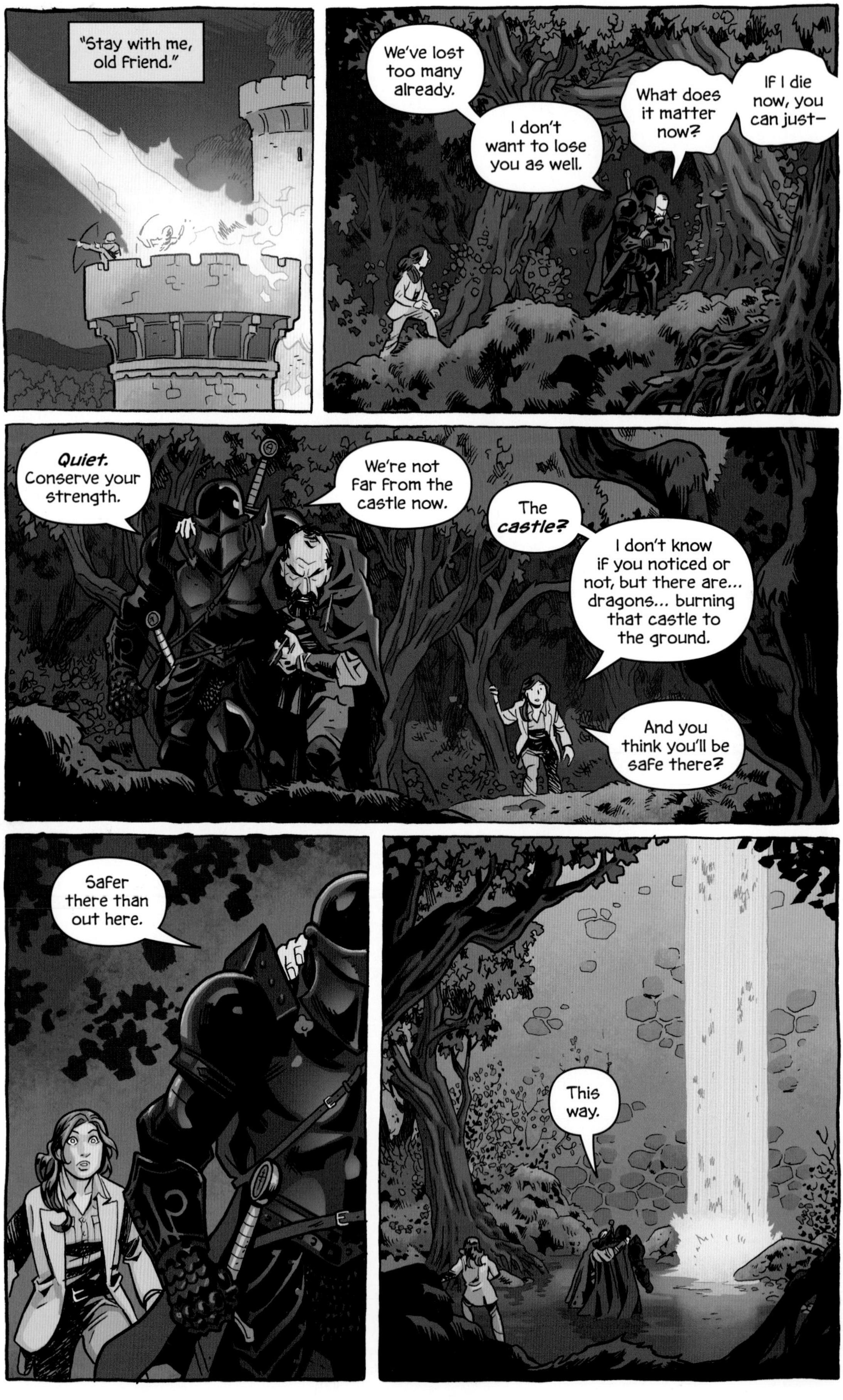
"Stay with me, old friend."
We've lost too many already.
I don't want to lose you as well.
What does it matter now?
If I die now, you can just—
Quiet. Conserve your strength.
We're not far from the castle now.
The *castle?*
I don't know if you noticed or not, but there are... dragons... burning that castle to the ground.
And you think you'll be safe there?
Safer there than out here.
This way.

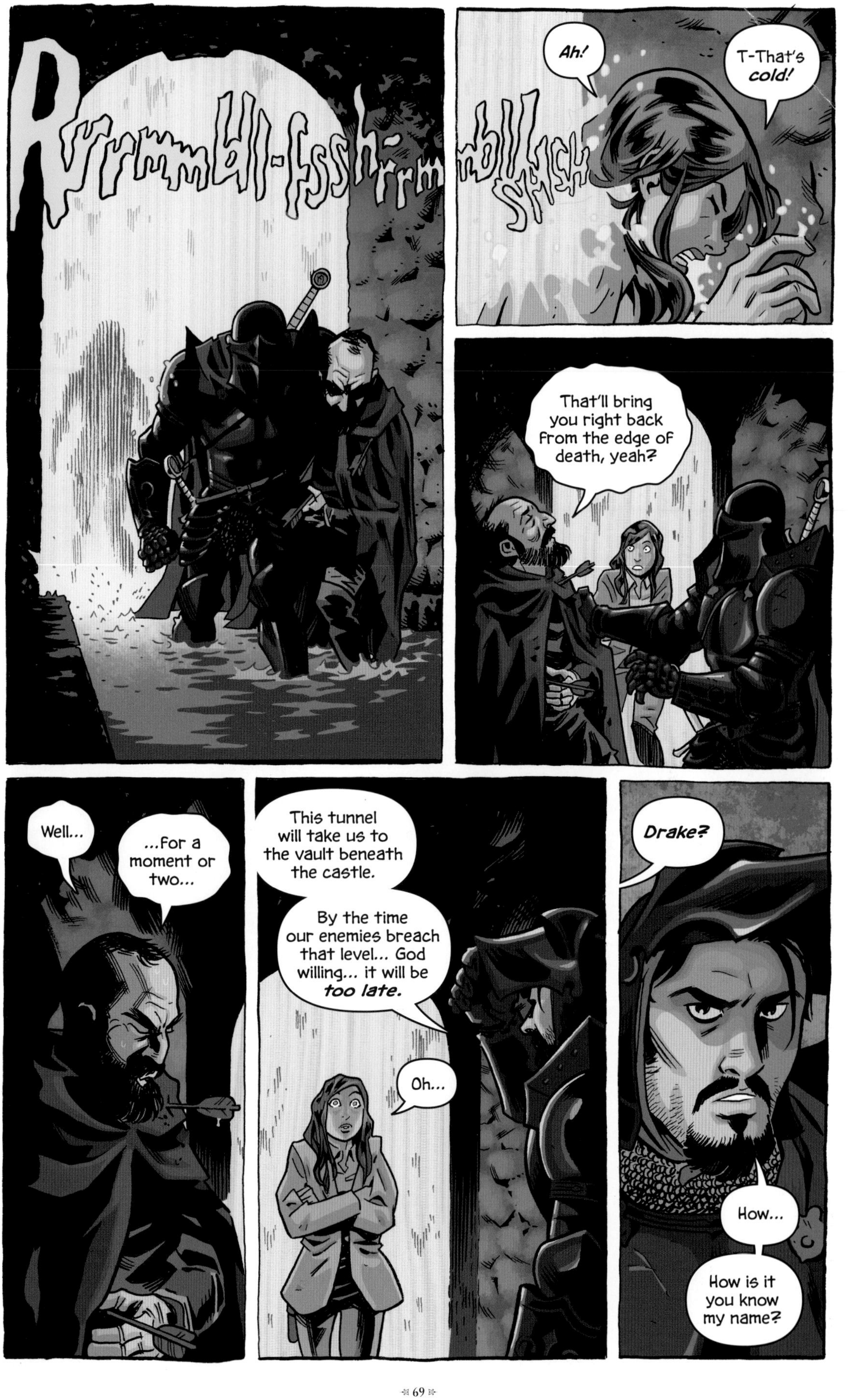
Rrrrmmbll-fssh-rrmmbll-splash
Ah!
T-That's cold!
That'll bring you right back from the edge of death, yeah?
Well...
...For a moment or two...
This tunnel will take us to the vault beneath the castle.
By the time our enemies breach that level... God willing... it will be too late.
Oh...
Drake?
How...
How is it you know my name?

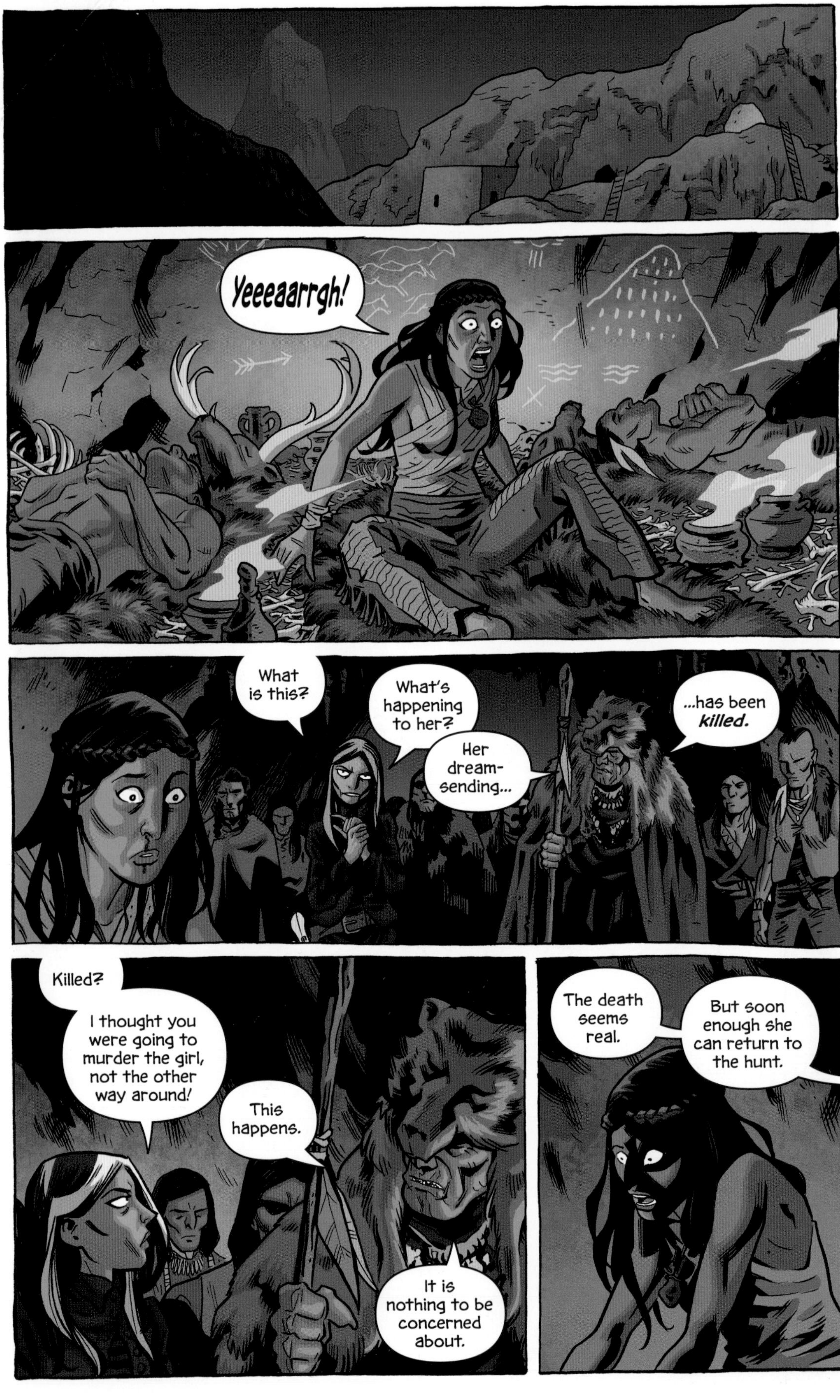

Yeeeaarrgh!
What is this?
What's happening to her?
Her dream-sending...
...has been *killed.*
Killed?
I thought you were going to murder the girl, not the other way around!
This happens.
It is nothing to be concerned about.
The death seems real.
But soon enough she can return to the hunt.

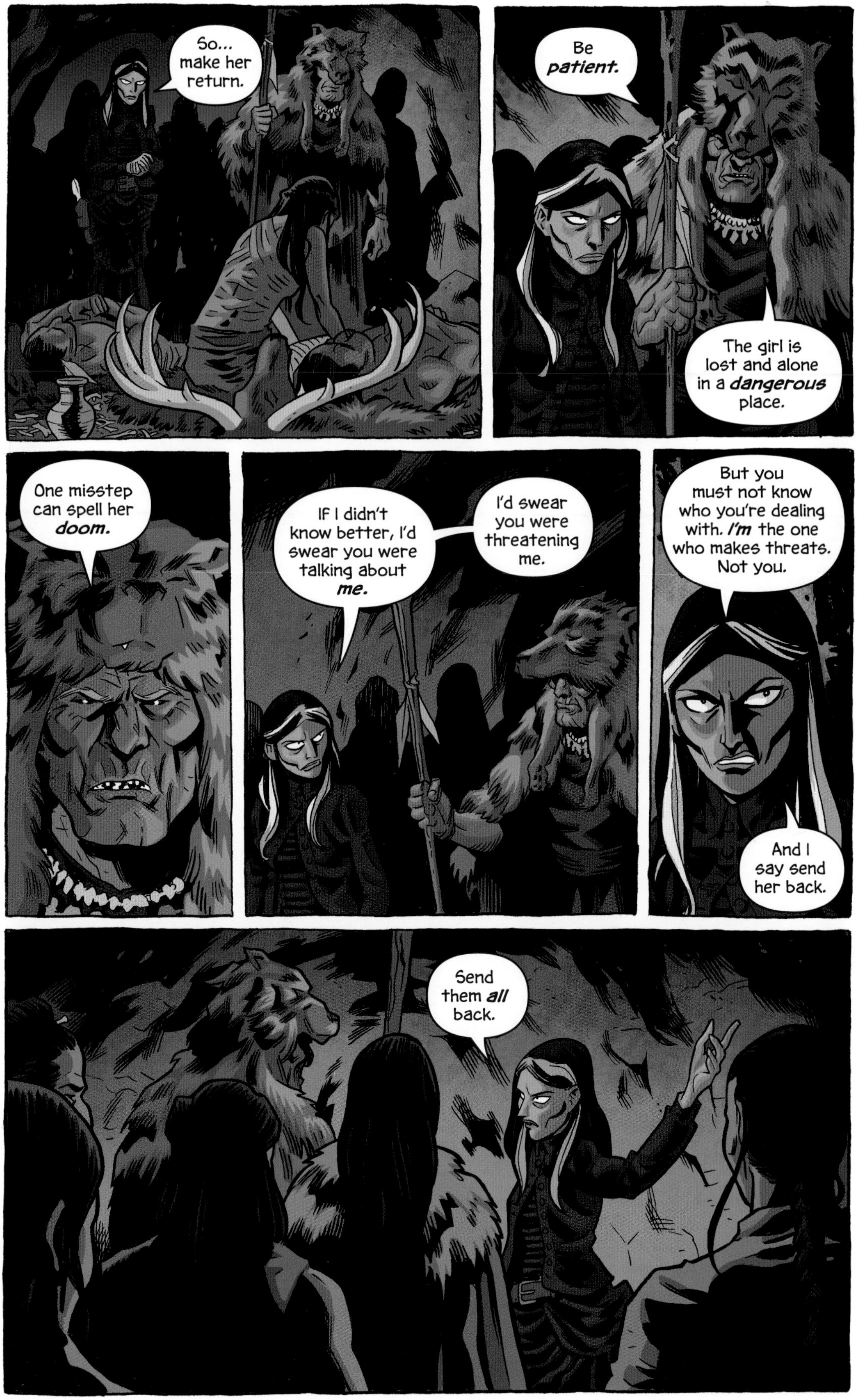
So... make her return.
Be *patient.*
The girl is lost and alone in a *dangerous* place.
One misstep can spell her *doom.*
If I didn't know better, I'd swear you were talking about *me.*
I'd swear you were threatening me.
But you must not know who you're dealing with. *I'm* the one who makes threats. Not you.
And I say send her back.
Send them *all* back.

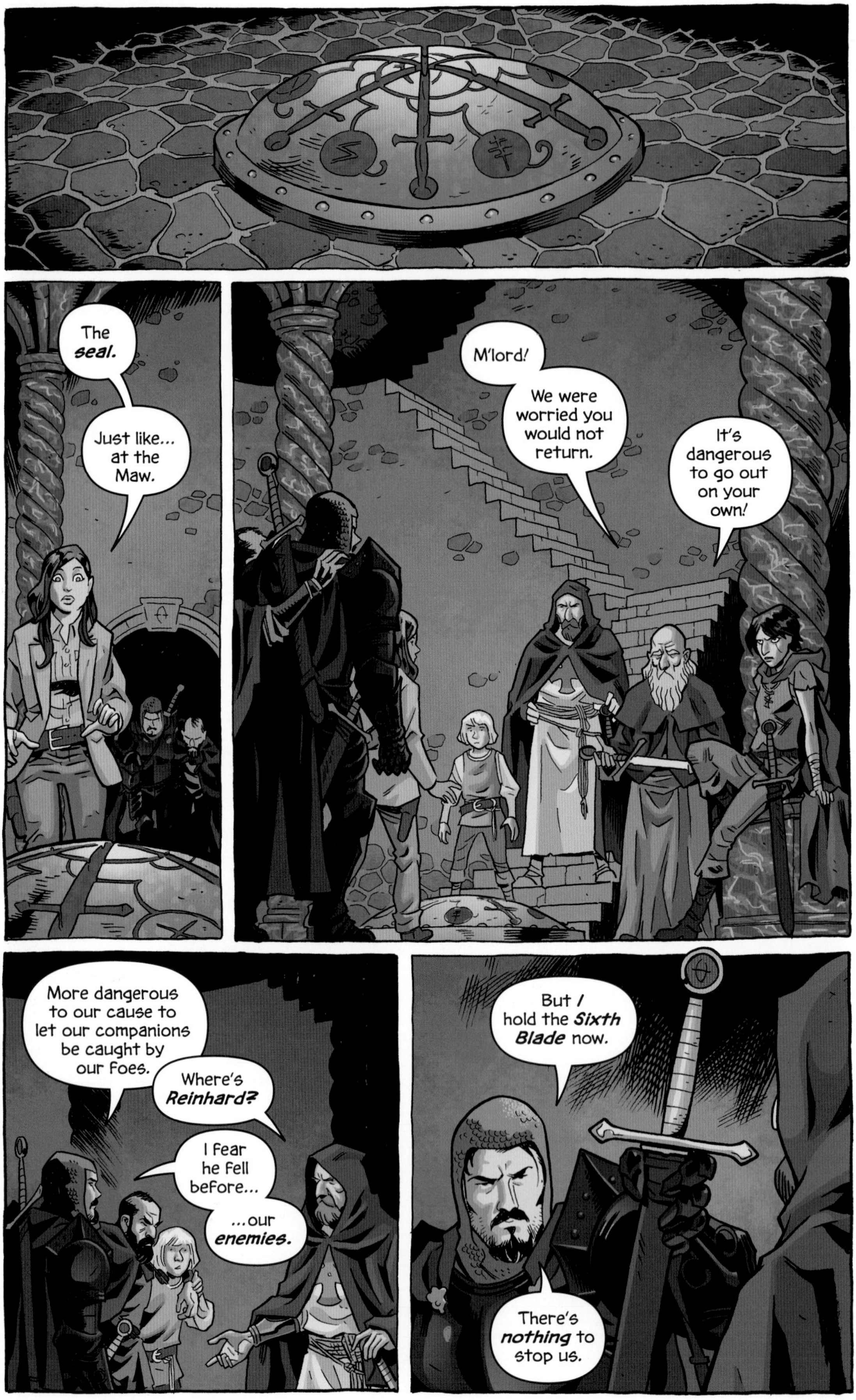
The *seal.*
Just like... at the Maw.
M'lord!
We were worried you would not return.
It's dangerous to go out on your own!
More dangerous to our cause to let our companions be caught by our Foes.
Where's *Reinhard?*
I fear he fell before...
...our *enemies.*
But *I* hold the *Sixth Blade* now.
There's *nothing* to stop us.

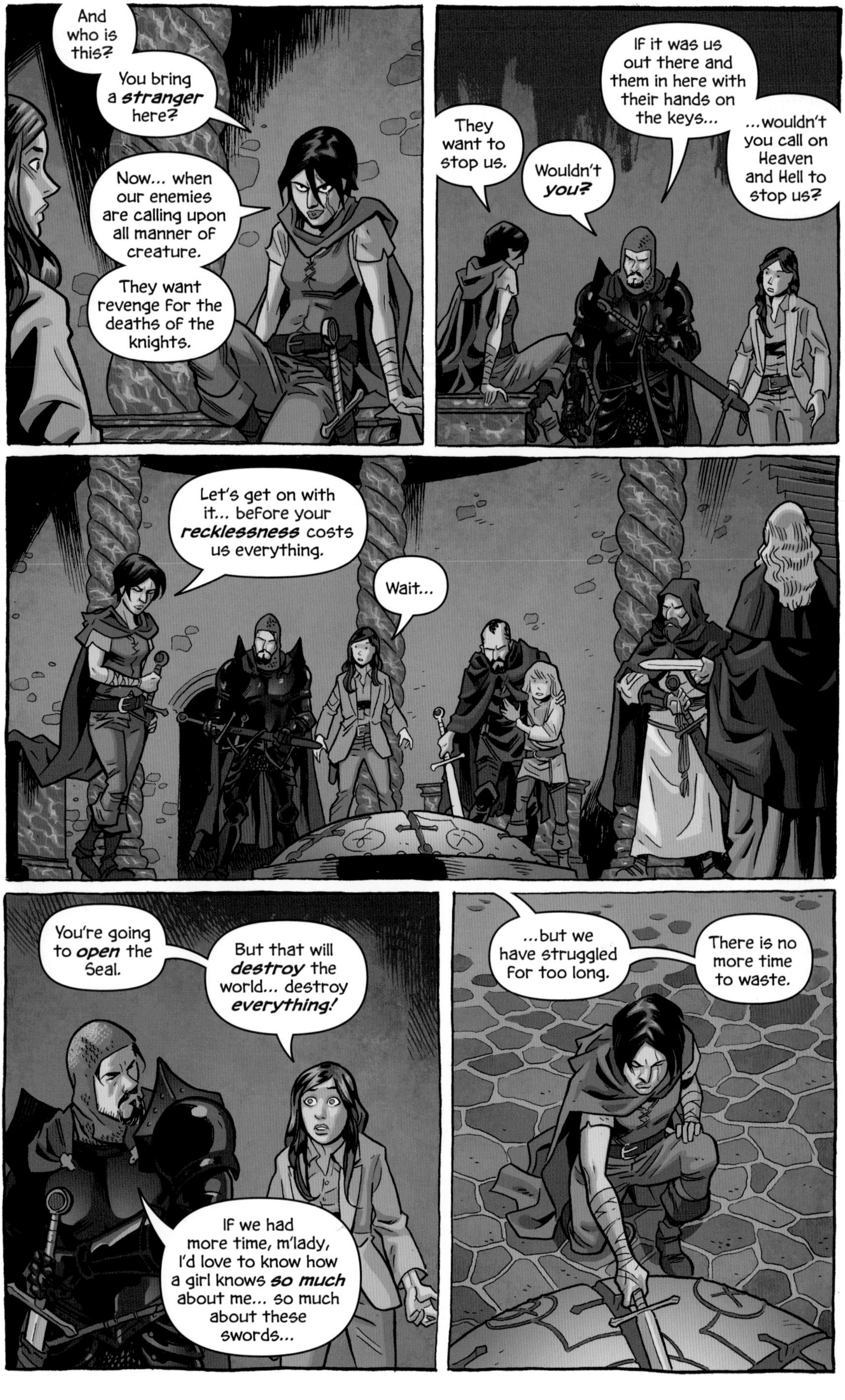
And who is this?
You bring a *stranger* here?
Now... when our enemies are calling upon all manner of creature.
They want revenge for the deaths of the knights.
They want to stop us.
Wouldn't *you?*
If it was us out there and them in here with their hands on the keys...
...wouldn't you call on Heaven and Hell to stop us?
Let's get on with it... before your *recklessness* costs us everything.
Wait...
You're going to *open* the Seal.
But that will *destroy* the world... destroy *everything!*
If we had more time, m'lady, I'd love to know how a girl knows *so much* about me... so much about these swords...
...but we have struggled for too long.
There is no more time to waste.

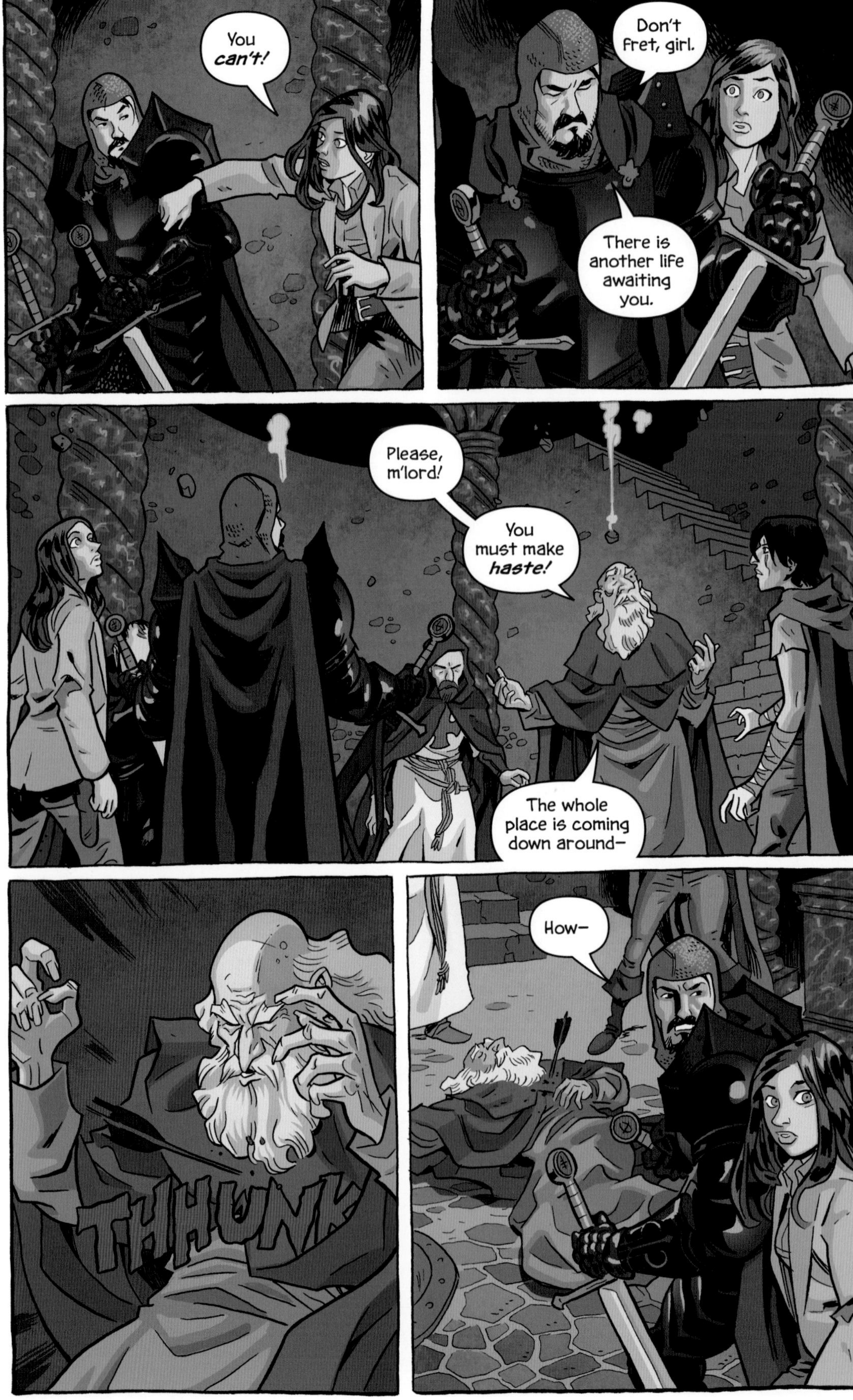
You *can't!*
Don't fret, girl.
There is another life awaiting you.
Please, m'lord!
You must make *haste!*
The whole place is coming down around–
THUNK
How–

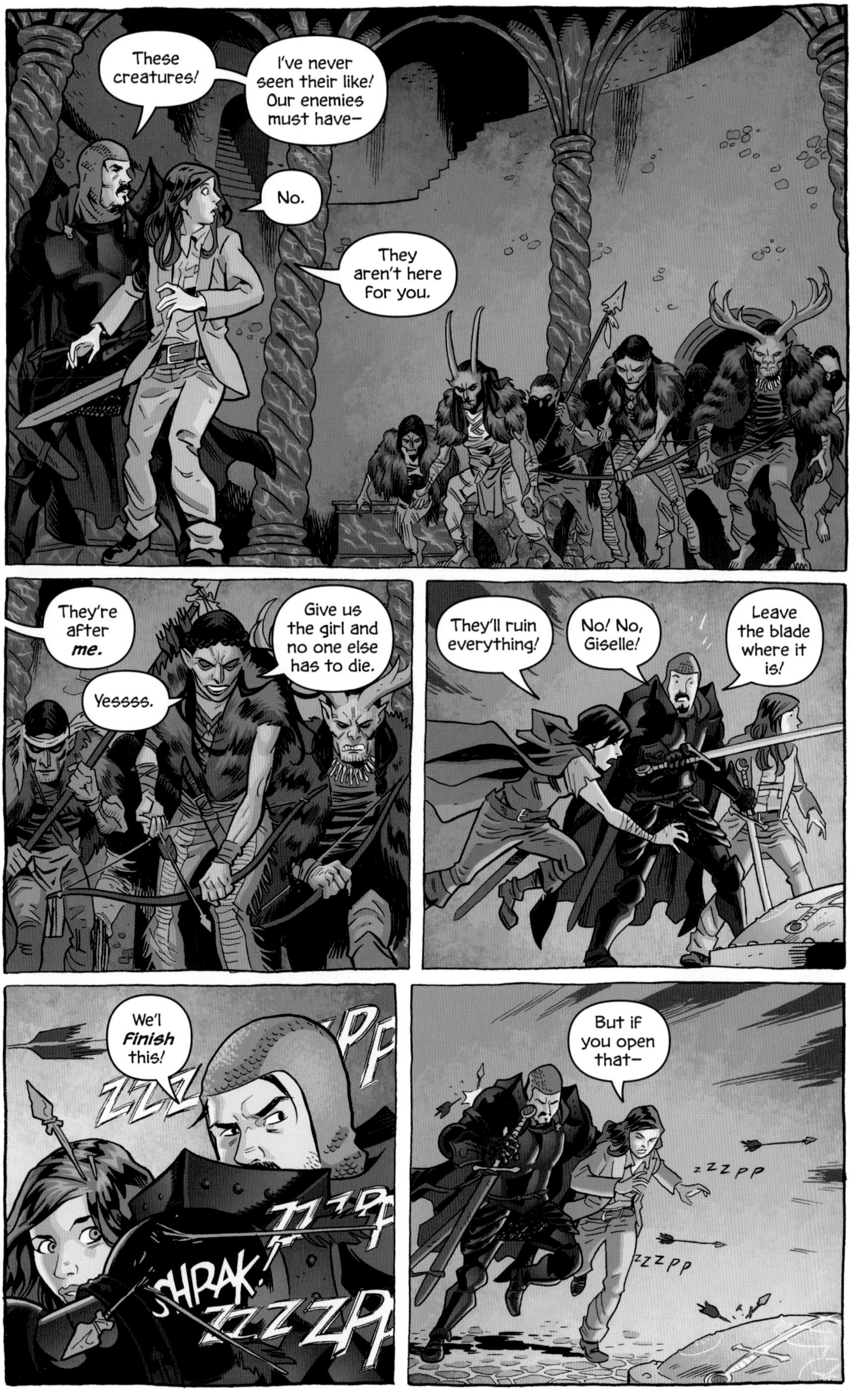
These creatures!
I've never seen their like! Our enemies must have–
No.
They aren't here for you.
They're after *me.*
Give us the girl and no one else has to die.
Yessss.
They'll ruin everything!
No! No, Giselle!
Leave the blade where it is!
We'l *Finish* this!
ZZZ
ZZZ
SHRAK!
ZZZZP
But if you open that–
zzzpp
zzzpp

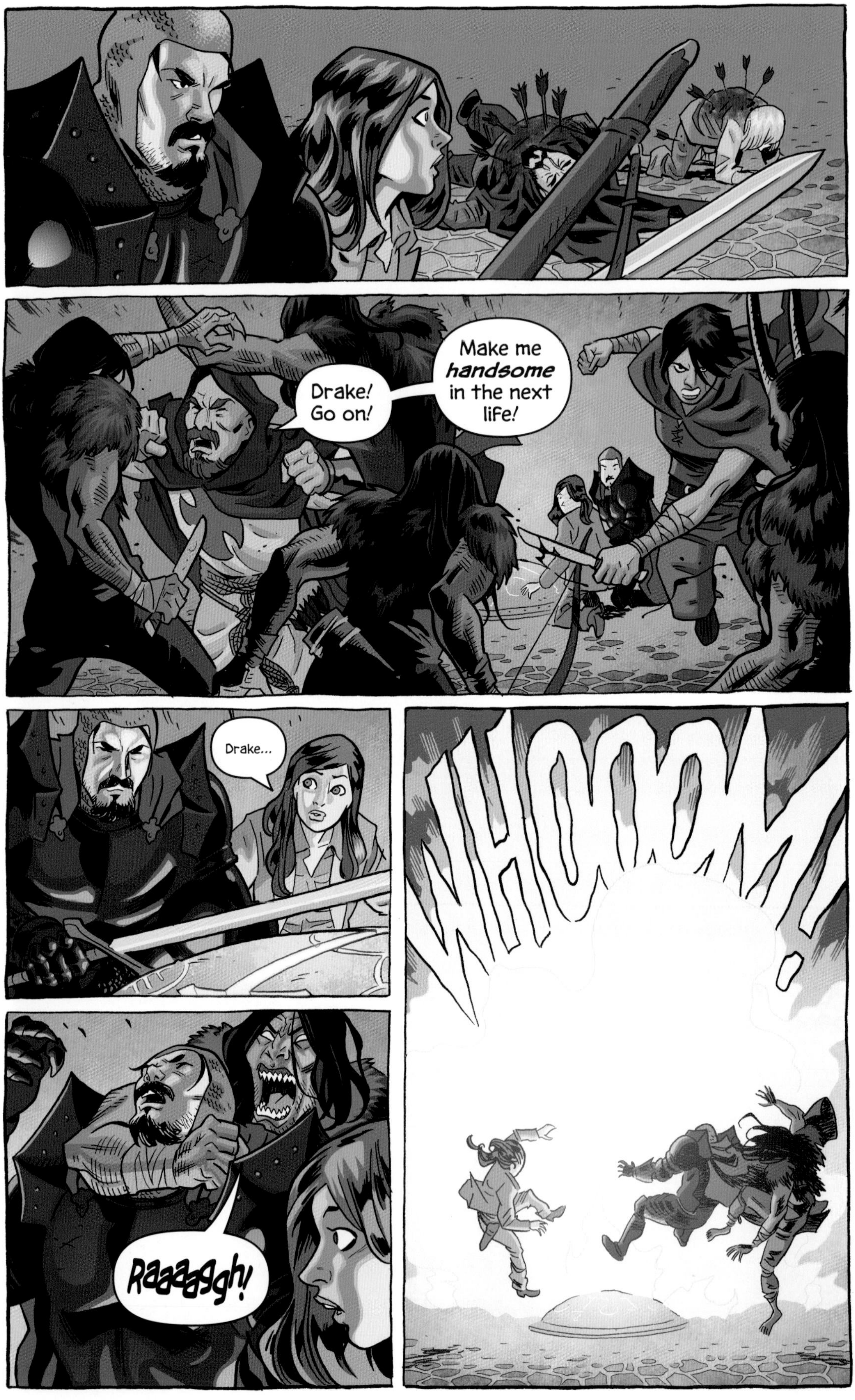
Drake! Go on!
Make me *handsome* in the next life!
Drake...
Raaaagh!
WHOOOM!

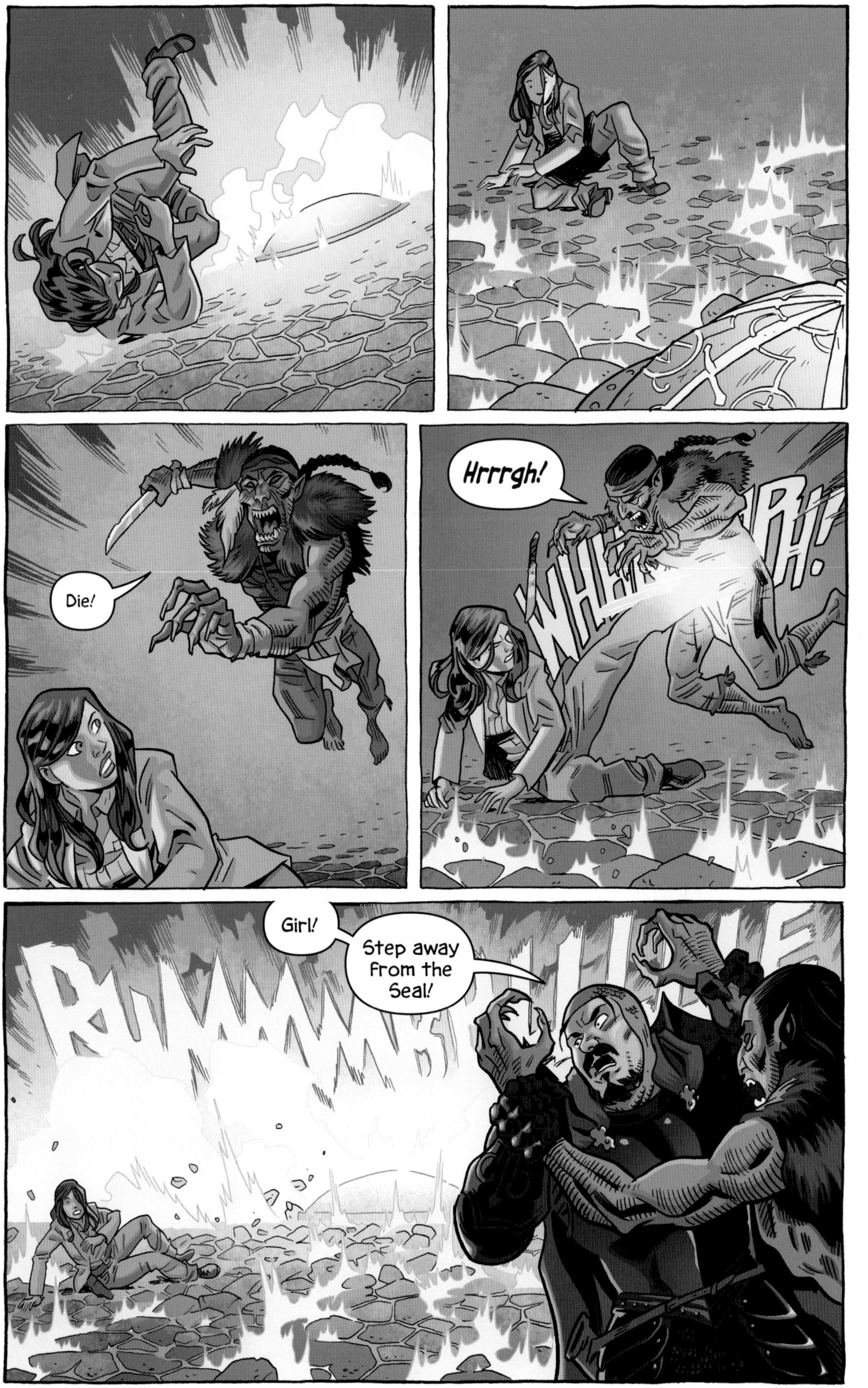

Die!
Hrrrgh!
Girl!
Step away from the Seal!

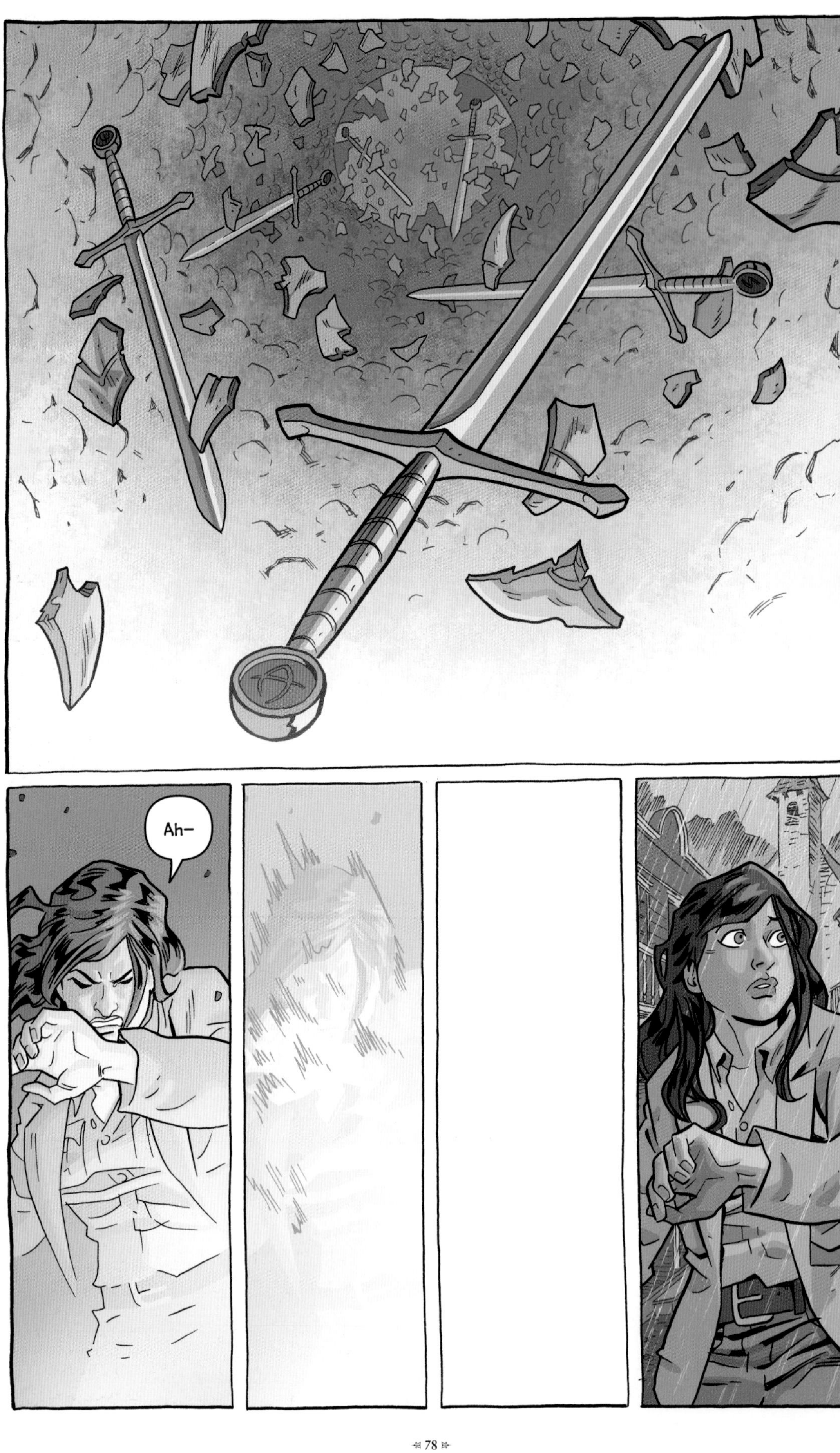
Ah–

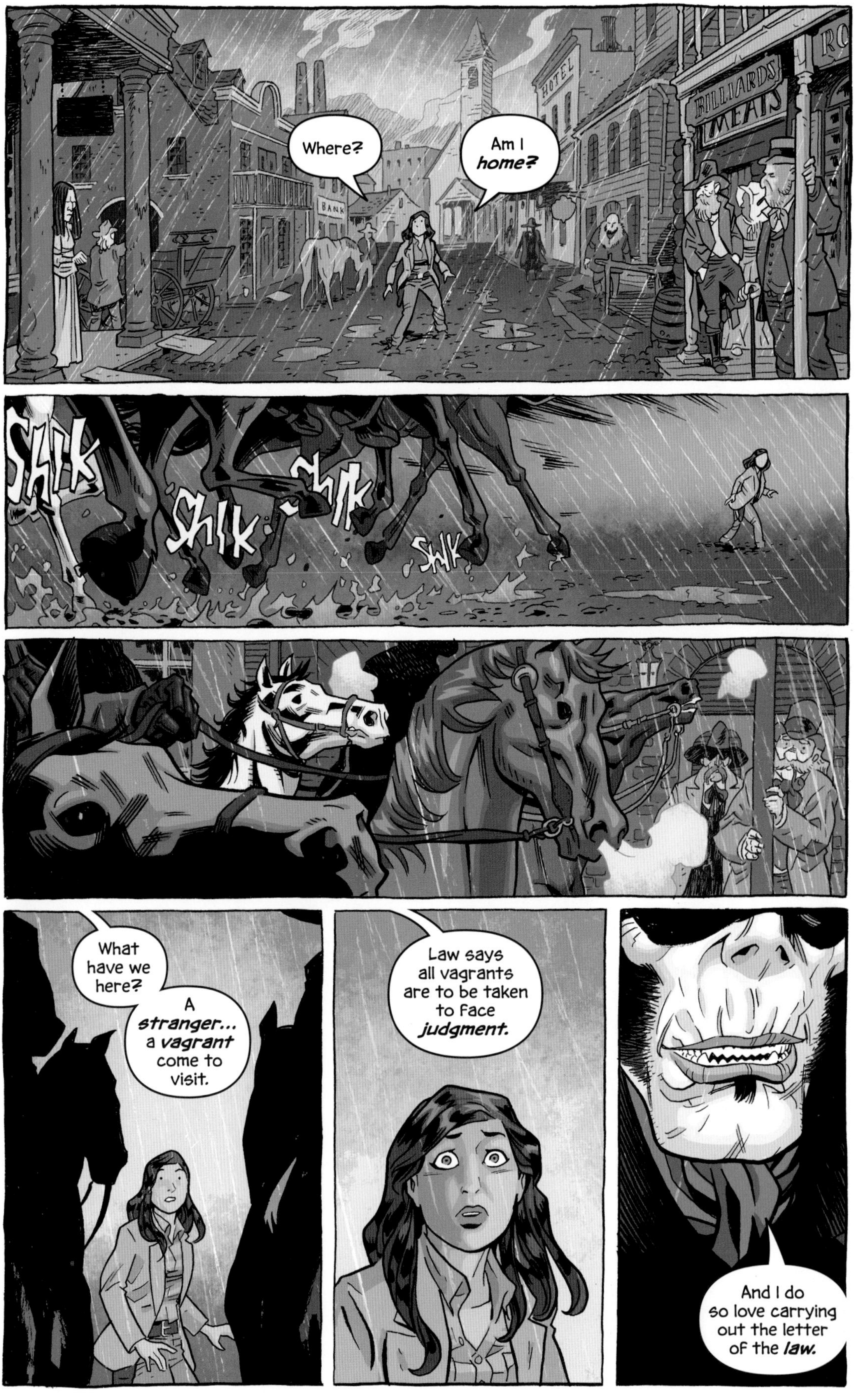

HOTEL
BILLIARDS
MEATS
BANK
Where?
Am I *home?*
SHIK
SHIK
SHIK
SHIK
What have we here?
A *stranger...* a *vagrant* come to visit.
Law says all vagrants are to be taken to face *judgment.*
And I do so love carrying out the letter of the *law.*

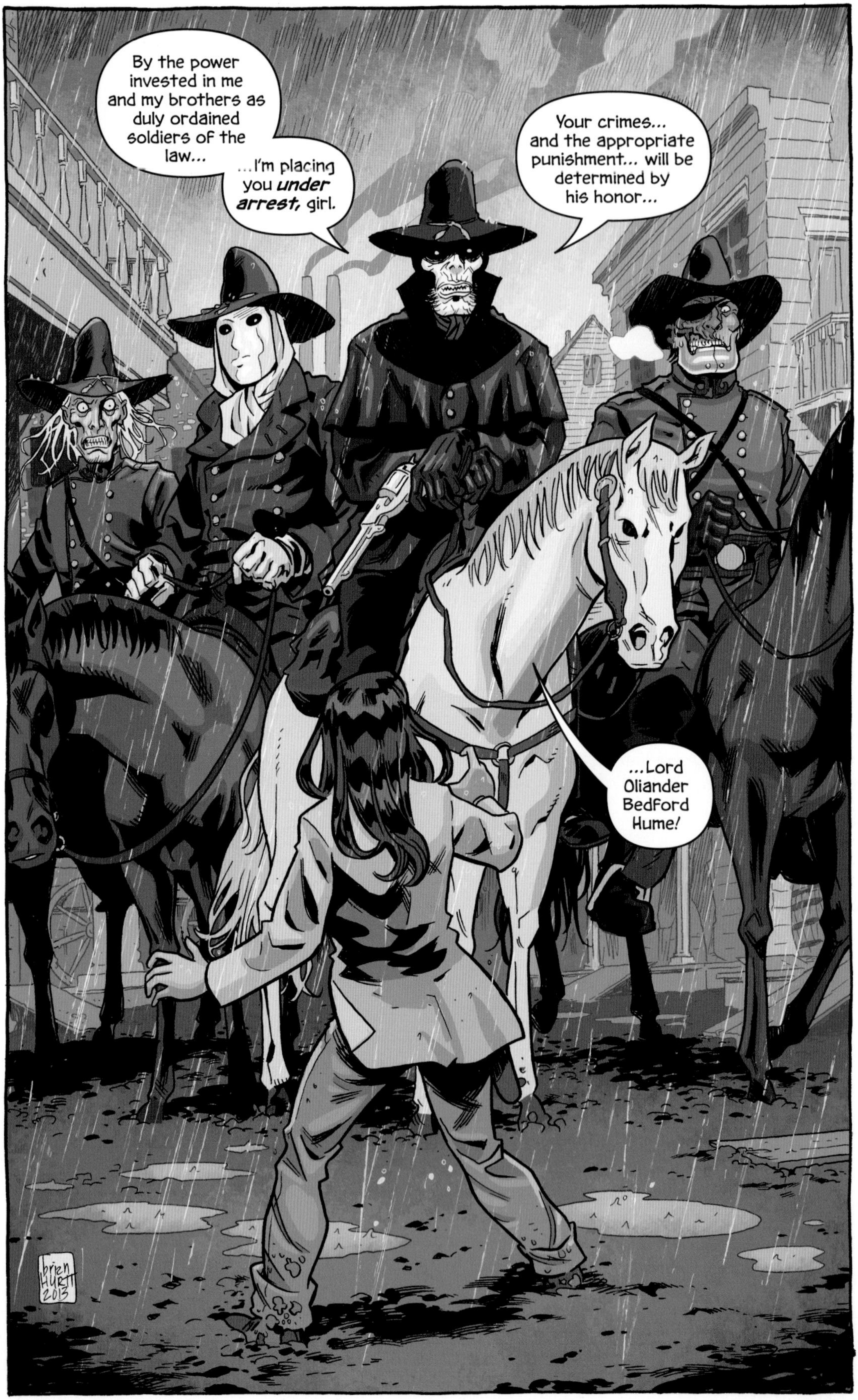

By the power invested in me and my brothers as duly ordained soldiers of the law...
...I'm placing you ***under arrest,*** girl.
Your crimes... and the appropriate punishment... will be determined by his honor...
...Lord Oliander Bedford Hume!
brien HURTT 2013

CHAPTER
FOUR

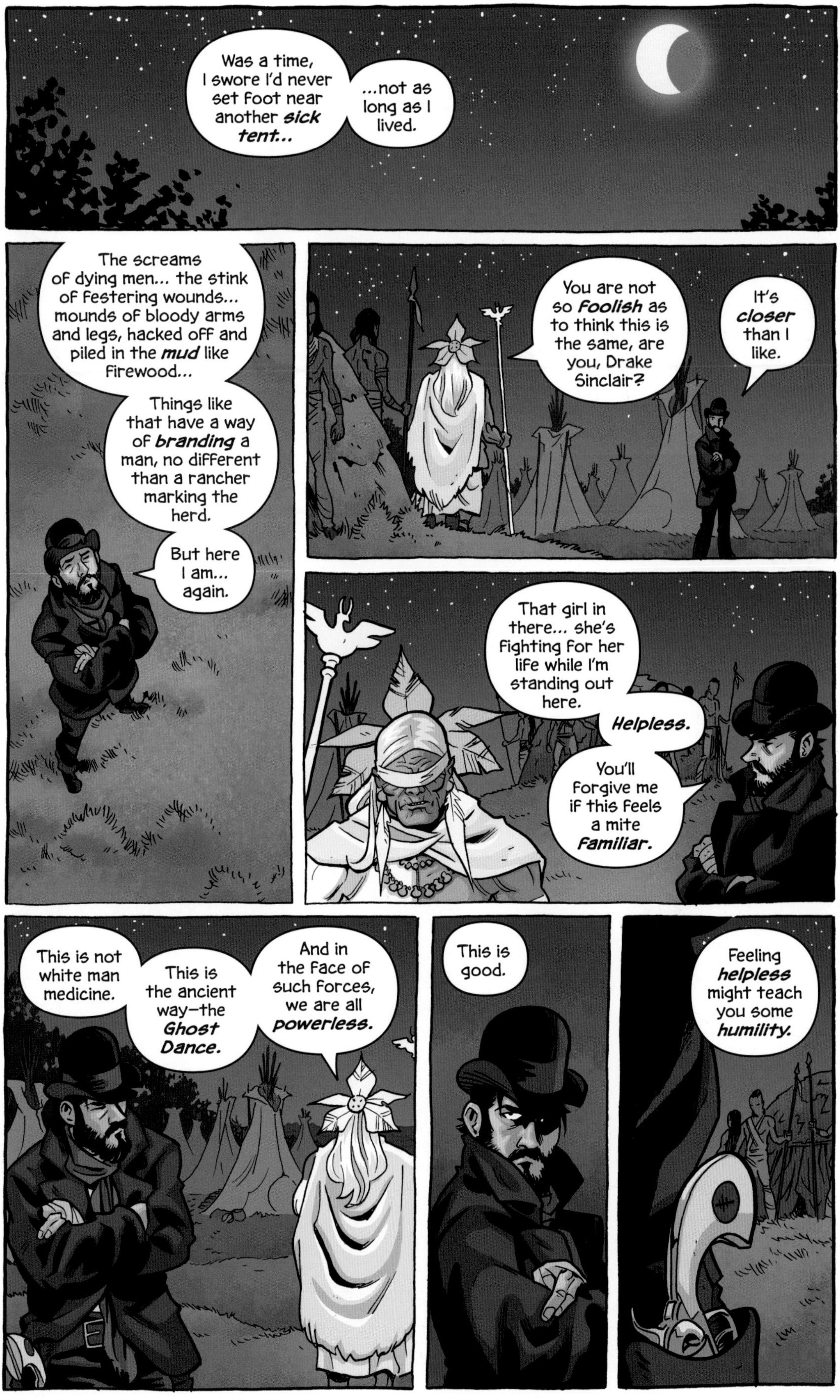

Was a time, I swore I'd never set foot near another *sick tent...*
...not as long as I lived.
The screams of dying men... the stink of festering wounds... mounds of bloody arms and legs, hacked off and piled in the *mud* like firewood...
Things like that have a way of *branding* a man, no different than a rancher marking the herd.
But here I am... again.
You are not so *foolish* as to think this is the same, are you, Drake Sinclair?
It's *closer* than I like.
That girl in there... she's fighting for her life while I'm standing out here.
Helpless.
You'll forgive me if this feels a mite *familiar.*
This is not white man medicine.
This is the ancient way—the *Ghost Dance.*
And in the face of such forces, we are all *powerless.*
This is good.
Feeling *helpless* might teach you some *humility.*

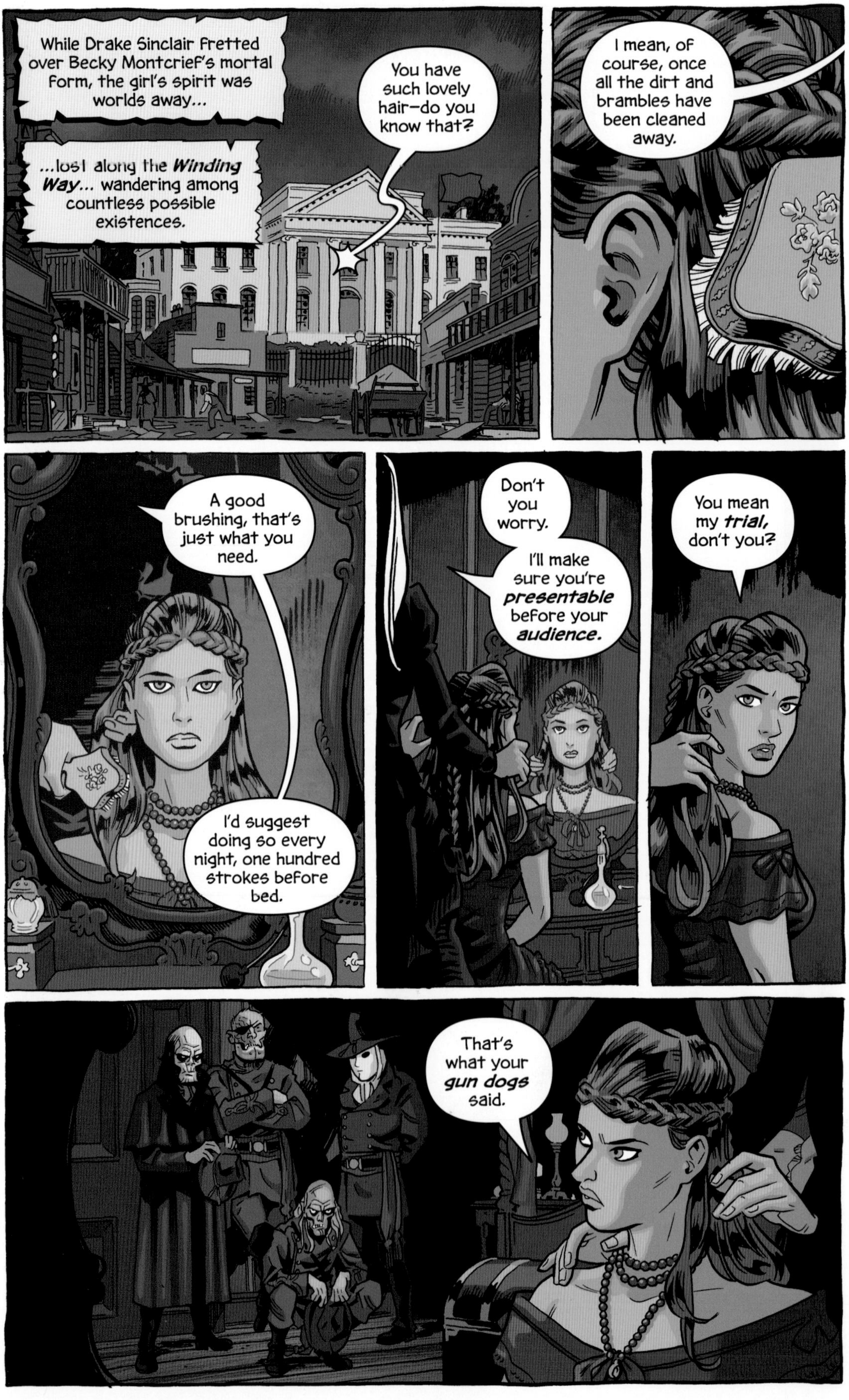

While Drake Sinclair fretted over Becky Montcrief's mortal form, the girl's spirit was worlds away...
...lost along the *Winding Way*... wandering among countless possible existences.
You have such lovely hair—do you know that?
I mean, of course, once all the dirt and brambles have been cleaned away.
A good brushing, that's just what you need.
I'd suggest doing so every night, one hundred strokes before bed.
Don't you worry.
I'll make sure you're *presentable* before your *audience.*
You mean my *trial,* don't you?
That's what your *gun dogs* said.

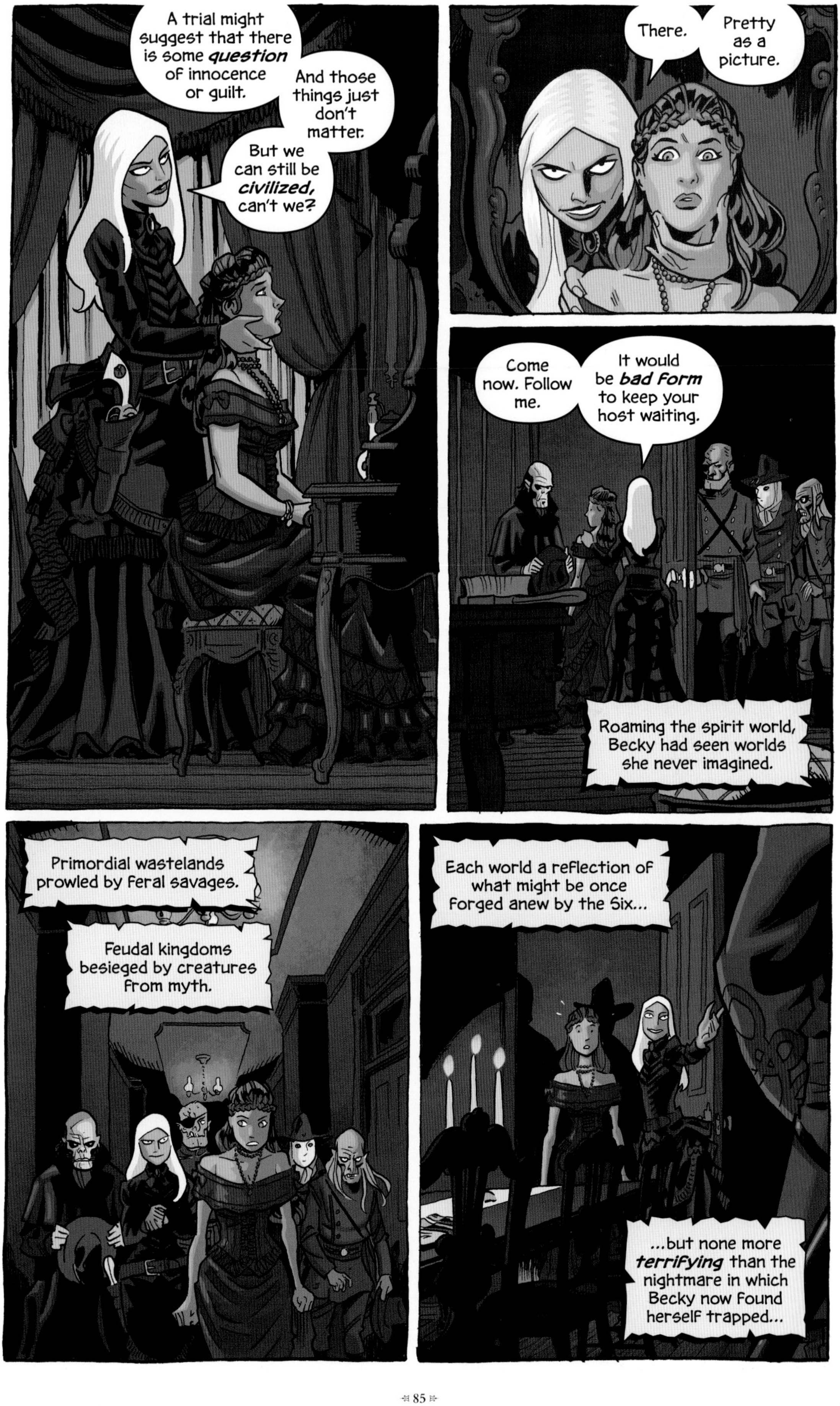
A trial might suggest that there is some *question* of innocence or guilt.
And those things just don't matter.
But we can still be *civilized,* can't we?
There.
Pretty as a picture.
Come now. Follow me.
It would be *bad form* to keep your host waiting.
Roaming the spirit world, Becky had seen worlds she never imagined.
Primordial wastelands prowled by feral savages.
Feudal kingdoms besieged by creatures from myth.
Each world a reflection of what might be once forged anew by the Six...
...but none more *terrifying* than the nightmare in which Becky now found herself trapped...

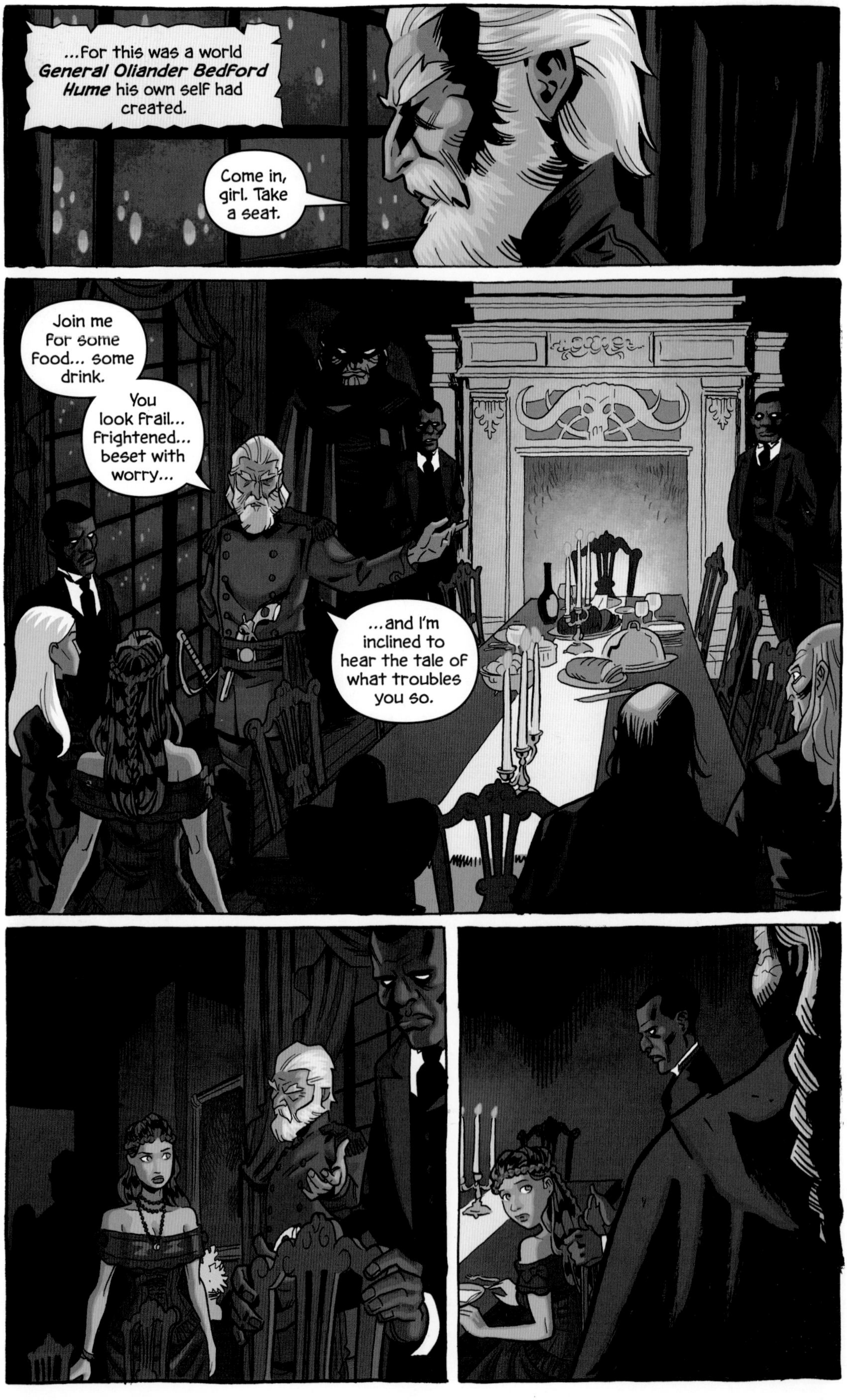
...For this was a world *General Oliander Bedford Hume* his own self had created.
Come in, girl. Take a seat.
Join me for some food... some drink.
You look frail... frightened... beset with worry...
...and I'm inclined to hear the tale of what troubles you so.

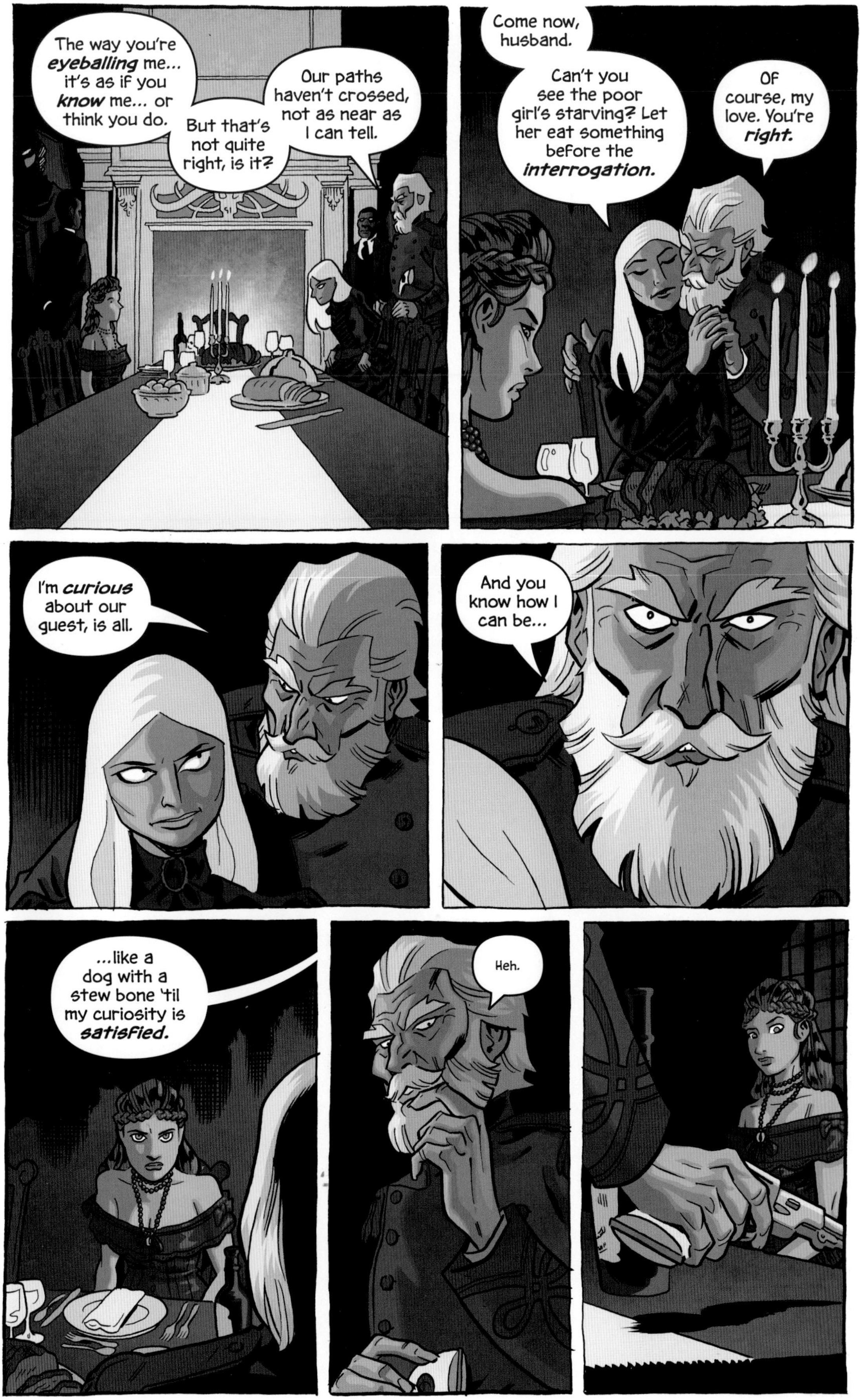
The way you're *eyeballing* me... it's as if you *know* me... or think you do.
But that's not quite right, is it?
Our paths haven't crossed, not as near as I can tell.
Come now, husband.
Can't you see the poor girl's starving? Let her eat something before the *interrogation.*
Of course, my love. You're *right.*
I'm *curious* about our guest, is all.
And you know how I can be...
...like a dog with a stew bone 'til my curiosity is *satisfied.*
Heh.

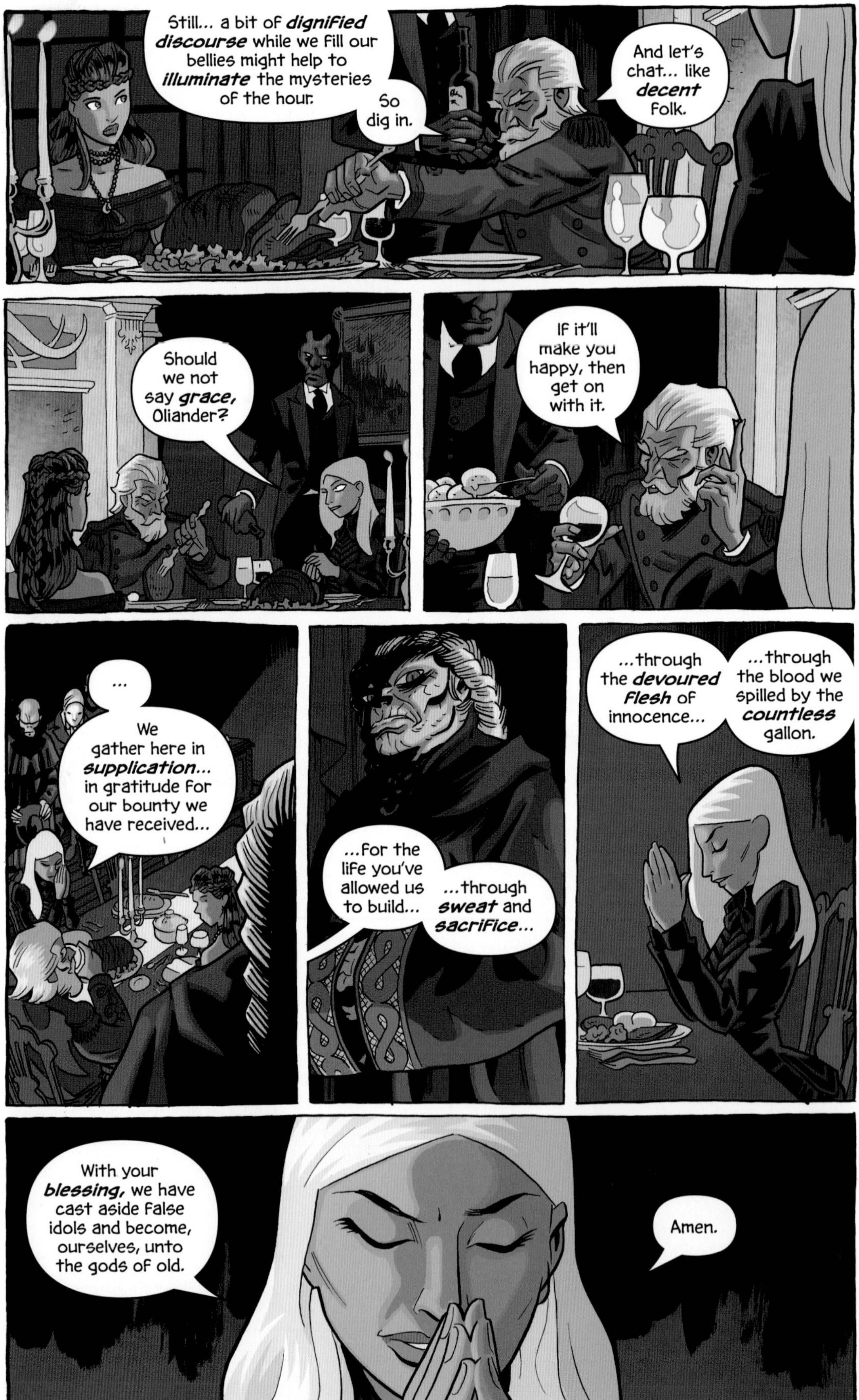

Still... a bit of dignified discourse while we fill our bellies might help to illuminate the mysteries of the hour.
So dig in.
And let's chat... like decent folk.
Should we not say grace, Oliander?
If it'll make you happy, then get on with it.
...
We gather here in supplication... in gratitude for our bounty we have received...
...for the life you've allowed us to build...
...through sweat and sacrifice...
...through the devoured flesh of innocence...
...through the blood we spilled by the countless gallon.
With your blessing, we have cast aside false idols and become, ourselves, unto the gods of old.
Amen.

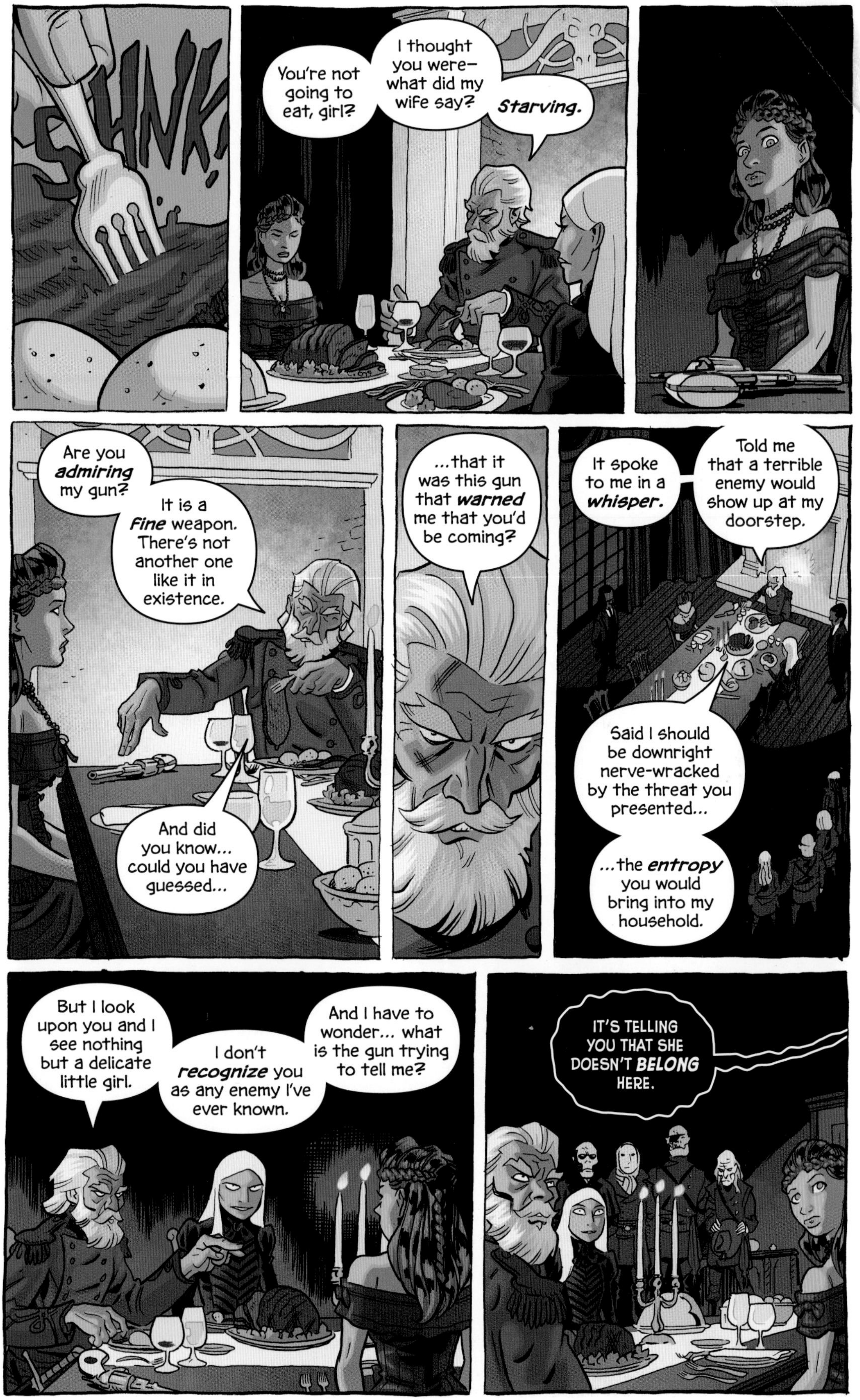
SHUNK!
You're not going to eat, girl?
I thought you were— what did my wife say?
Starving.
Are you admiring my gun?
It is a fine weapon. There's not another one like it in existence.
And did you know... could you have guessed...
...that it was this gun that warned me that you'd be coming?
It spoke to me in a whisper.
Told me that a terrible enemy would show up at my doorstep.
Said I should be downright nerve-wracked by the threat you presented...
...the entropy you would bring into my household.
But I look upon you and I see nothing but a delicate little girl.
I don't recognize you as any enemy I've ever known.
And I have to wonder... what is the gun trying to tell me?
IT'S TELLING YOU THAT SHE DOESN'T BELONG HERE.

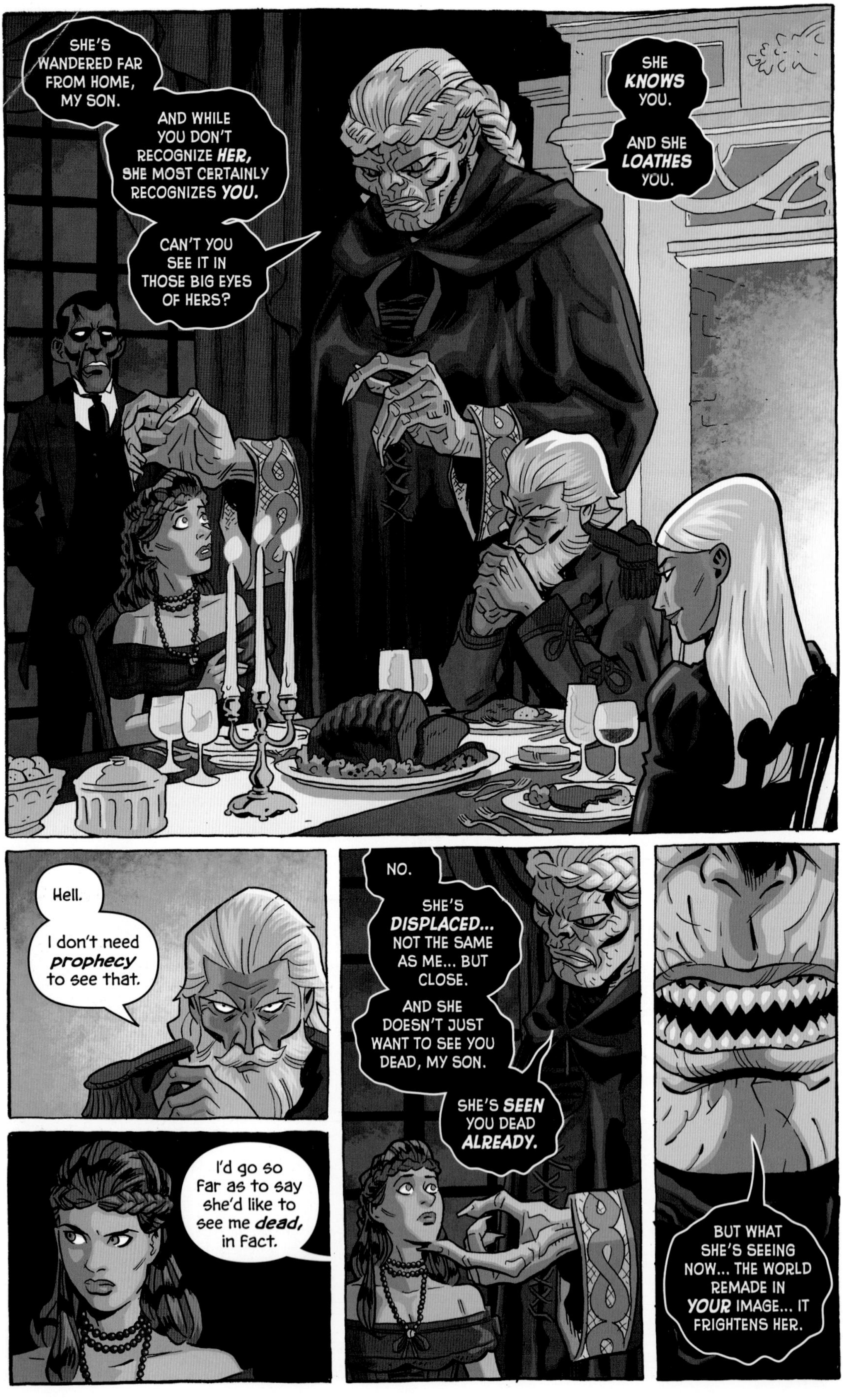
SHE'S WANDERED FAR FROM HOME, MY SON.
AND WHILE YOU DON'T RECOGNIZE HER, SHE MOST CERTAINLY RECOGNIZES YOU.
CAN'T YOU SEE IT IN THOSE BIG EYES OF HERS?
SHE KNOWS YOU.
AND SHE LOATHES YOU.
Hell.
I don't need prophecy to see that.
I'd go so far as to say she'd like to see me dead, in fact.
NO.
SHE'S DISPLACED... NOT THE SAME AS ME... BUT CLOSE.
AND SHE DOESN'T JUST WANT TO SEE YOU DEAD, MY SON.
SHE'S SEEN YOU DEAD ALREADY.
BUT WHAT SHE'S SEEING NOW... THE WORLD REMADE IN YOUR IMAGE... IT FRIGHTENS HER.

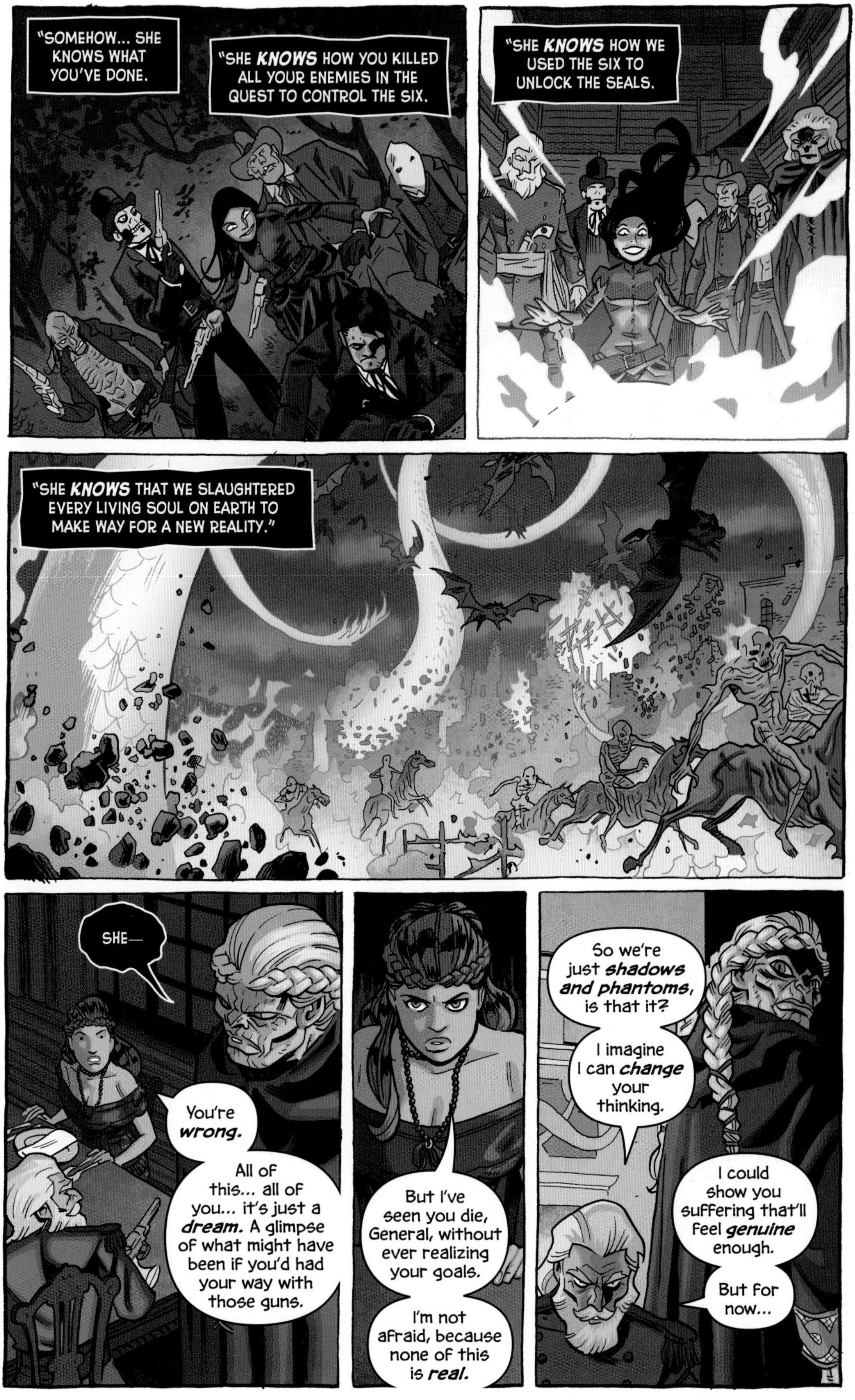
"SOMEHOW... SHE KNOWS WHAT YOU'VE DONE.
"SHE KNOWS HOW YOU KILLED ALL YOUR ENEMIES IN THE QUEST TO CONTROL THE SIX.
"SHE KNOWS HOW WE USED THE SIX TO UNLOCK THE SEALS.
"SHE KNOWS THAT WE SLAUGHTERED EVERY LIVING SOUL ON EARTH TO MAKE WAY FOR A NEW REALITY."
SHE—
You're wrong.
All of this... all of you... it's just a dream. A glimpse of what might have been if you'd had your way with those guns.
But I've seen you die, General, without ever realizing your goals.
I'm not afraid, because none of this is real.
So we're just shadows and phantoms, is that it?
I imagine I can change your thinking.
I could show you suffering that'll feel genuine enough.
But for now...

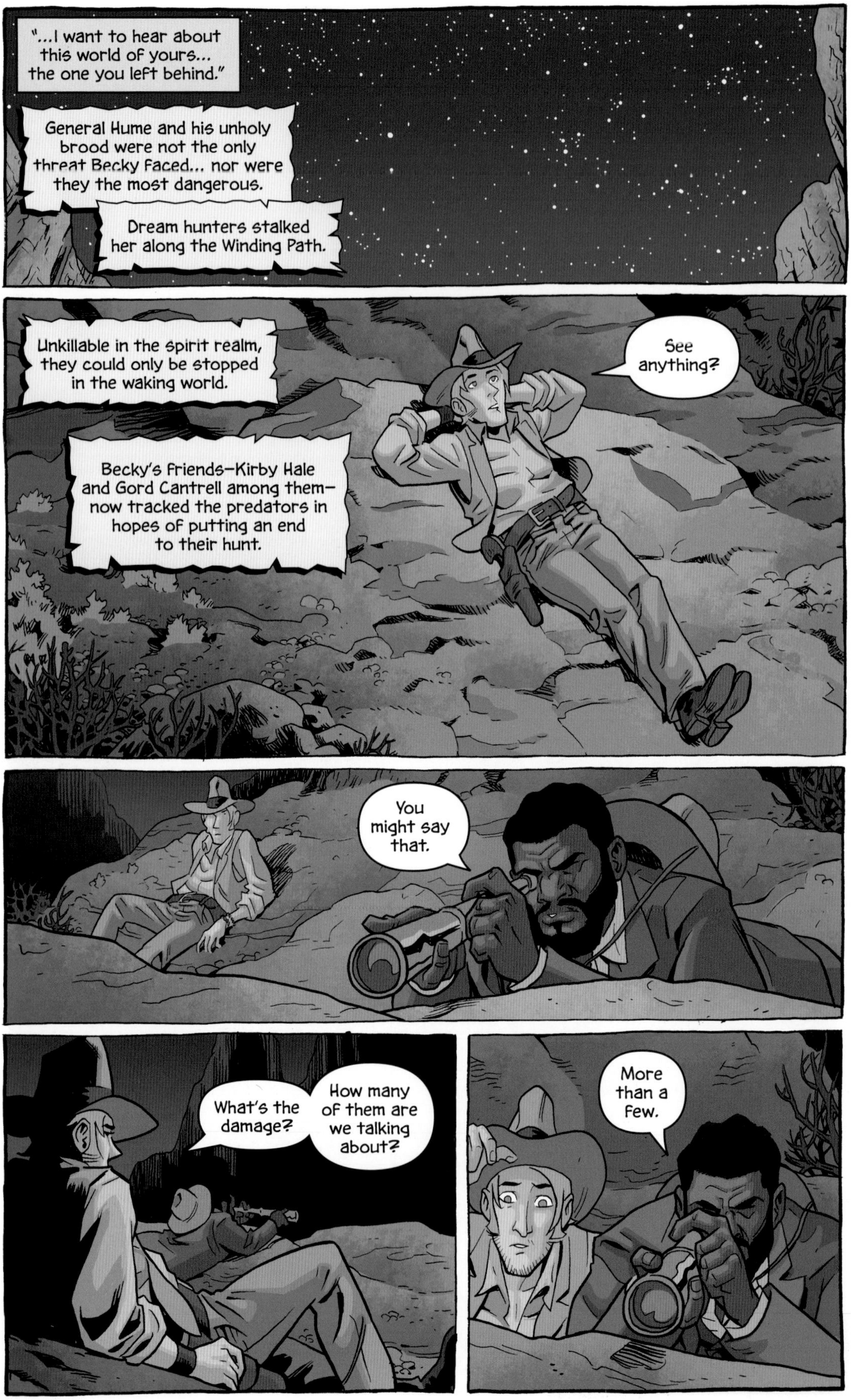
"...I want to hear about this world of yours... the one you left behind."
General Hume and his unholy brood were not the only threat Becky faced... nor were they the most dangerous.
Dream hunters stalked her along the Winding Path.
Unkillable in the spirit realm, they could only be stopped in the waking world.
Becky's friends—Kirby Hale and Gord Cantrell among them—now tracked the predators in hopes of putting an end to their hunt.
See anything?
You might say that.
What's the damage?
How many of them are we talking about?
More than a few.

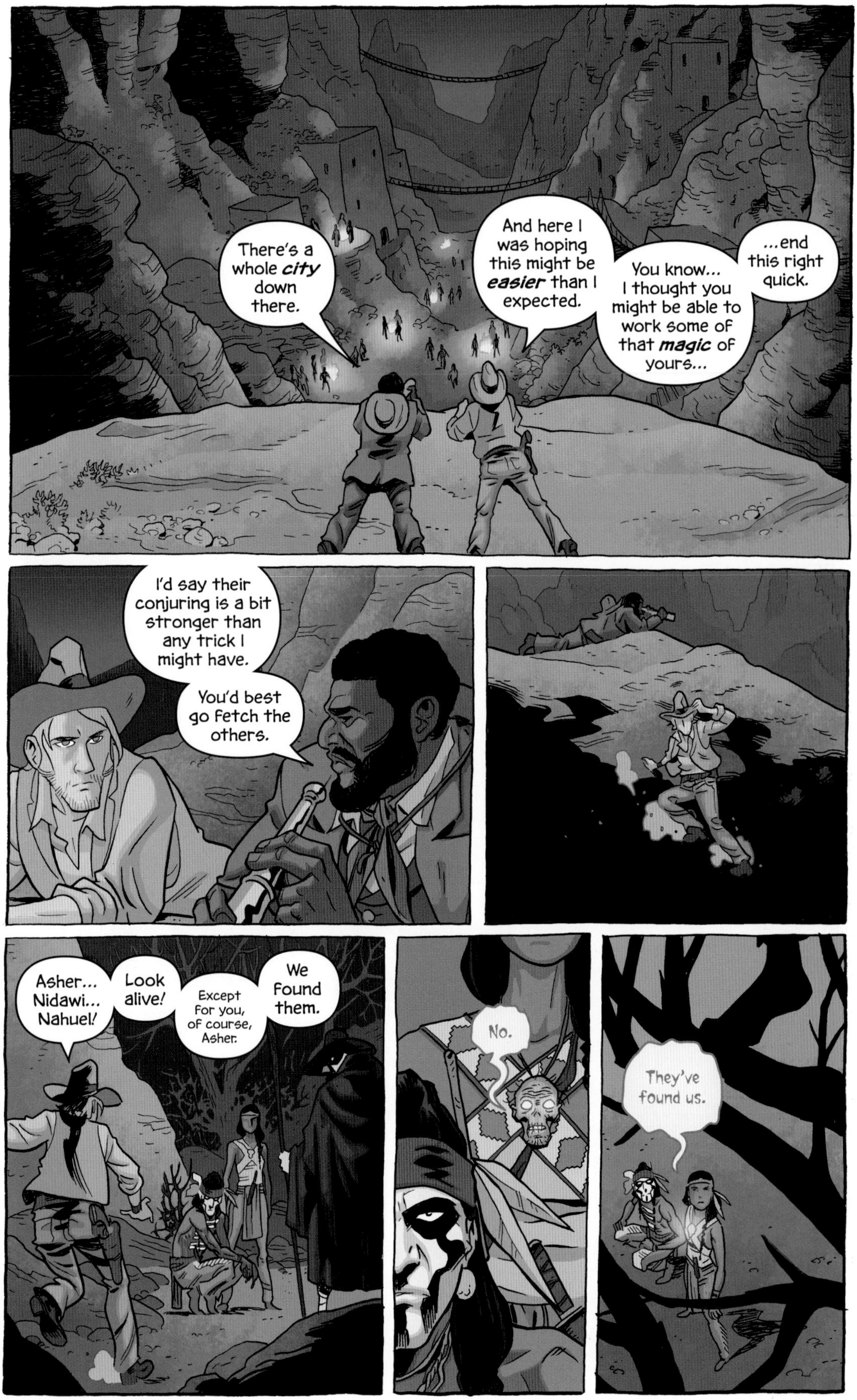
There's a whole *city* down there.
And here I was hoping this might be *easier* than I expected.
You know... I thought you might be able to work some of that *magic* of yours...
...end this right quick.
I'd say their conjuring is a bit stronger than any trick I might have.
You'd best go fetch the others.
Asher... Nidawi... Nahuel!
Look alive!
Except for you, of course, Asher.
We found them.
No.
They've found us.

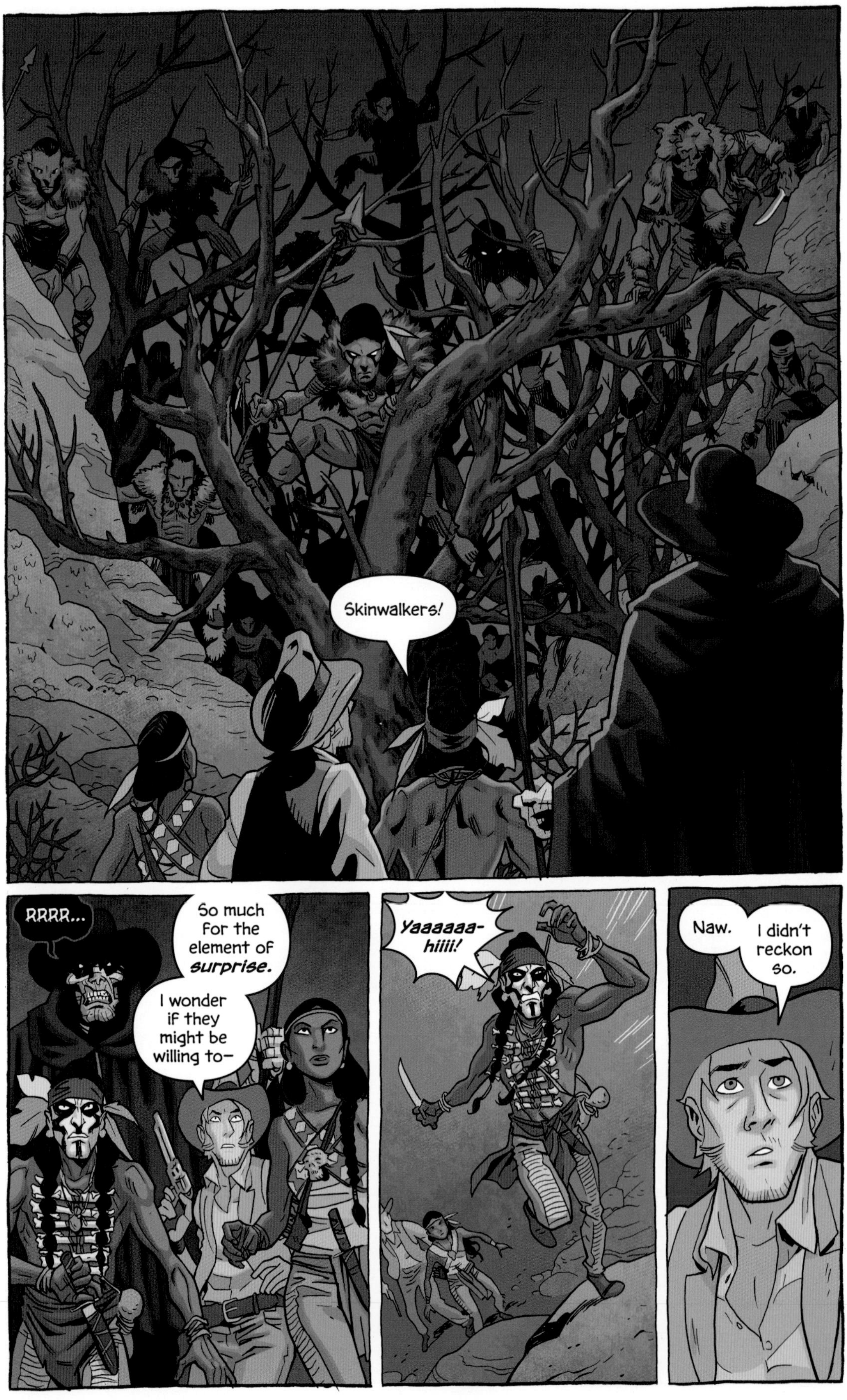
Skinwalkers!
RRRR...
So much for the element of *surprise.*
I wonder if they might be willing to–
Yaaaaaa-hiiii!
Naw.
I didn't reckon so.

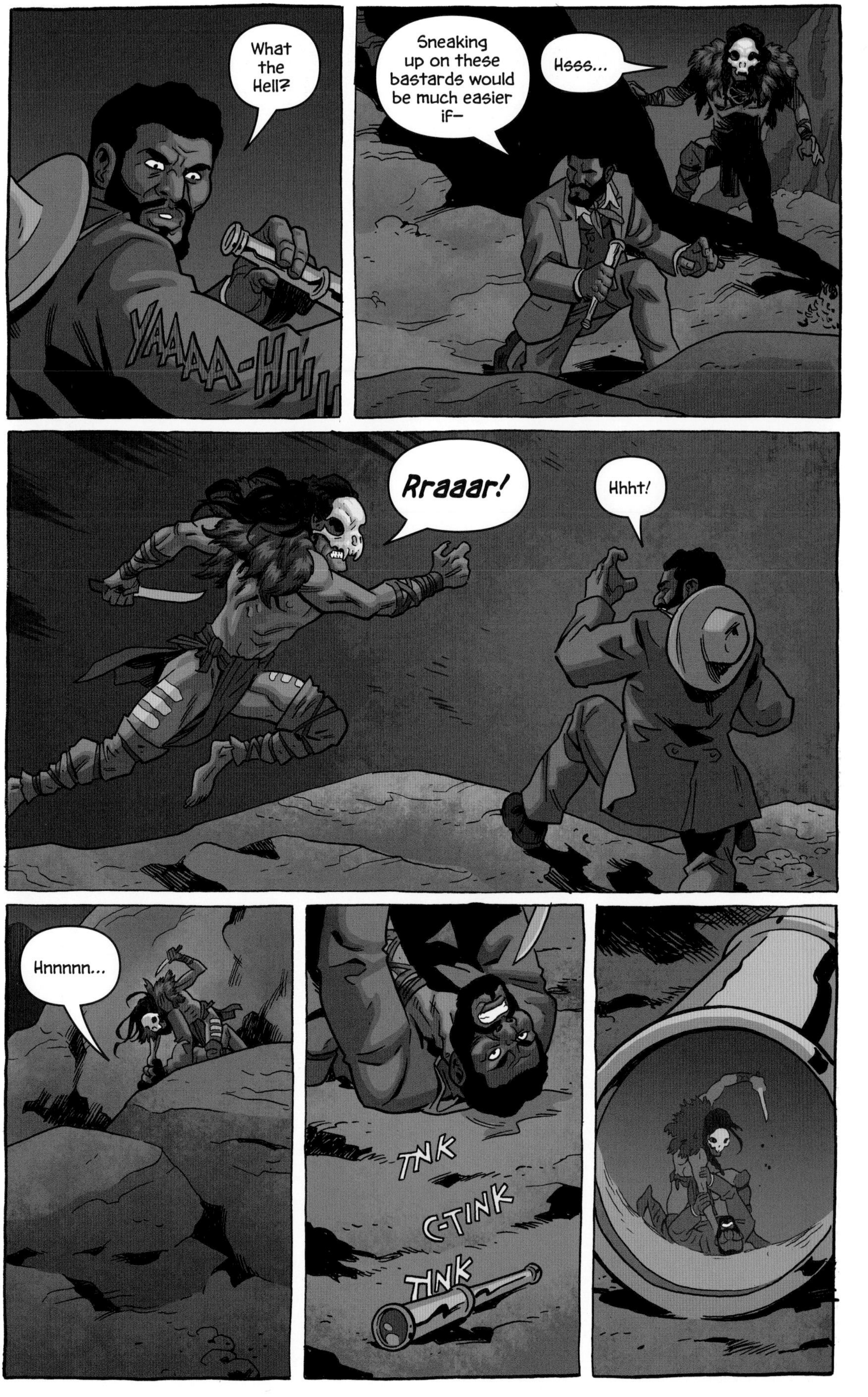

What the Hell?
YAAAA-HIII
Sneaking up on these bastards would be much easier if—
Hsss...
Rraaar!
Hhht!
Hnnnnn...
TNK
C-TINK
TNK

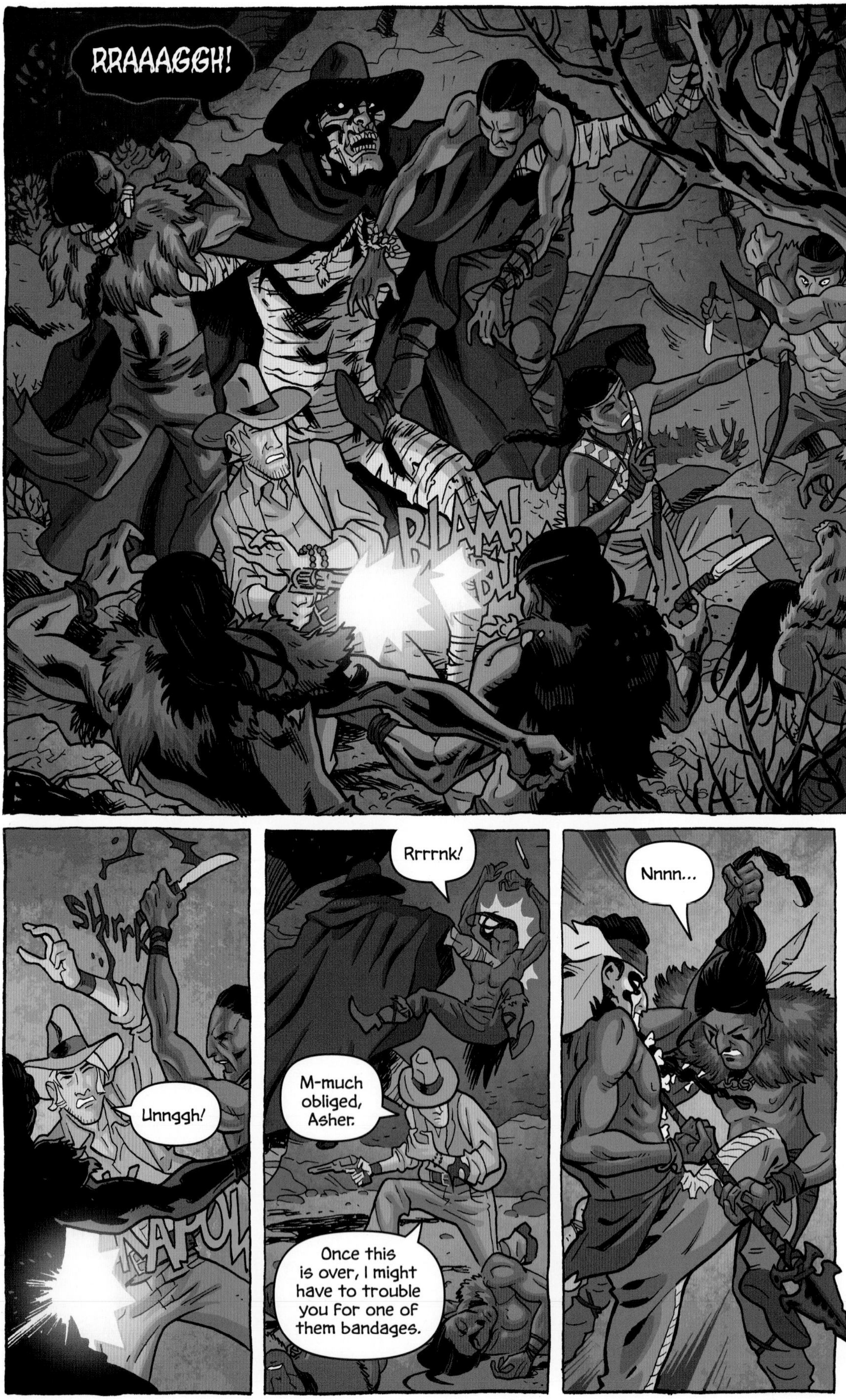
RRAAAGGH!
Unnggh!
Rrrrnk!
M-much obliged, Asher.
Once this is over, I might have to trouble you for one of them bandages.
Nnnn...

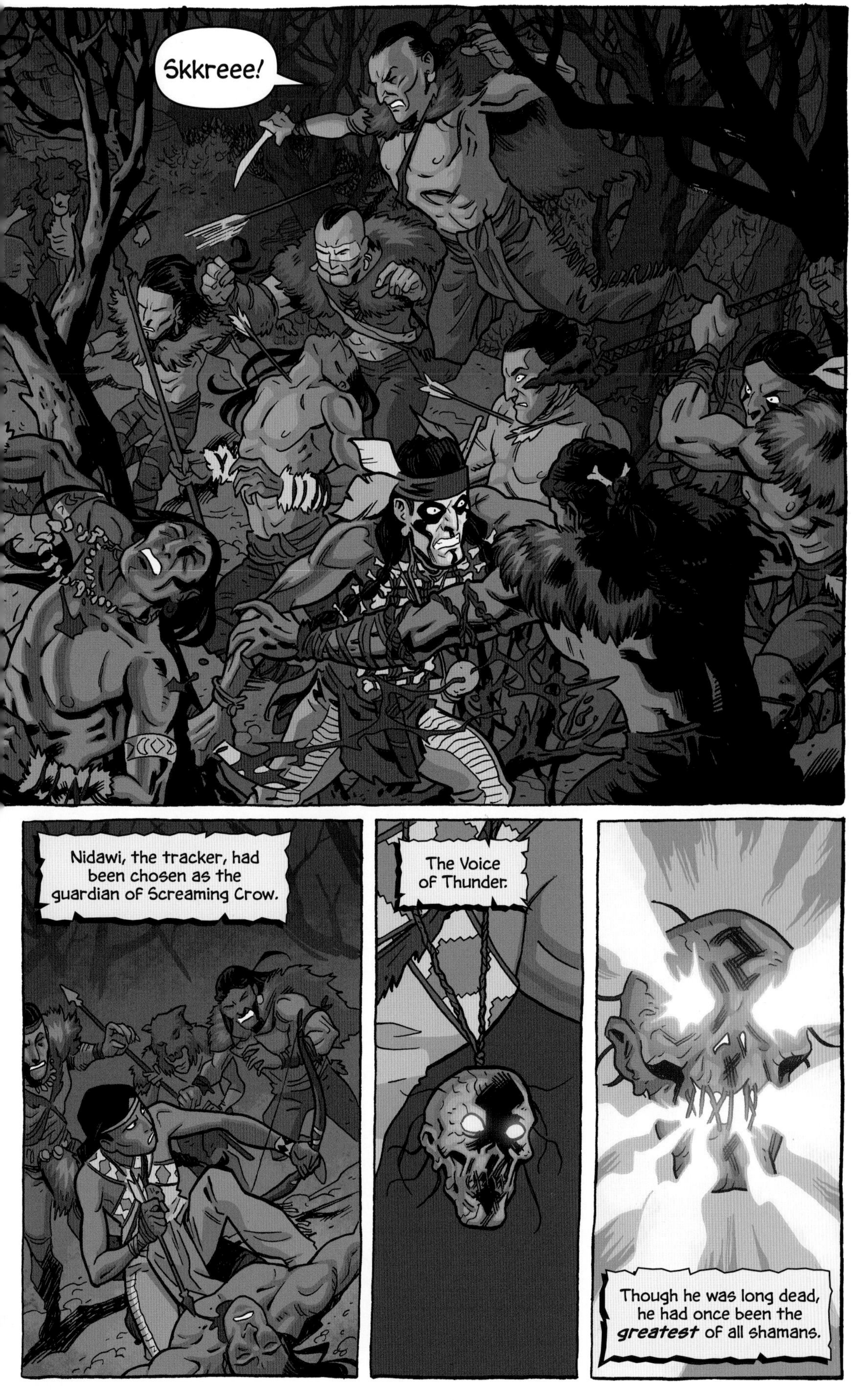
Skkreee!
Nidawi, the tracker, had been chosen as the guardian of Screaming Crow.
The Voice of Thunder.
Though he was long dead, he had once been the *greatest* of all shamans.

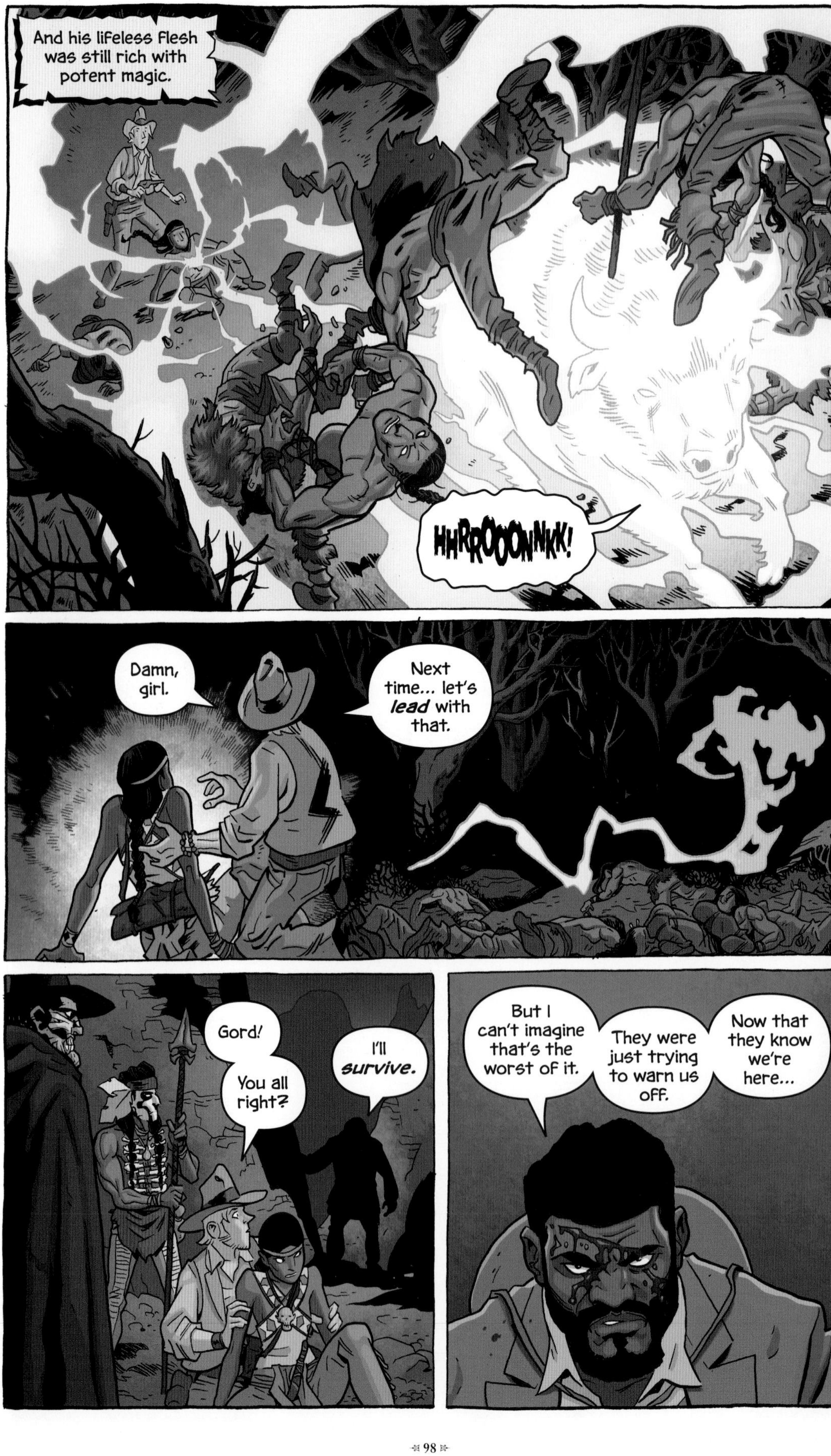
And his lifeless Flesh was still rich with potent magic.
HHRROOONNKK!
Damn, girl.
Next time... let's *lead* with that.
Gord!
You all right?
I'll *survive.*
But I can't imagine that's the worst of it.
They were just trying to warn us off.
Now that they know we're here...

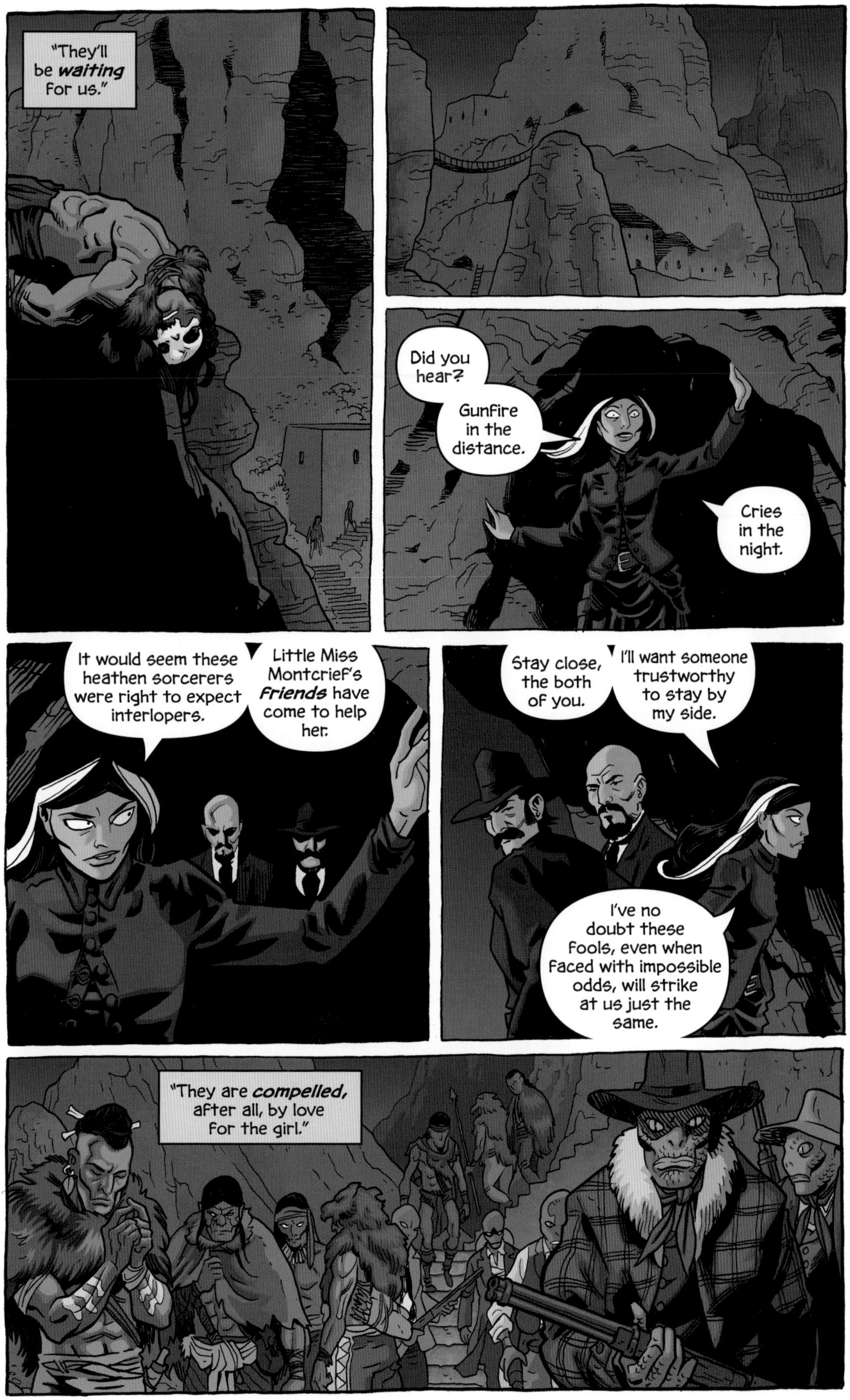
"They'll be *waiting* for us."
Did you hear?
Gunfire in the distance.
Cries in the night.
It would seem these heathen sorcerers were right to expect interlopers.
Little Miss Montcrief's *Friends* have come to help her.
Stay close, the both of you.
I'll want someone trustworthy to stay by my side.
I've no doubt these fools, even when faced with impossible odds, will strike at us just the same.
"They are *compelled*, after all, by love for the girl."

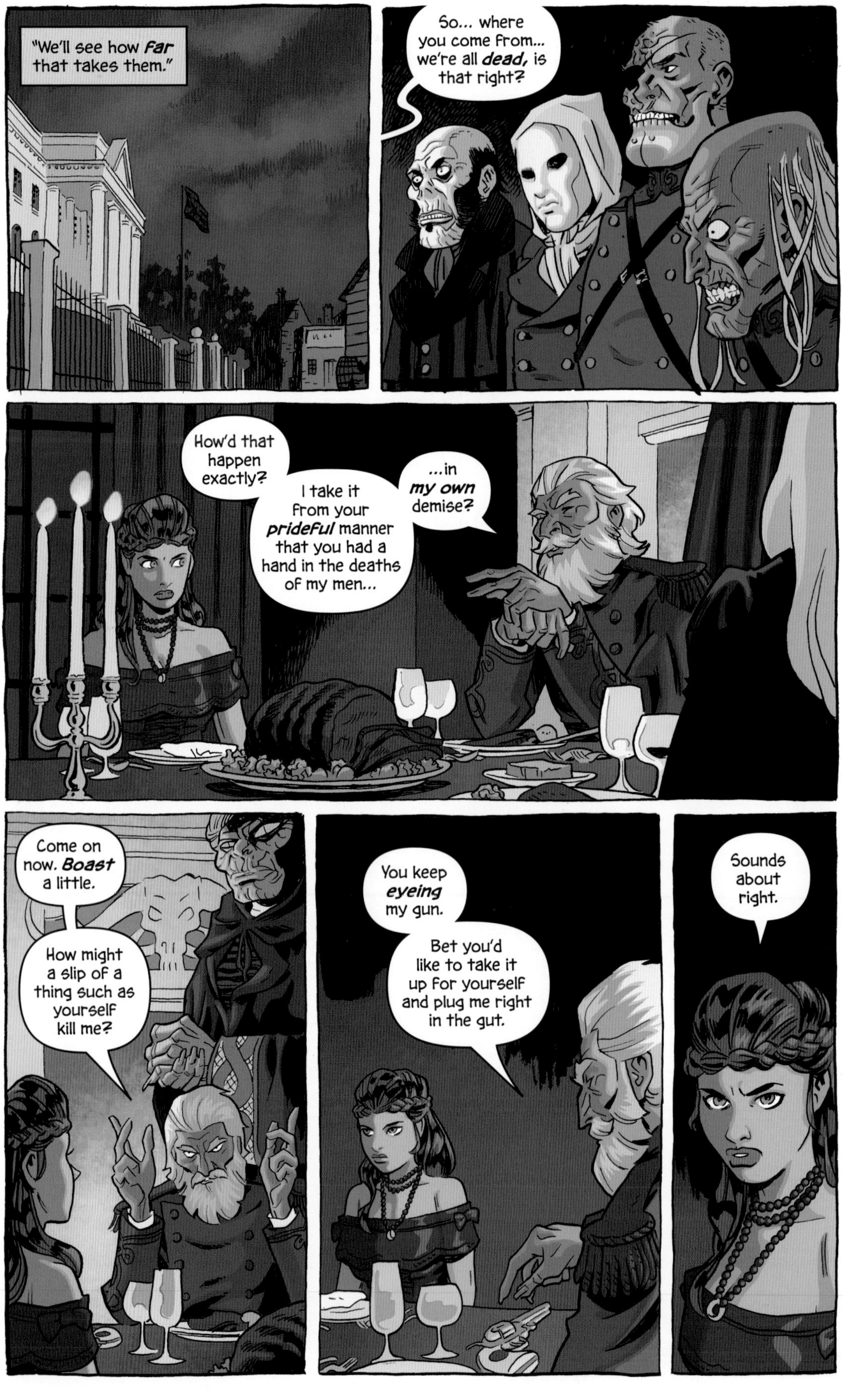
"We'll see how *far* that takes them."
So... where you come from... we're all *dead,* is that right?
How'd that happen exactly?
I take it from your *prideful* manner that you had a hand in the deaths of my men...
...in *my own* demise?
Come on now. *Boast* a little.
How might a slip of a thing such as yourself kill me?
You keep *eyeing* my gun.
Bet you'd like to take it up for yourself and plug me right in the gut.
Sounds about right.

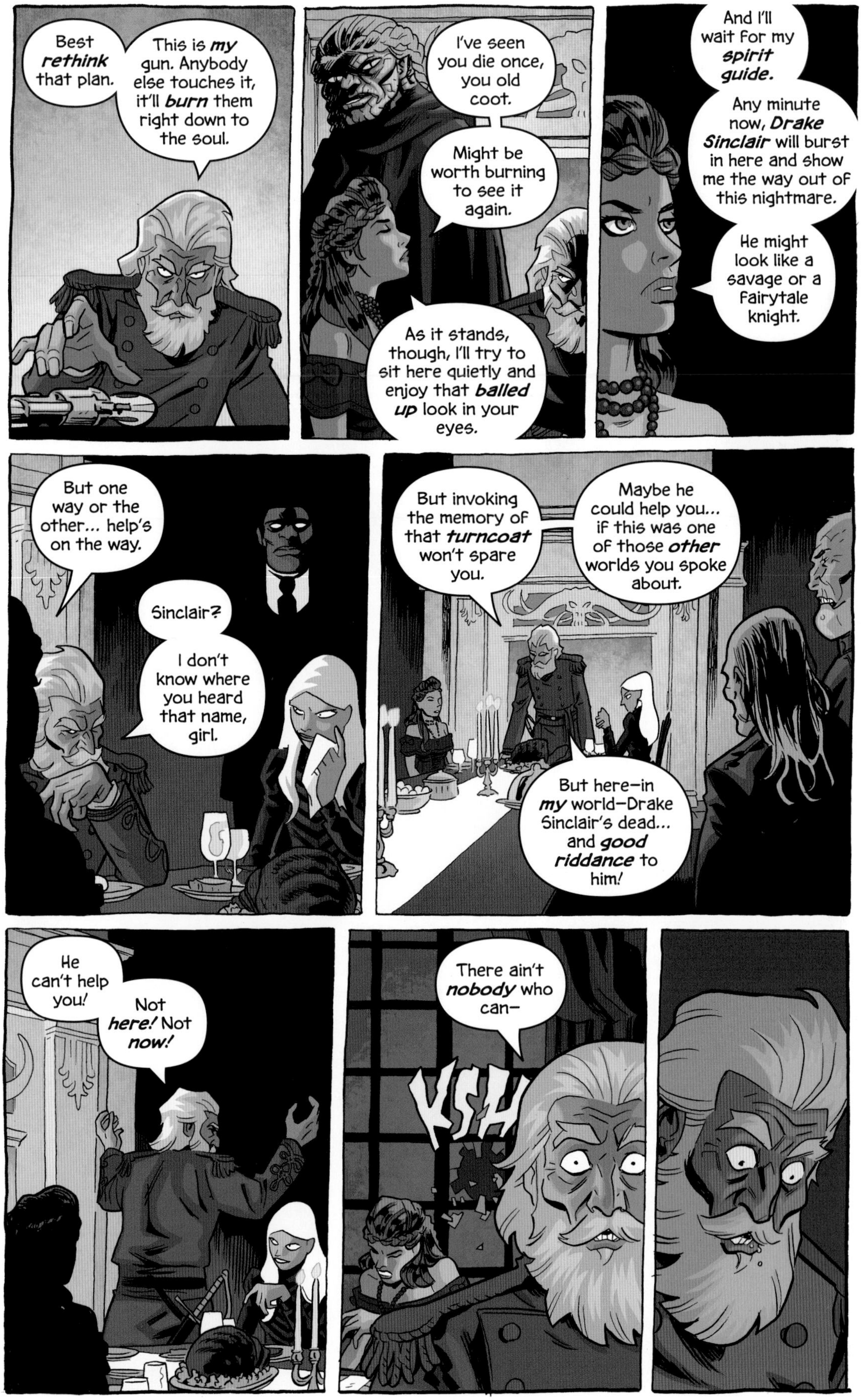
Best *rethink* that plan.
This is *my* gun. Anybody else touches it, it'll *burn* them right down to the soul.
I've seen you die once, you old coot.
Might be worth burning to see it again.
As it stands, though, I'll try to sit here quietly and enjoy that *balled up* look in your eyes.
And I'll wait for my *spirit guide.*
Any minute now, *Drake Sinclair* will burst in here and show me the way out of this nightmare.
He might look like a savage or a fairytale knight.
But one way or the other... help's on the way.
Sinclair?
I don't know where you heard that name, girl.
But invoking the memory of that *turncoat* won't spare you.
Maybe he could help you... if this was one of those *other* worlds you spoke about.
But here—in *my* world—Drake Sinclair's dead... and *good riddance* to him!
He can't help you!
Not *here!* Not *now!*
There ain't *nobody* who can—
KSH

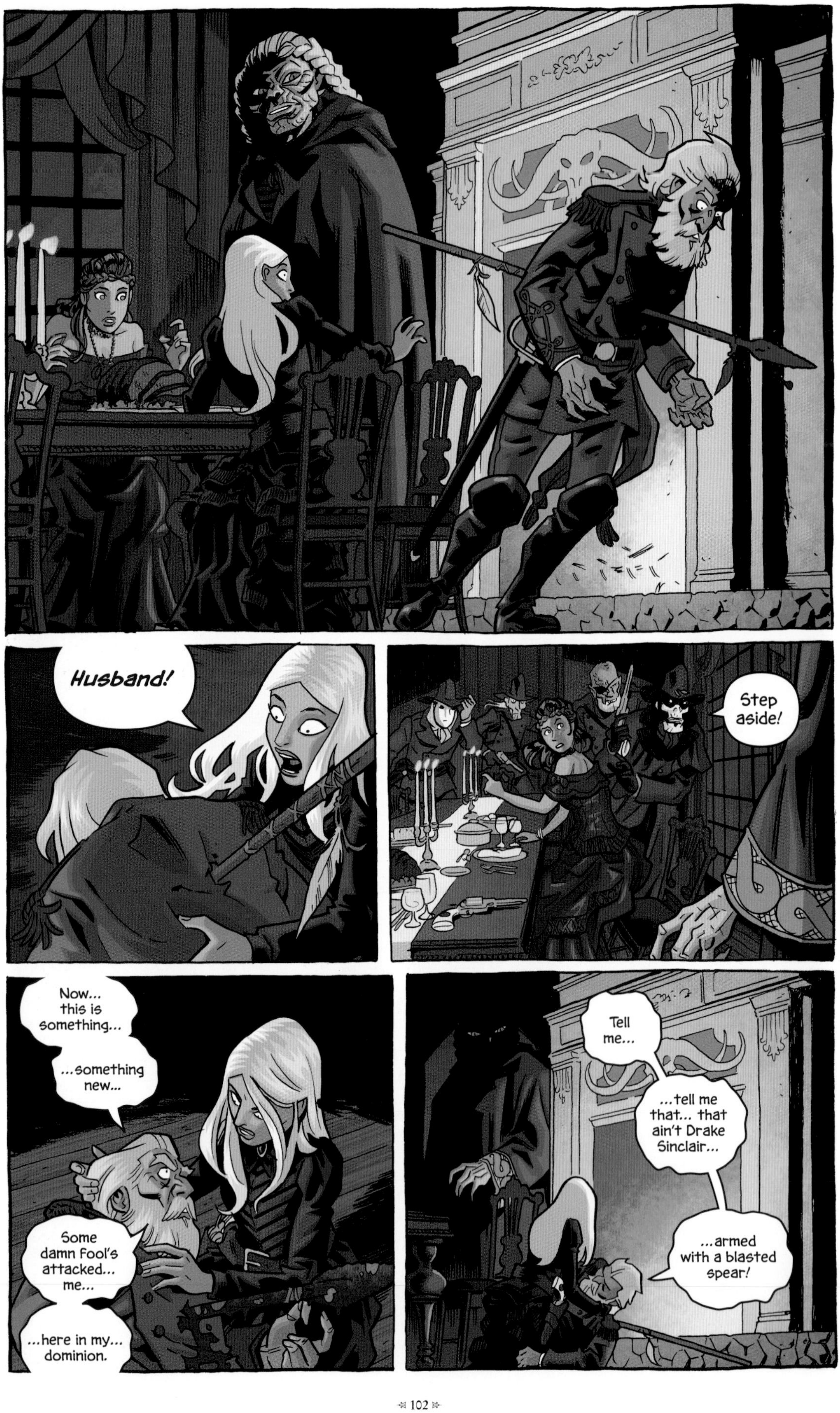
Husband!
Step aside!
Now... this is something...
...something new...
Some damn fool's attacked... me...
...here in my... dominion.
Tell me...
...tell me that... that ain't Drake Sinclair...
...armed with a blasted spear!

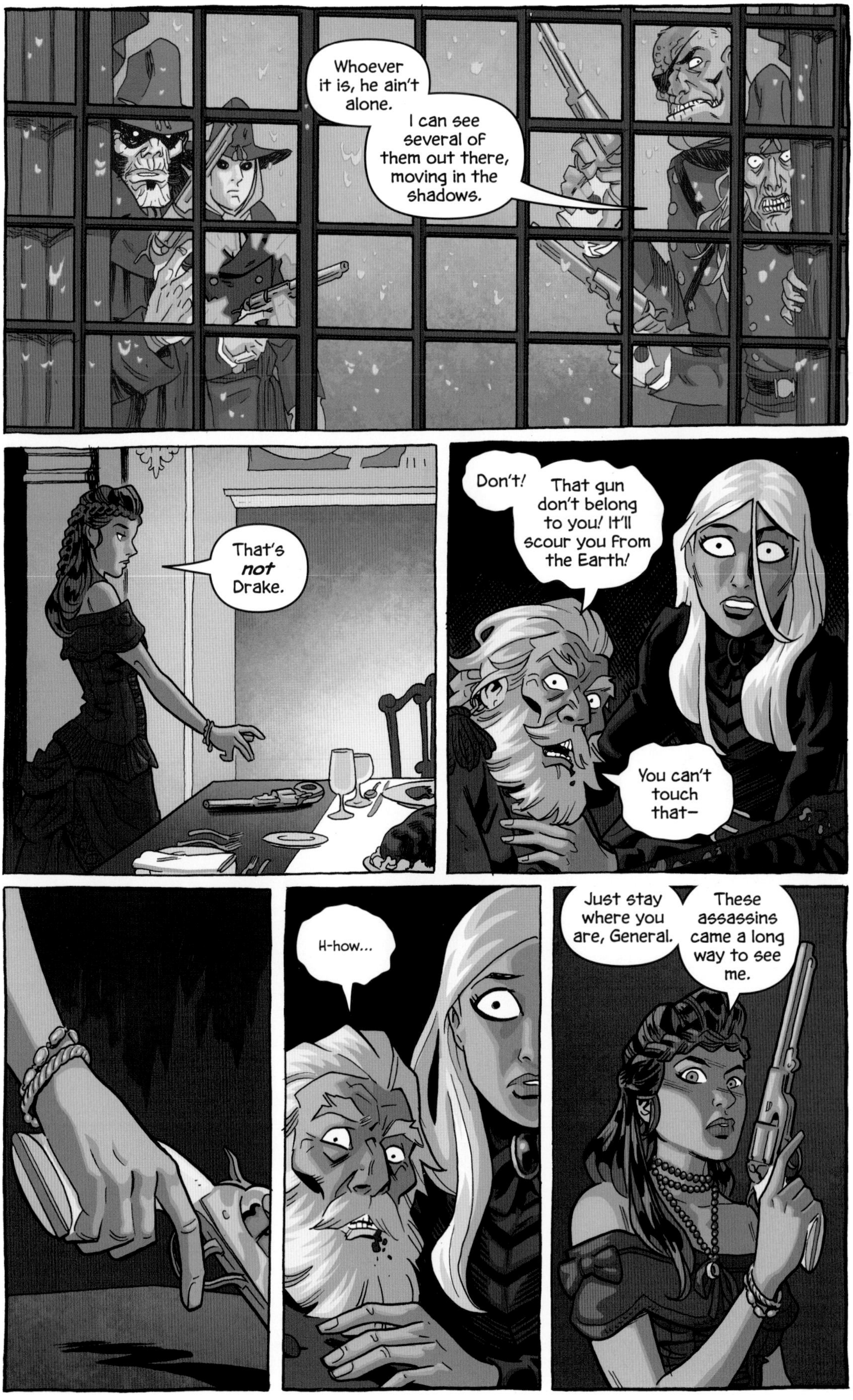

Whoever it is, he ain't alone.
I can see several of them out there, moving in the shadows.
That's *not* Drake.
Don't!
That gun don't belong to you! It'll scour you from the Earth!
You can't touch that–
H-how...
Just stay where you are, General.
These assassins came a long way to see me.

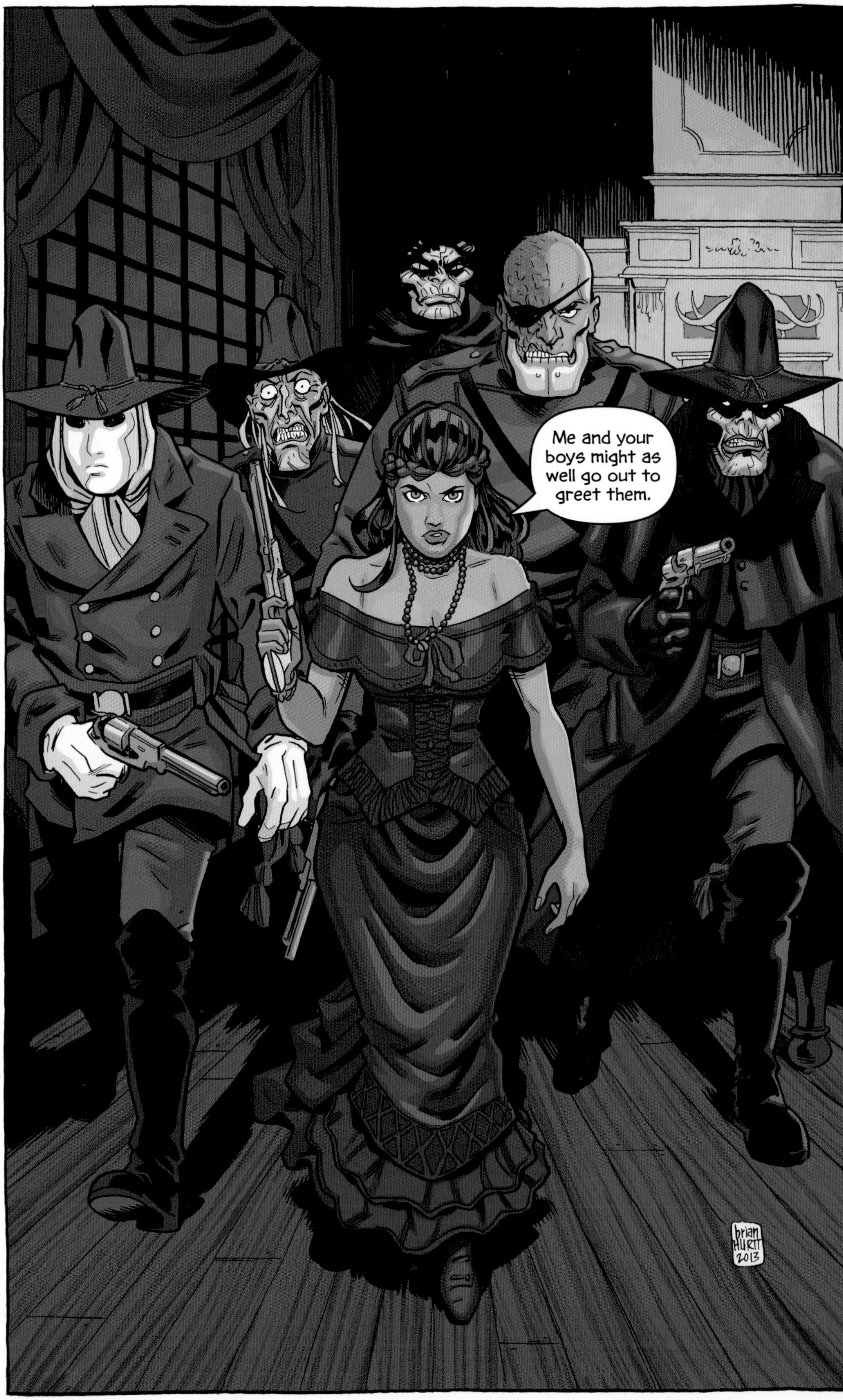
Me and your boys might as well go out to greet them.
brian HURTT 2013

CHAPTER
FIVE

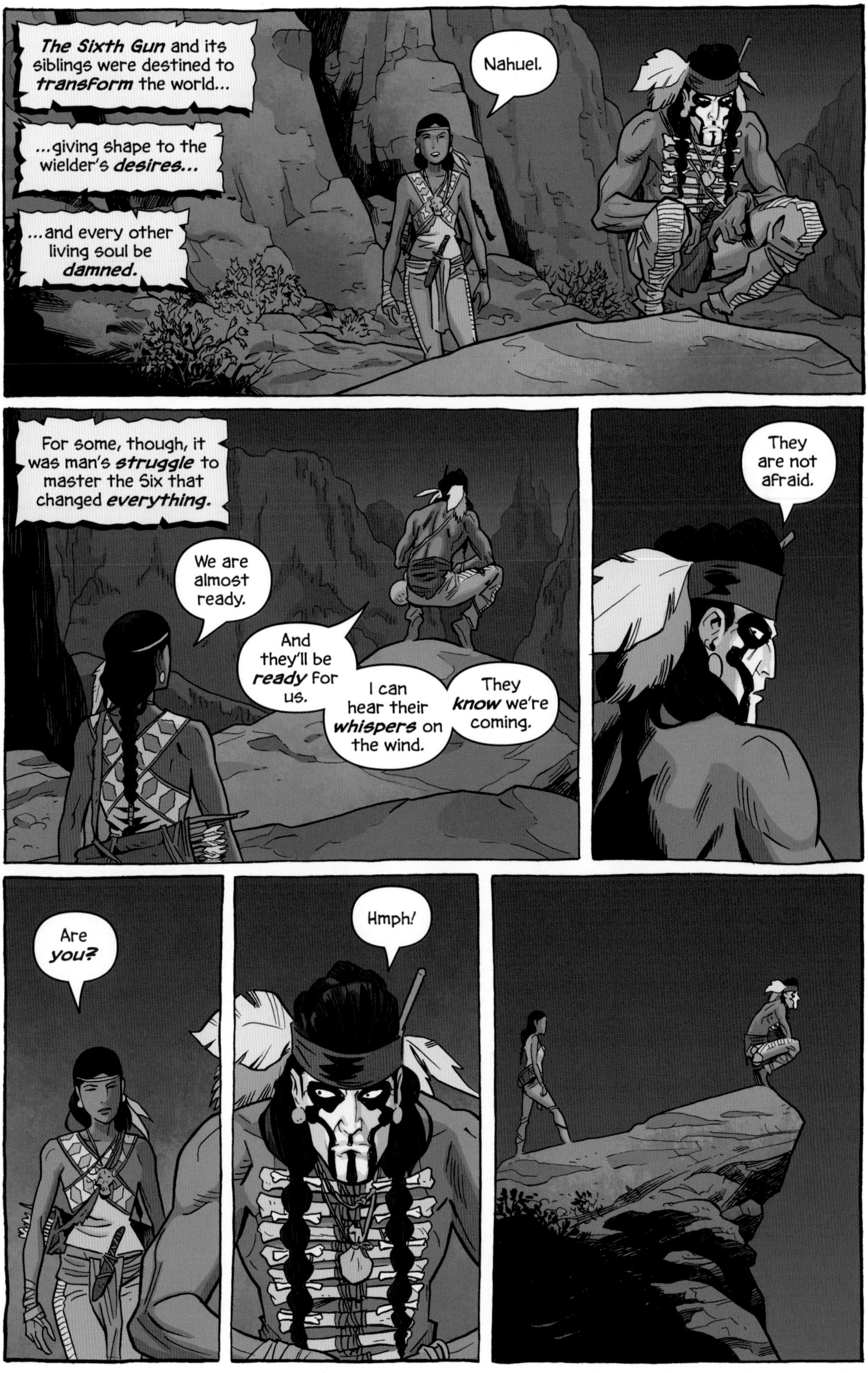
The Sixth Gun and its siblings were destined to transform the world...
...giving shape to the wielder's desires...
...and every other living soul be damned.
Nahuel.
For some, though, it was man's struggle to master the Six that changed everything.
We are almost ready.
And they'll be ready for us.
I can hear their whispers on the wind.
They know we're coming.
They are not afraid.
Are you?
Hmph!

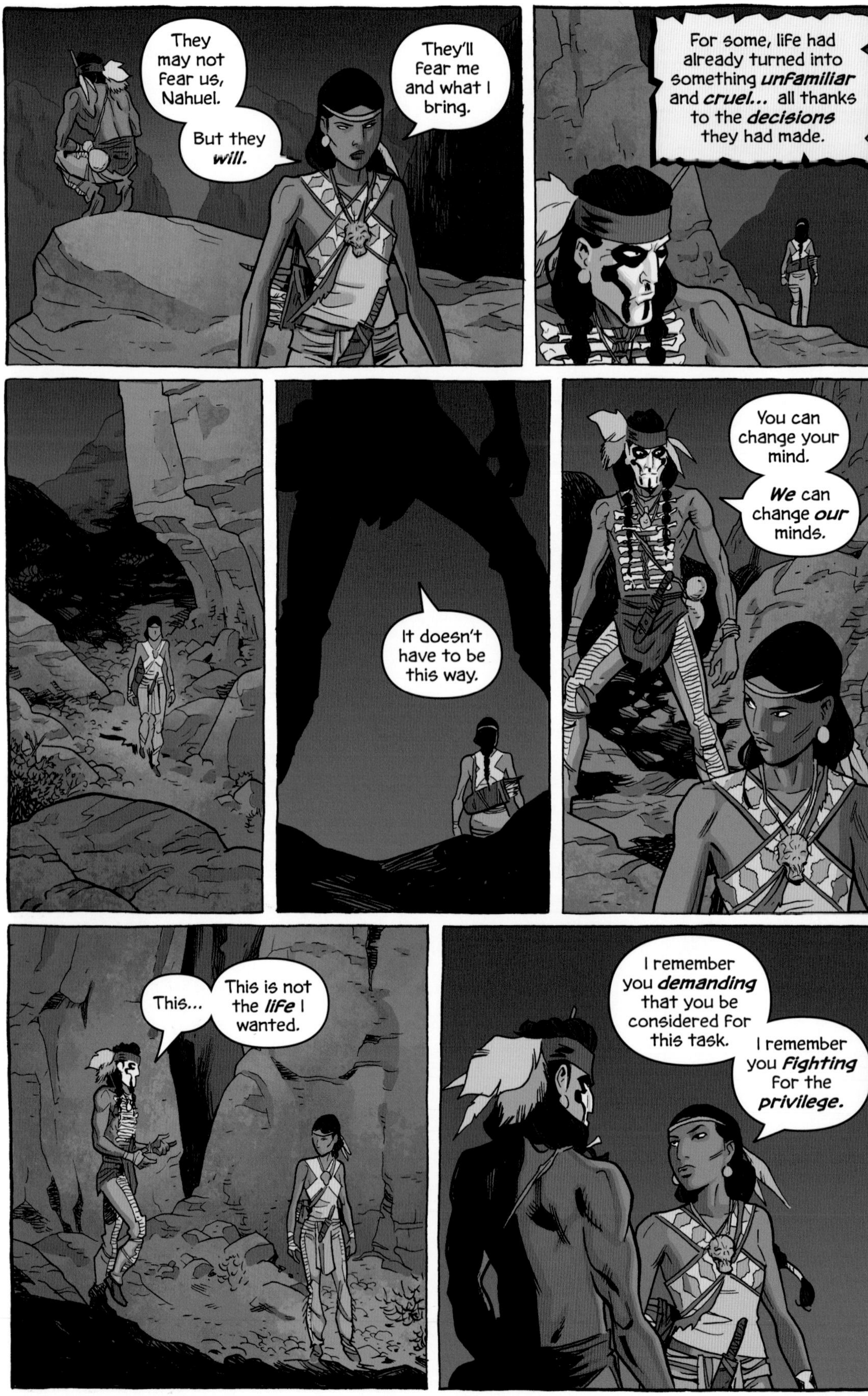

They may not fear us, Nahuel.
But they *will.*
They'll fear me and what I bring.
For some, life had already turned into something *unfamiliar* and *cruel...* all thanks to the *decisions* they had made.
It doesn't have to be this way.
You can change your mind.
We can change *our* minds.
This...
This is not the *life* I wanted.
I remember you *demanding* that you be considered for this task.
I remember you *fighting* for the *privilege.*

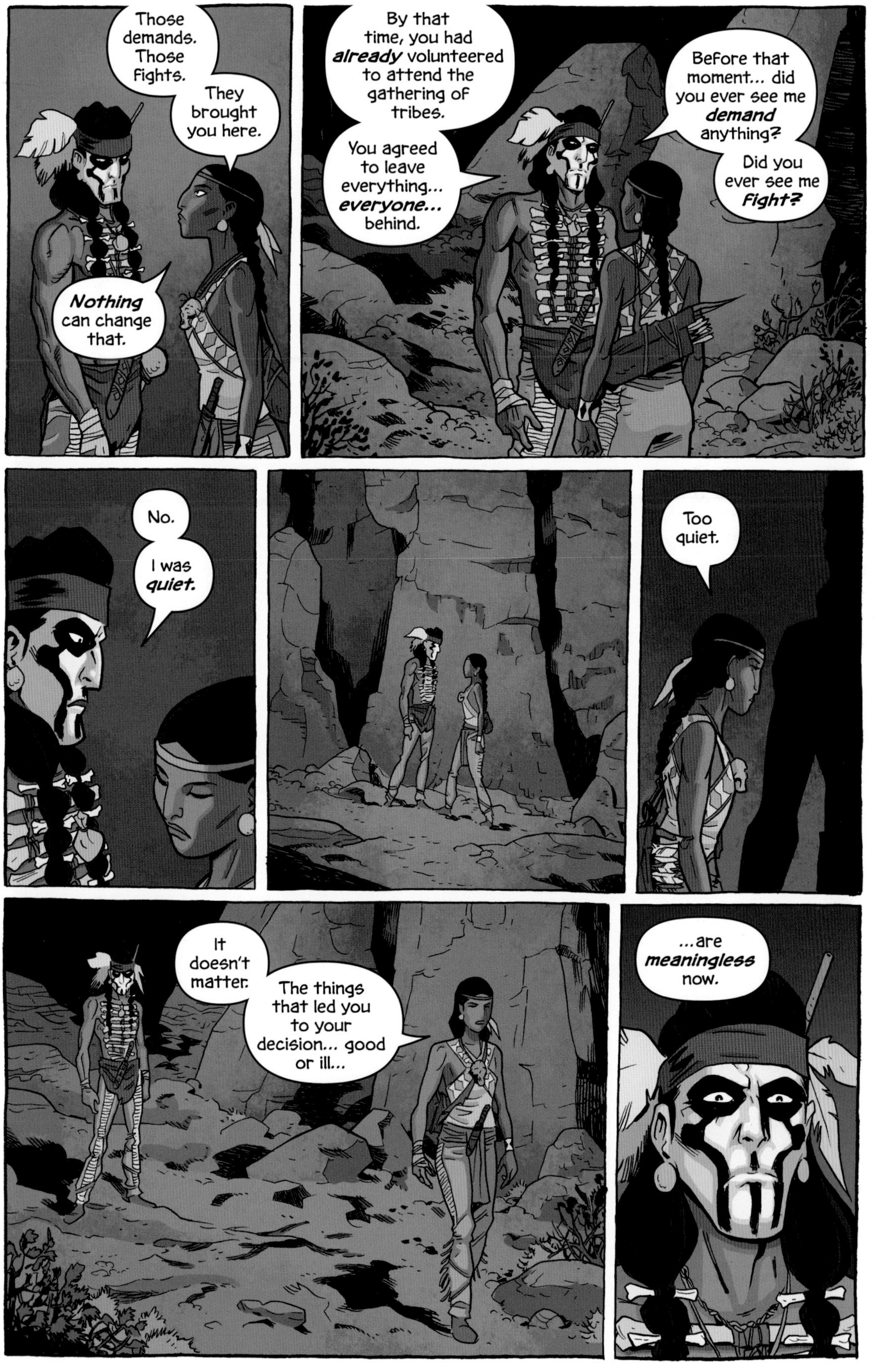
Those demands. Those fights.
They brought you here.
Nothing can change that.
By that time, you had already volunteered to attend the gathering of tribes.
You agreed to leave everything... everyone... behind.
Before that moment... did you ever see me demand anything?
Did you ever see me fight?
No.
I was quiet.
Too quiet.
It doesn't matter.
The things that led you to your decision... good or ill...
...are meaningless now.

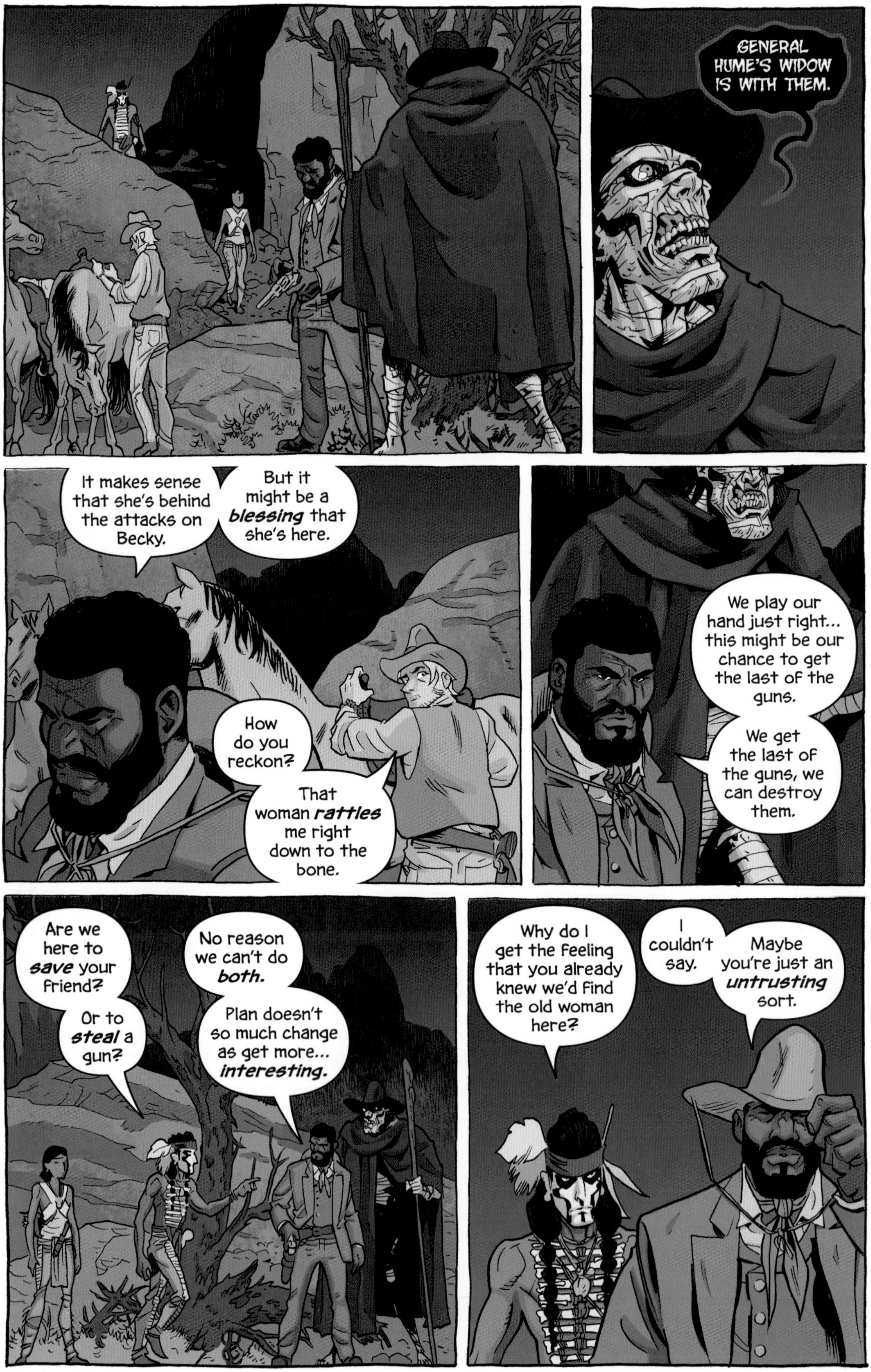
GENERAL HUME'S WIDOW IS WITH THEM.
It makes sense that she's behind the attacks on Becky.
But it might be a *blessing* that she's here.
How do you reckon?
That woman *rattles* me right down to the bone.
We play our hand just right... this might be our chance to get the last of the guns.
We get the last of the guns, we can destroy them.
Are we here to *save* your friend?
Or to *steal* a gun?
No reason we can't do *both.*
Plan doesn't so much change as get more... *interesting.*
Why do I get the feeling that you already knew we'd find the old woman here?
I couldn't say.
Maybe you're just an *untrusting* sort.

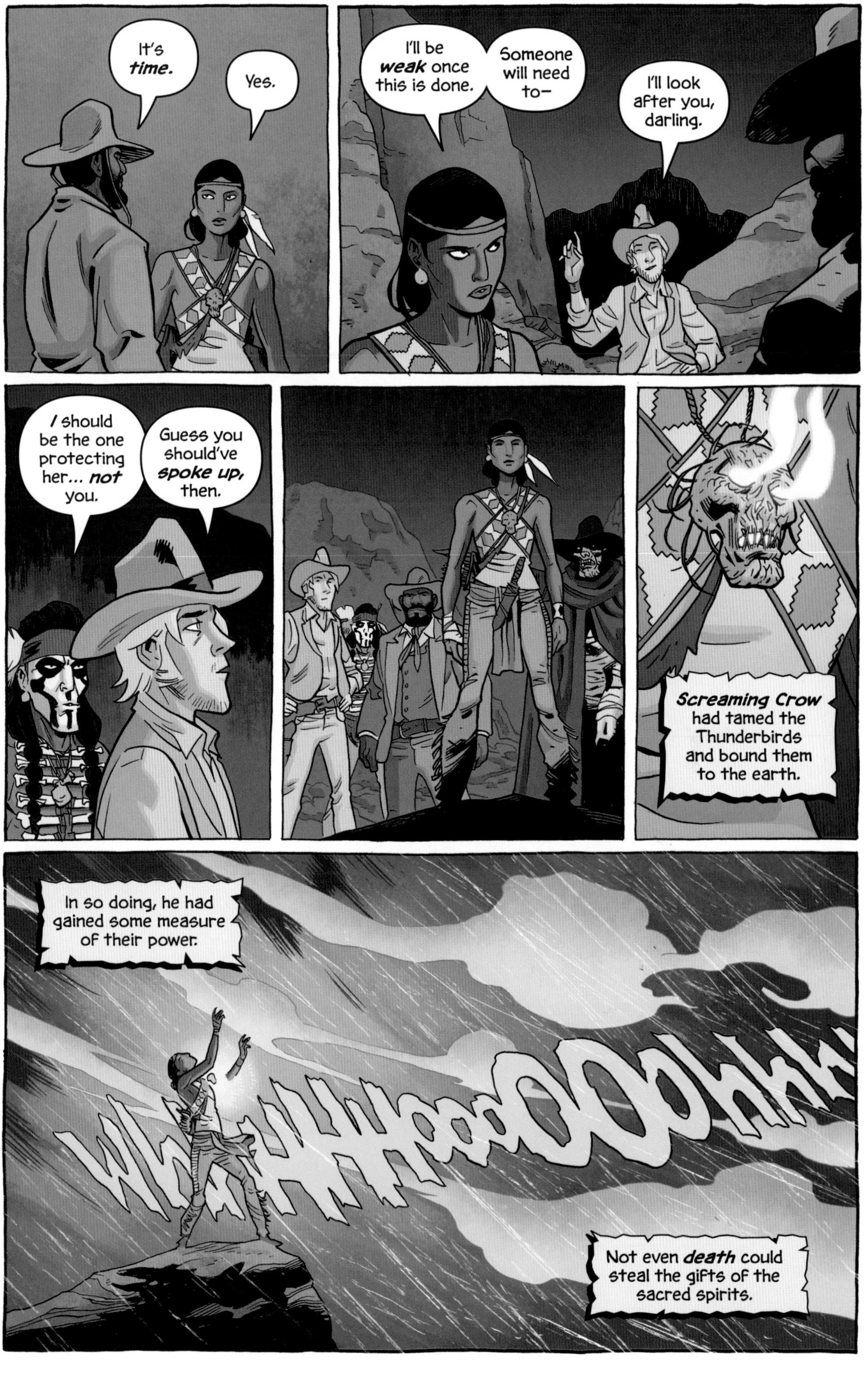

It's *time.*
Yes.
I'll be *weak* once this is done.
Someone will need to–
I'll look after you, darling.
I should be the one protecting her... *not* you.
Guess you should've *spoke up,* then.
Screaming Crow had tamed the Thunderbirds and bound them to the earth.
In so doing, he had gained some measure of their power.
WhhHHooOOhhh
Not even *death* could steal the gifts of the sacred spirits.

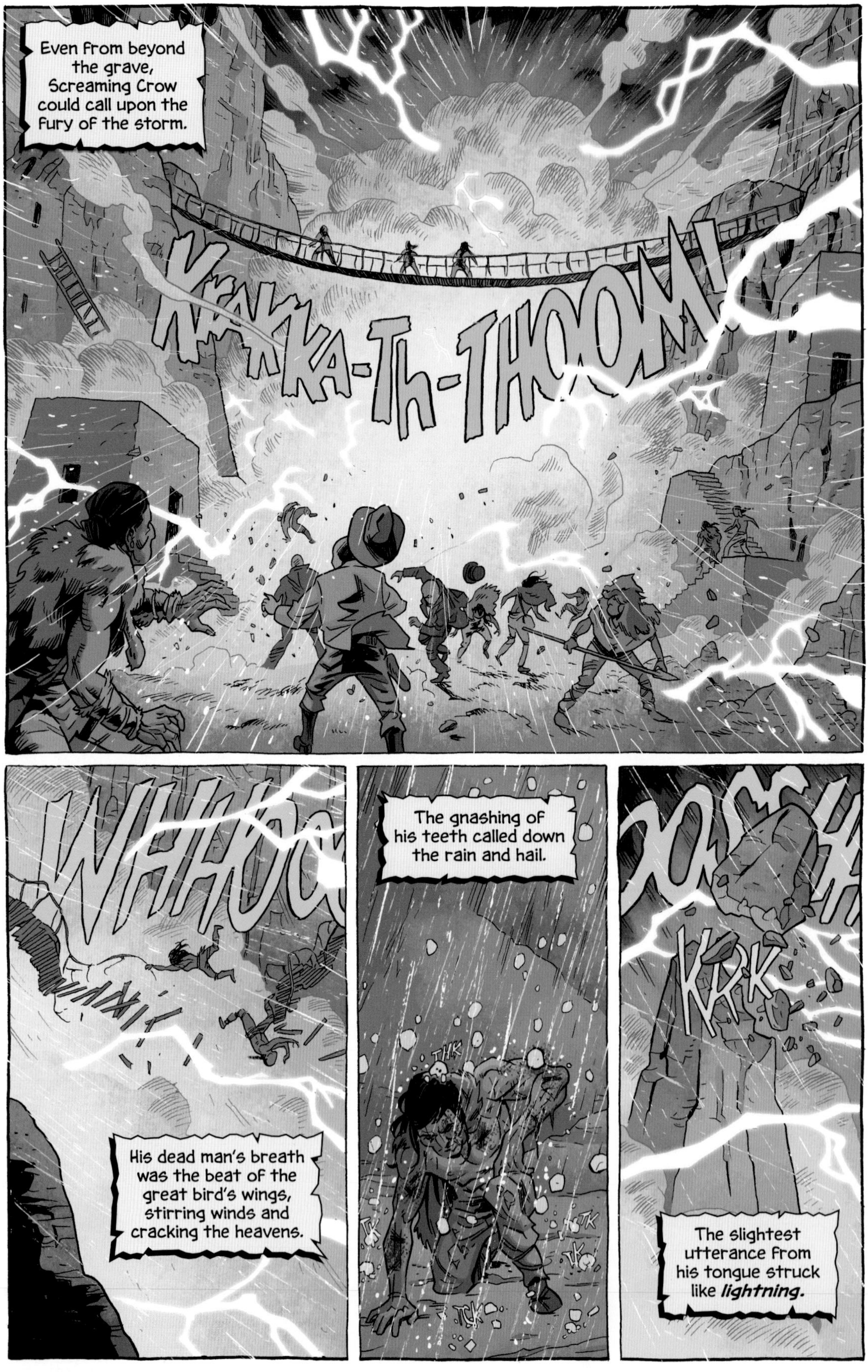
Even from beyond the grave, Screaming Crow could call upon the fury of the storm.
KRAKKA-Th-THOOM!
His dead man's breath was the beat of the great bird's wings, stirring winds and cracking the heavens.
The gnashing of his teeth called down the rain and hail.
THK
TK
TCK
KRK
The slightest utterance from his tongue struck like ***lightning.***

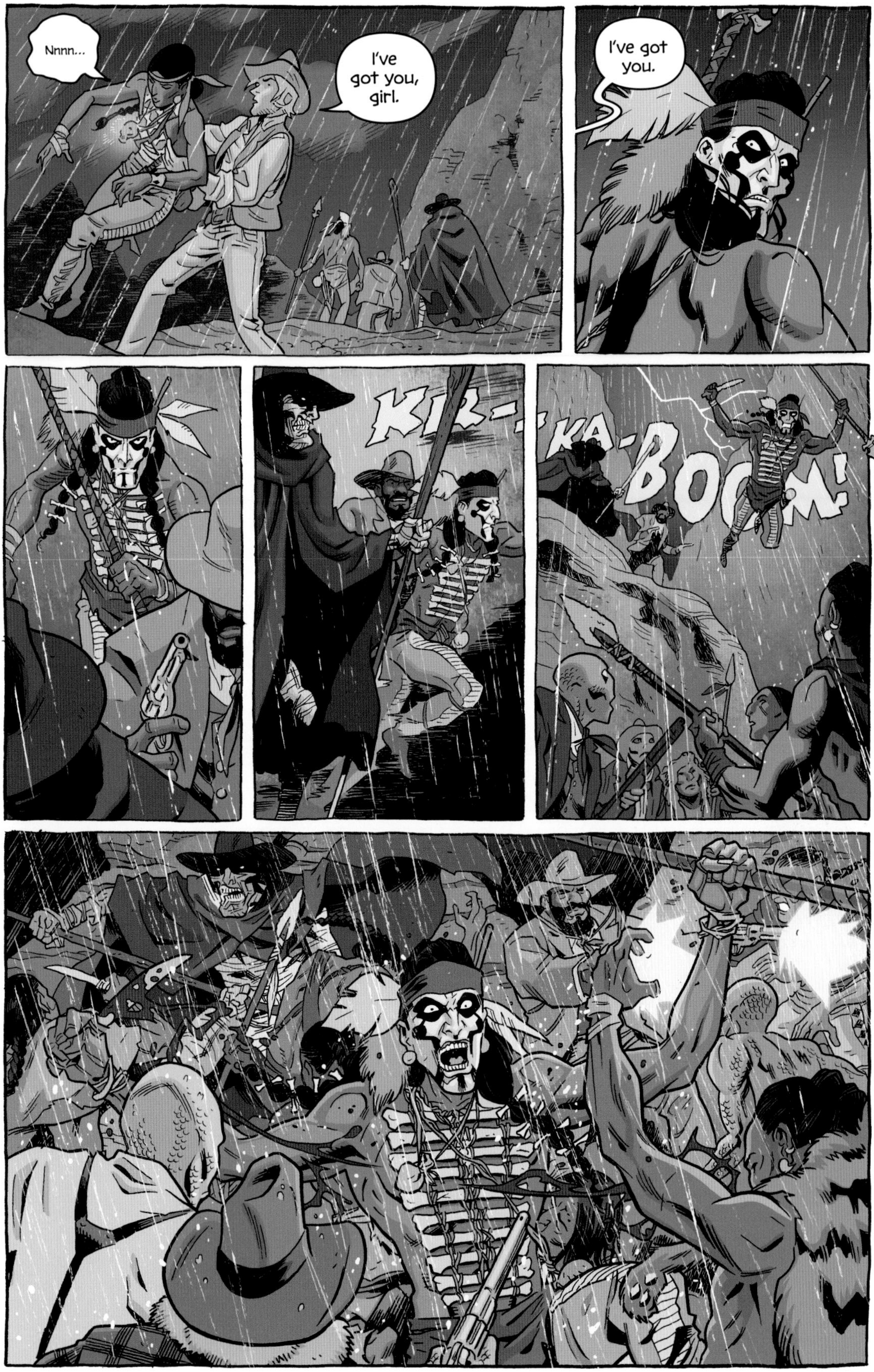
Nnnn...
I've got you, girl.
I've got you.
KIR-
KA-BOOM!

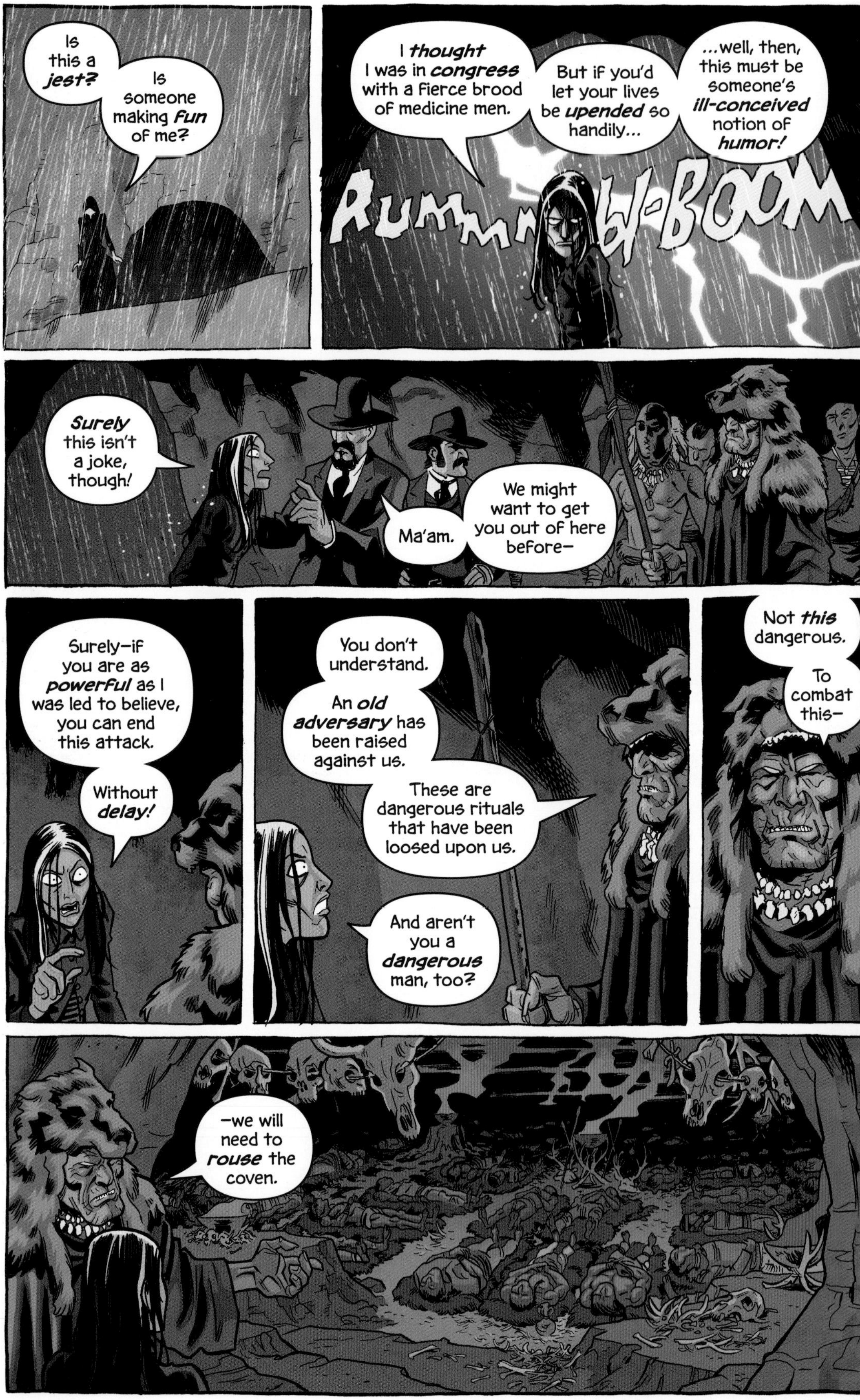

Is this a jest?
Is someone making fun of me?
I thought I was in congress with a fierce brood of medicine men.
But if you'd let your lives be upended so handily...
...well, then, this must be someone's ill-conceived notion of humor!
RUMMMBLY-BOOM
Surely this isn't a joke, though!
Ma'am.
We might want to get you out of here before—
Surely—if you are as powerful as I was led to believe, you can end this attack.
Without delay!
You don't understand.
An old adversary has been raised against us.
These are dangerous rituals that have been loosed upon us.
And aren't you a dangerous man, too?
Not this dangerous.
To combat this—
—we will need to rouse the coven.

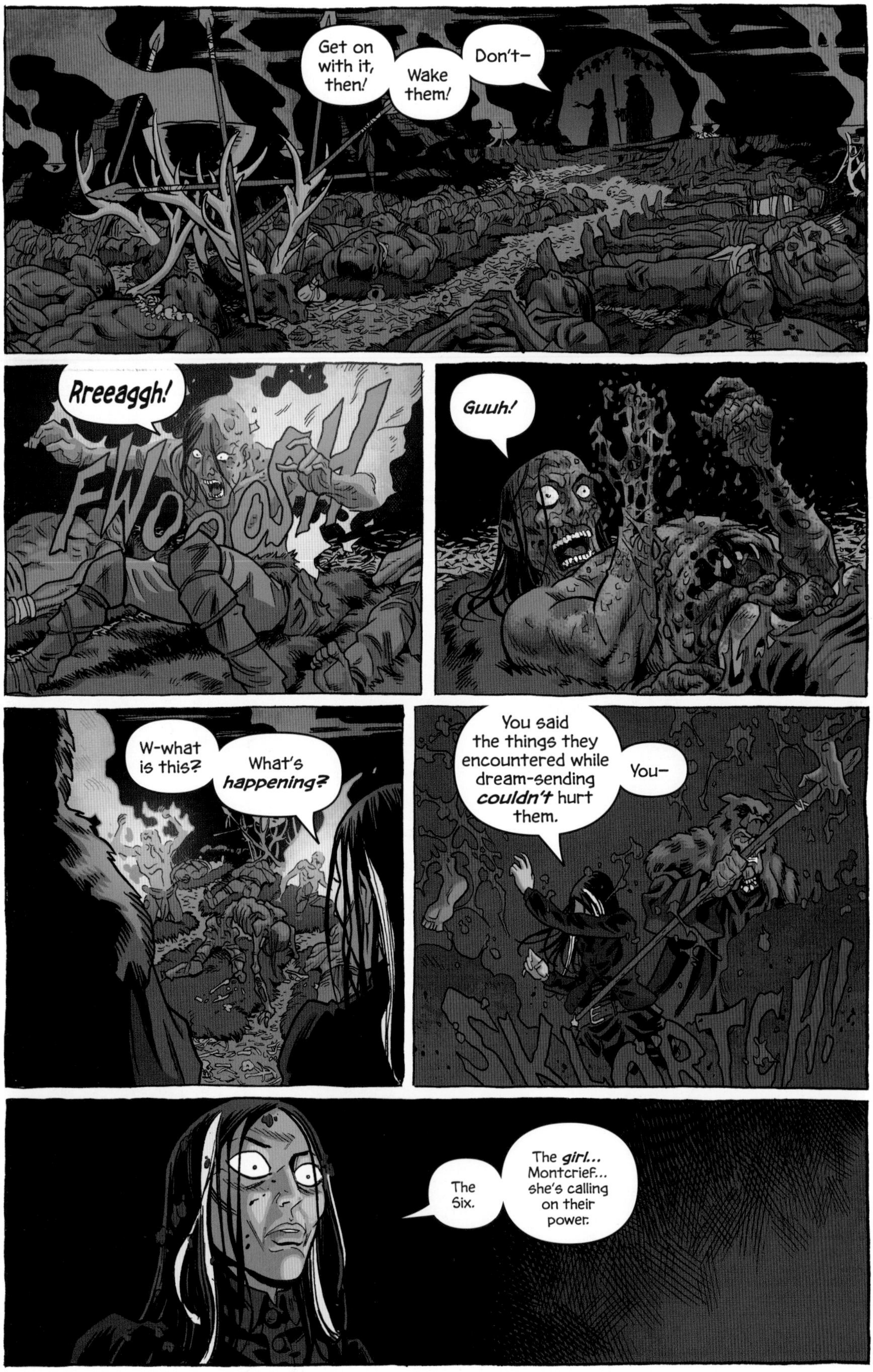
Get on with it, then!
Wake them!
Don't—
Rreeaggh!
FWOOSH
Guuh!
W-what is this?
What's *happening?*
You said the things they encountered while dream-sending *couldn't* hurt them.
You—
SPLORTCH!!
The Six.
The *girl...* Montcrief... she's calling on their power.

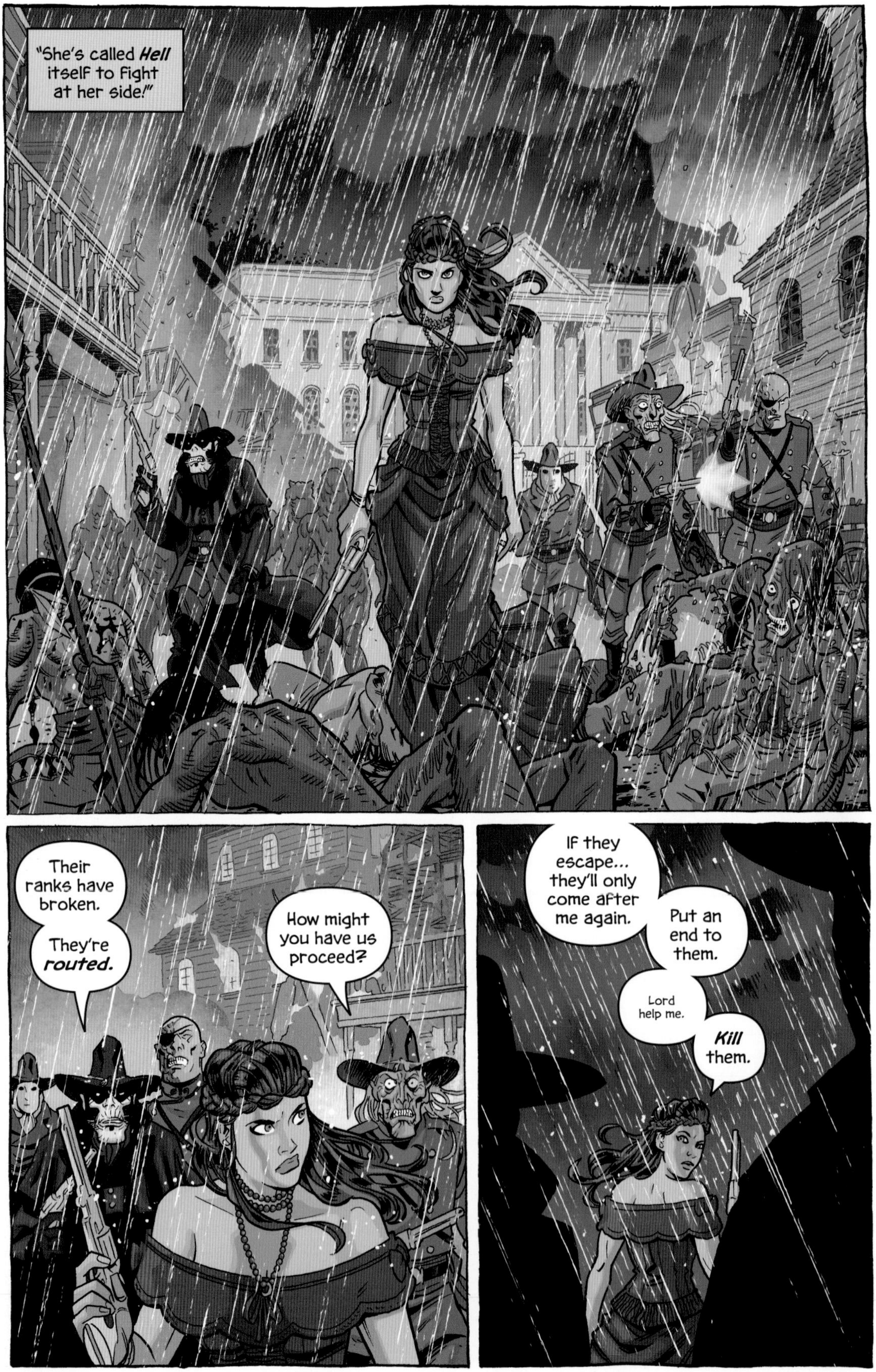
"She's called **Hell** itself to fight at her side!"
Their ranks have broken.
They're ***routed.***
How might you have us proceed?
If they escape... they'll only come after me again.
Put an end to them.
Lord help me.
Kill them.

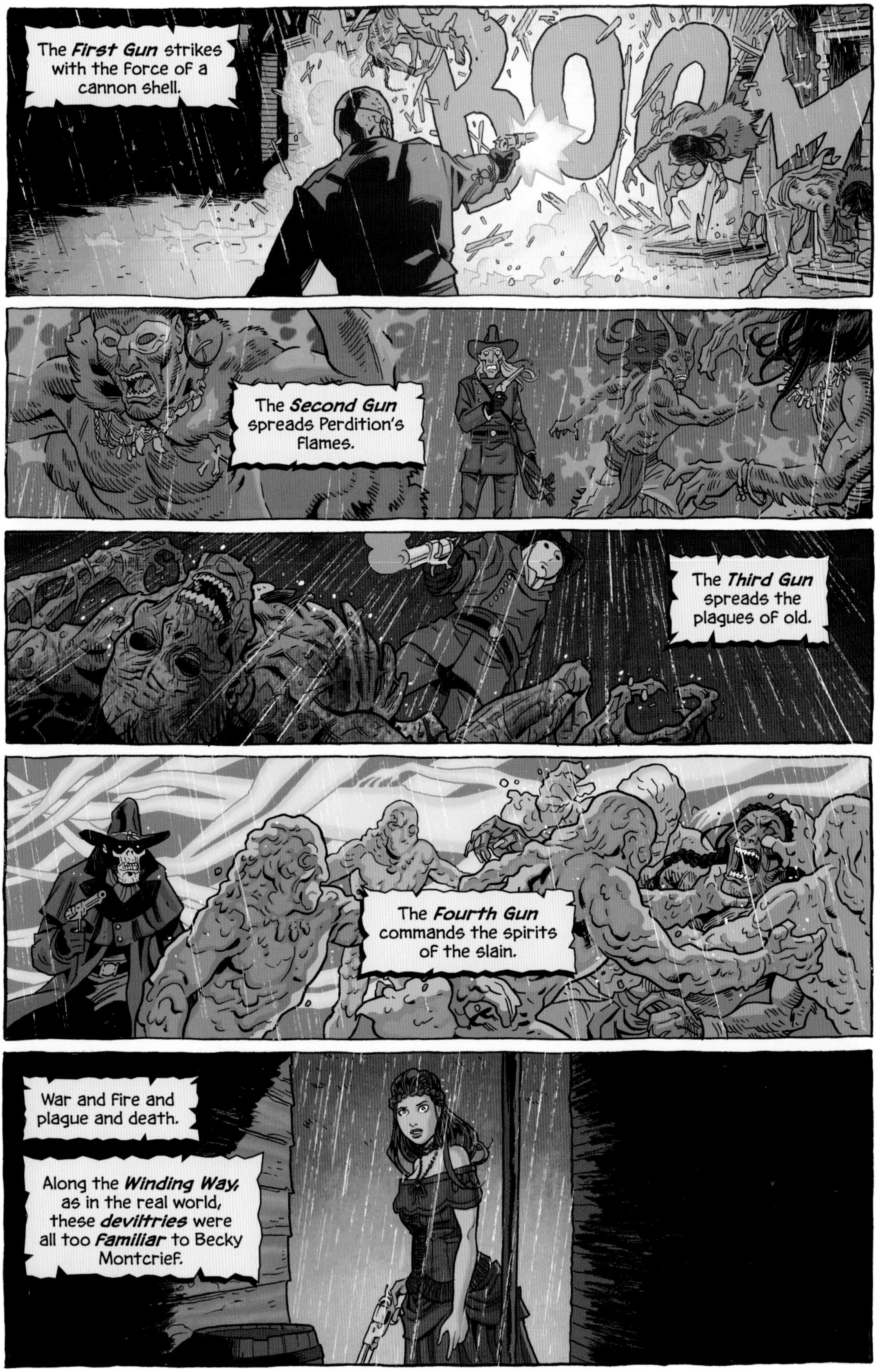
The *First Gun* strikes with the force of a cannon shell.
BOOM
The *Second Gun* spreads Perdition's flames.
The *Third Gun* spreads the plagues of old.
The *Fourth Gun* commands the spirits of the slain.
War and fire and plague and death.
Along the *Winding Way,* as in the real world, these *deviltries* were all too *familiar* to Becky Montcrief.

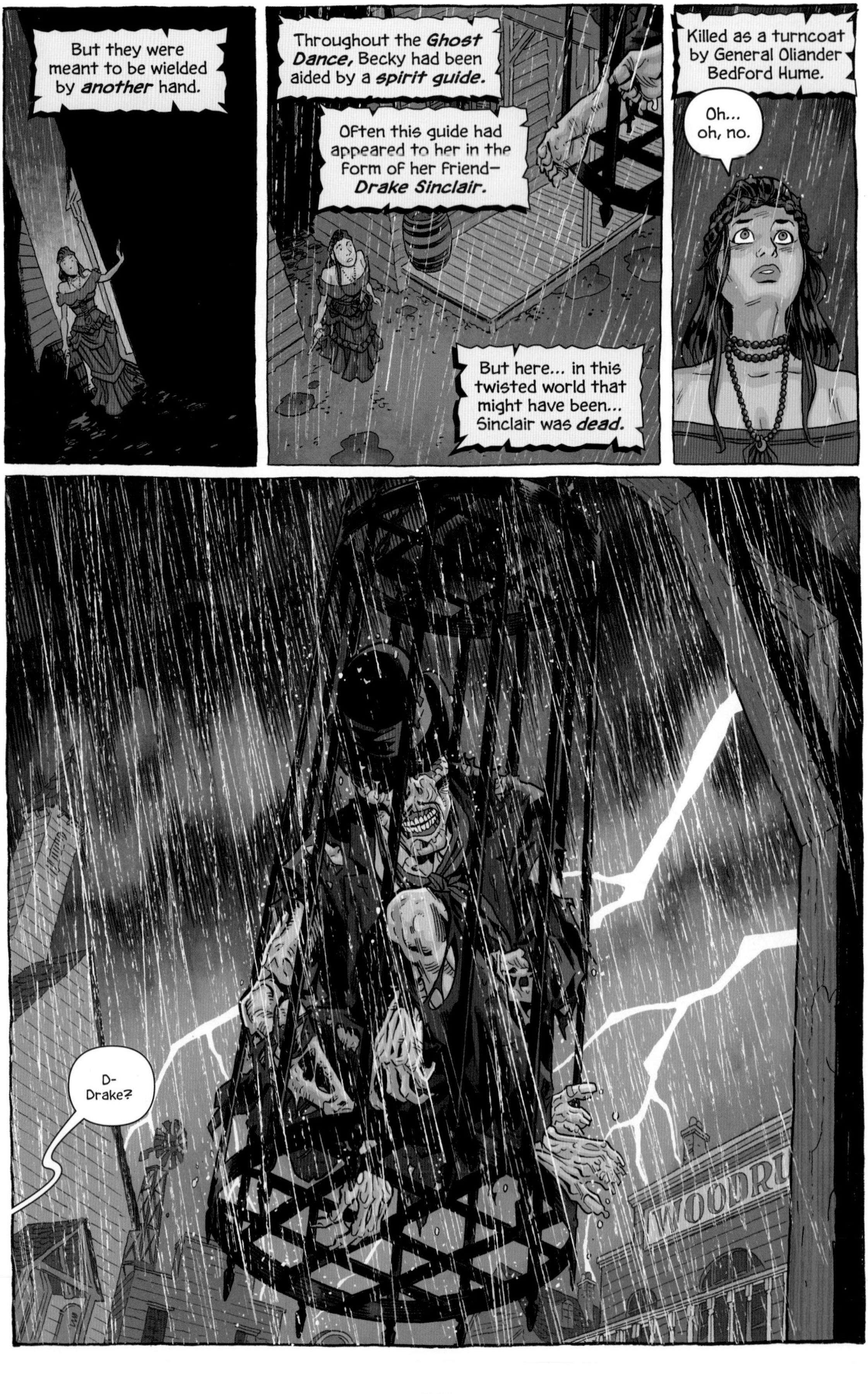
But they were meant to be wielded by *another* hand.
Throughout the *Ghost Dance,* Becky had been aided by a *spirit guide.*
Often this guide had appeared to her in the form of her friend—*Drake Sinclair.*
But here... in this twisted world that might have been... Sinclair was *dead.*
Killed as a turncoat by General Oliander Bedford Hume.
Oh... oh, no.
D-Drake?

D-Drake?

I don't know *where* I am... *what* I'm seeing.

Everything's *wrong* here.

Lord... I wish you were with me.

I wish you could hear me...

Everywhere I turn... the world is *different*... and it keeps *changing*.

Different places... times... *possibilities,* I reckon.

But General Hume's here. And I think he's *won.*

The war... the world... *everything...*

I'm right *here,* Becky.

Can't you see me?

I'm *lost.*

I'm lost... and I thought you might help me find my way out...

I thought you'd find me again... or I'd find you.

But...

...I've got his gun... *my* gun... and I—

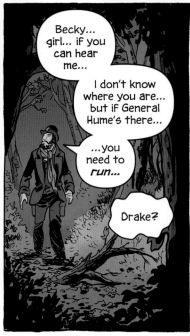

Becky... girl... if you can hear me...

I don't know where you are... but if General Hume's there...

...you need to *run...*

Drake?

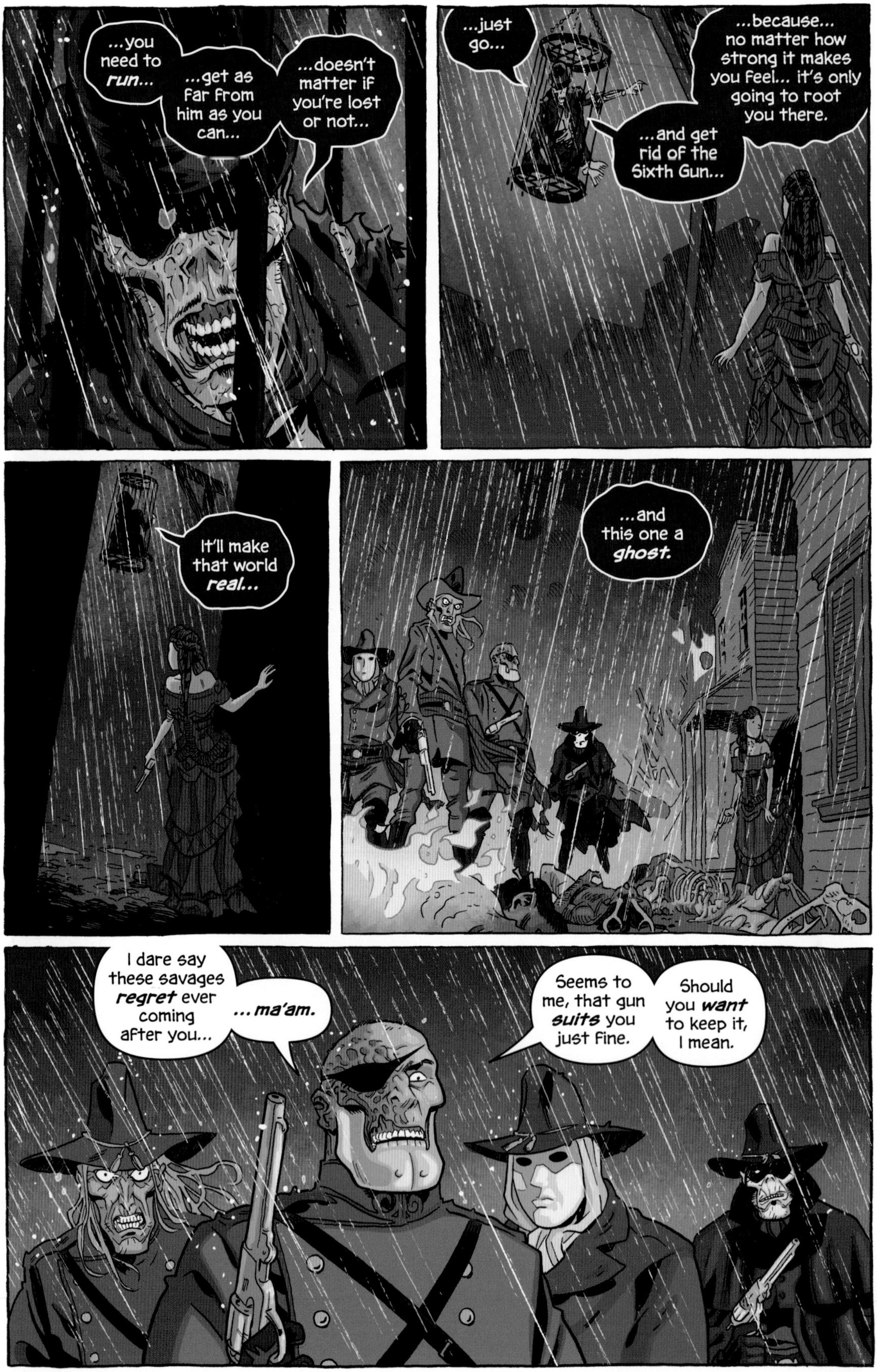
...you need to *run*...
...get as far from him as you can...
...doesn't matter if you're lost or not...
...just go...
...because... no matter how strong it makes you feel... it's only going to root you there.
...and get rid of the Sixth Gun...
It'll make that world *real...*
...and this one a *ghost.*
I dare say these savages *regret* ever coming after you...
...ma'am.
Seems to me, that gun *suits* you just fine.
Should you *want* to keep it, I mean.

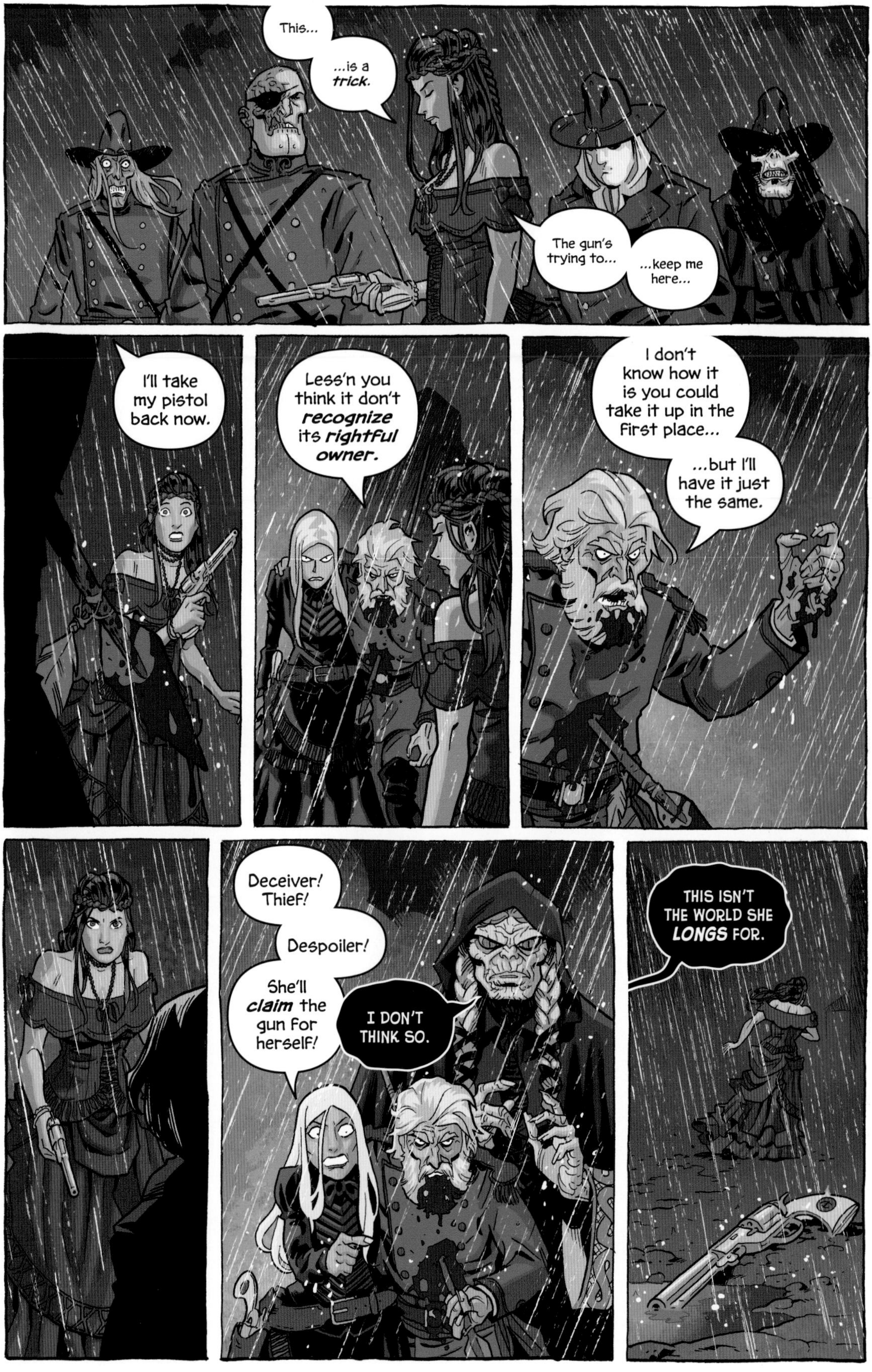

This...
...is a *trick.*
The gun's trying to...
...keep me here...
I'll take my pistol back now.
Less'n you think it don't *recognize* its *rightful owner.*
I don't know how it is you could take it up in the first place...
...but I'll have it just the same.
Deceiver! Thief!
Despoiler!
She'll *claim* the gun for herself!
I DON'T THINK SO.
THIS ISN'T THE WORLD SHE *LONGS* FOR.

"AND SHE'LL **RUN** UNTIL SHE FINDS IT."

RUMMBLL

CRMMB CRAK!

RMMBLL

The girl **lives** then?

She killed your **dream hunters?**

How—

The girl can **wait.**

This storm... it is the *Voice of Thunder* speaking... and it could bring *every-thing* crashing down around us.

We must stop our enemies here before we worry about killing the girl.

And how do you propose—

Augh!

Your blood is **potent,** Deathless One.

With it... we'll awaken the old things sleeping in these hills...

...those who wait for the **end of times...**

RRMMMBBLL BRMMMBLU

"They'll be **angry...**

"...and we'll **herd** them down upon our enemies!"

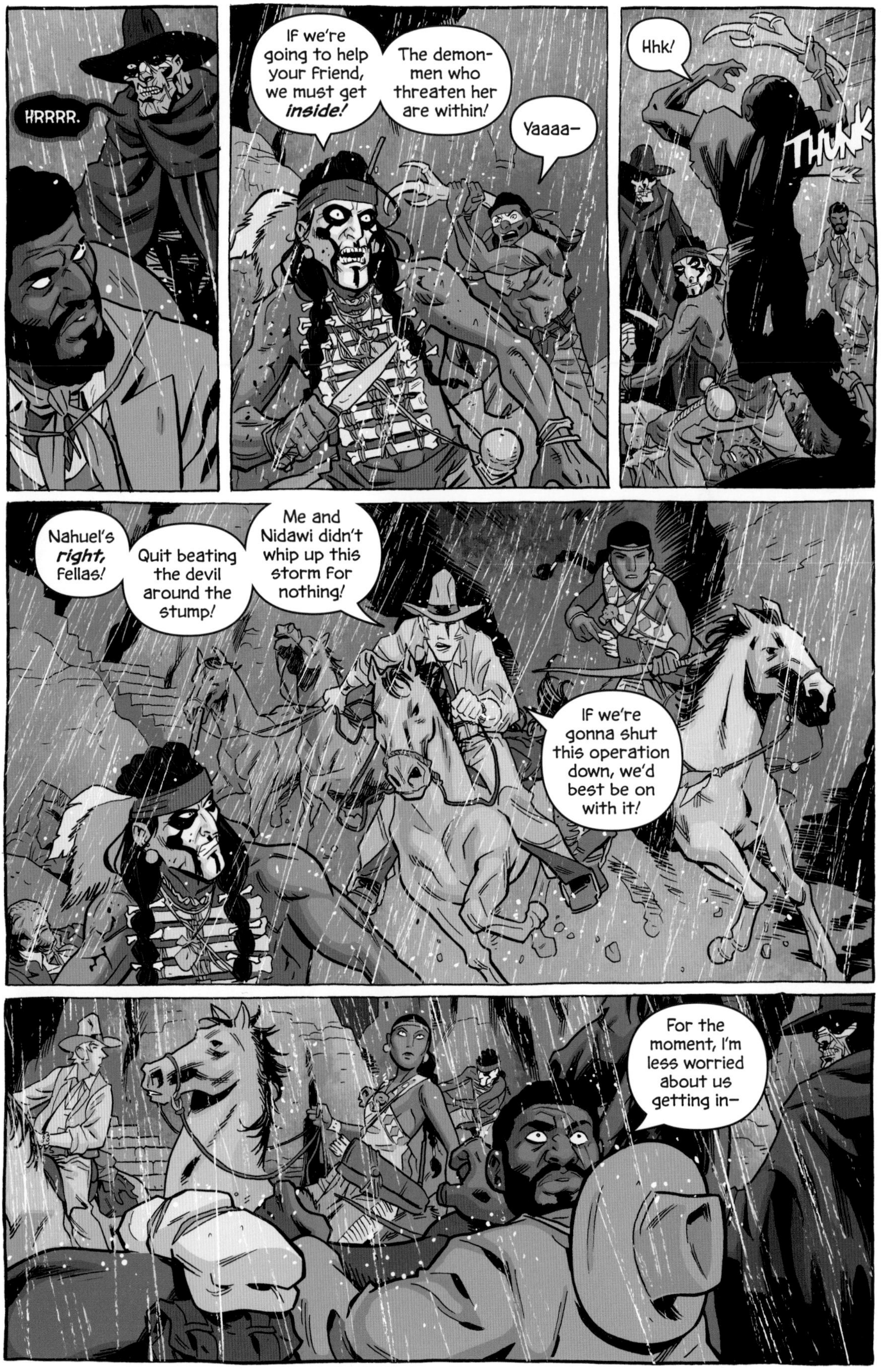
HRRRR.
If we're going to help your friend, we must get *inside!*
The demon-men who threaten her are within!
Yaaaa—
Hhk!
THUNK
Nahuel's *right,* Fellas!
Quit beating the devil around the stump!
Me and Nidawi didn't whip up this storm for nothing!
If we're gonna shut this operation down, we'd best be on with it!
For the moment, I'm less worried about us getting in—

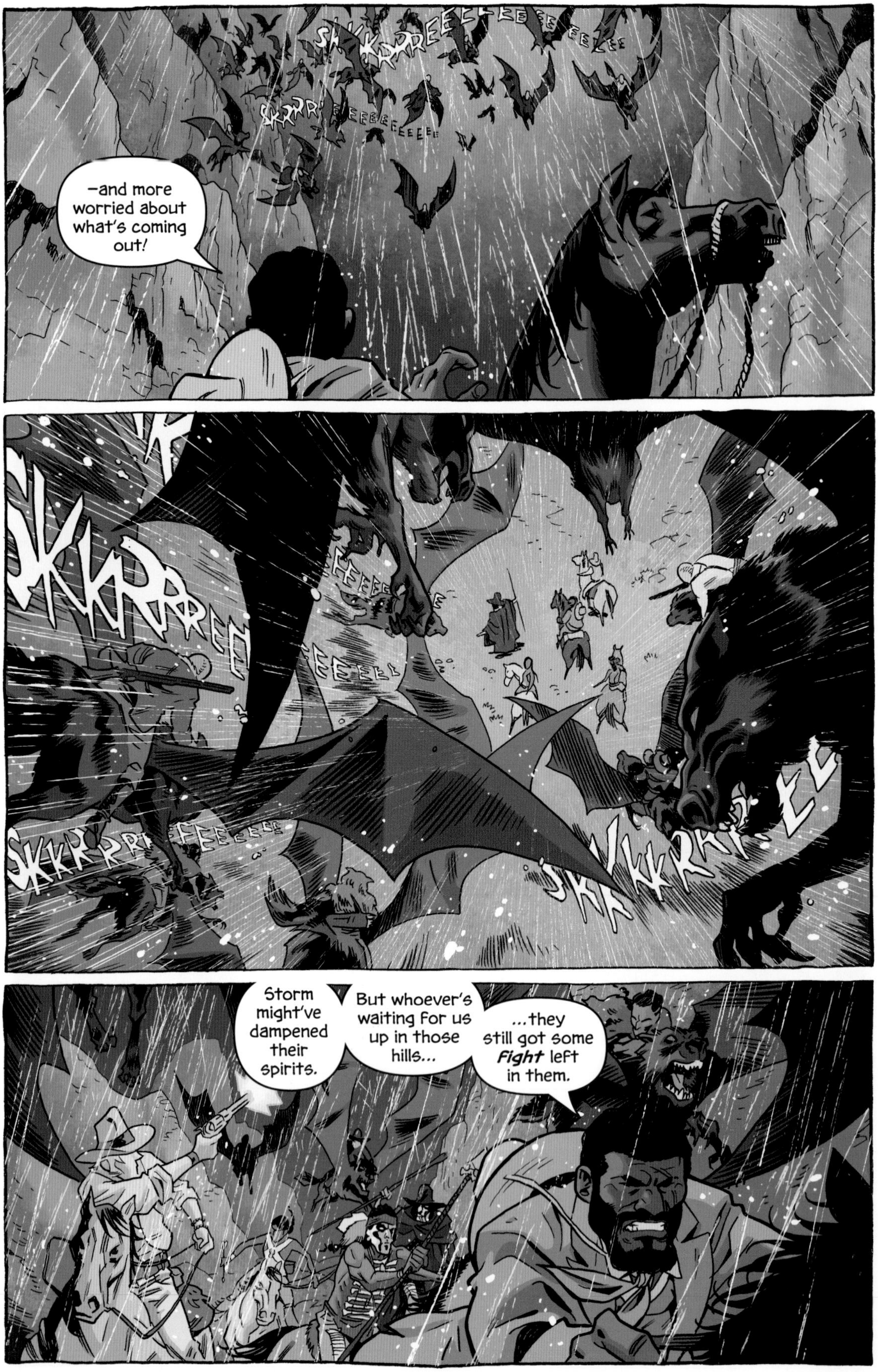
—and more worried about what's coming out!
Storm might've dampened their spirits.
But whoever's waiting for us up in those hills...
...they still got some *fight* left in them.

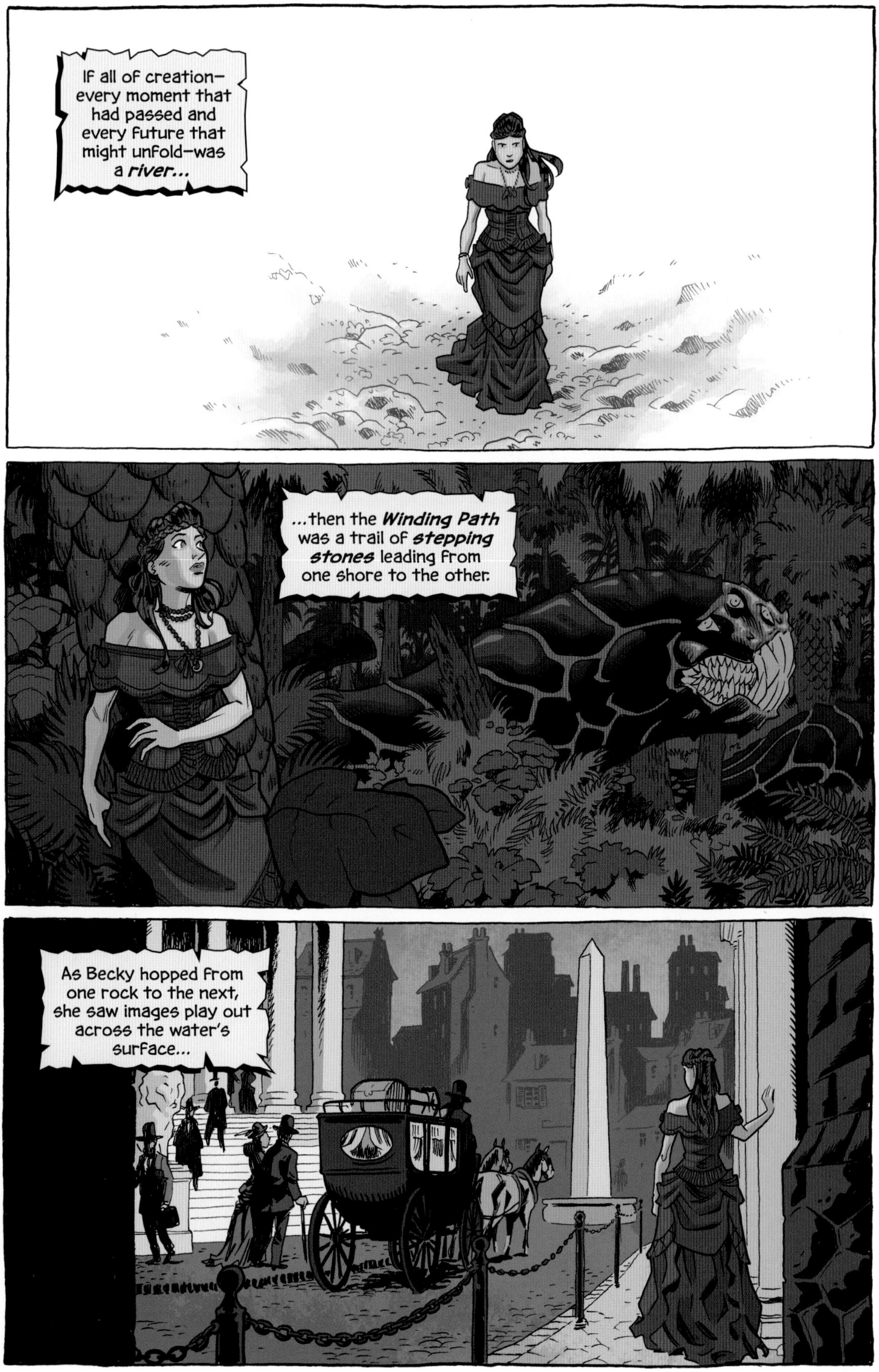
If all of creation—every moment that had passed and every future that might unfold—was a *river...*
...then the *Winding Path* was a trail of *stepping stones* leading from one shore to the other.
As Becky hopped from one rock to the next, she saw images play out across the water's surface...

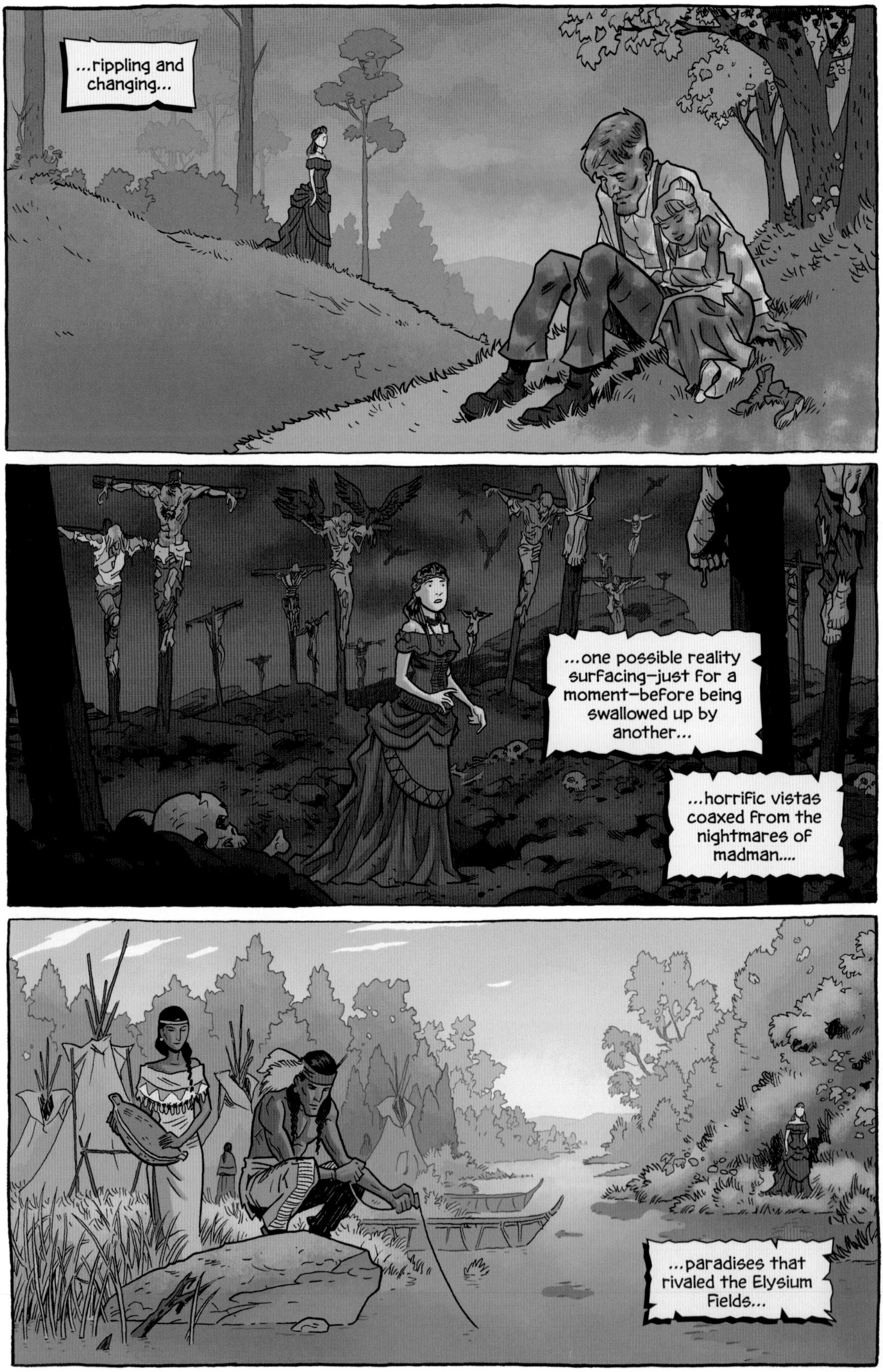
...rippling and changing...
...one possible reality surfacing—just for a moment—before being swallowed up by another...
...horrific vistas coaxed from the nightmares of madman....
...paradises that rivaled the Elysium Fields...

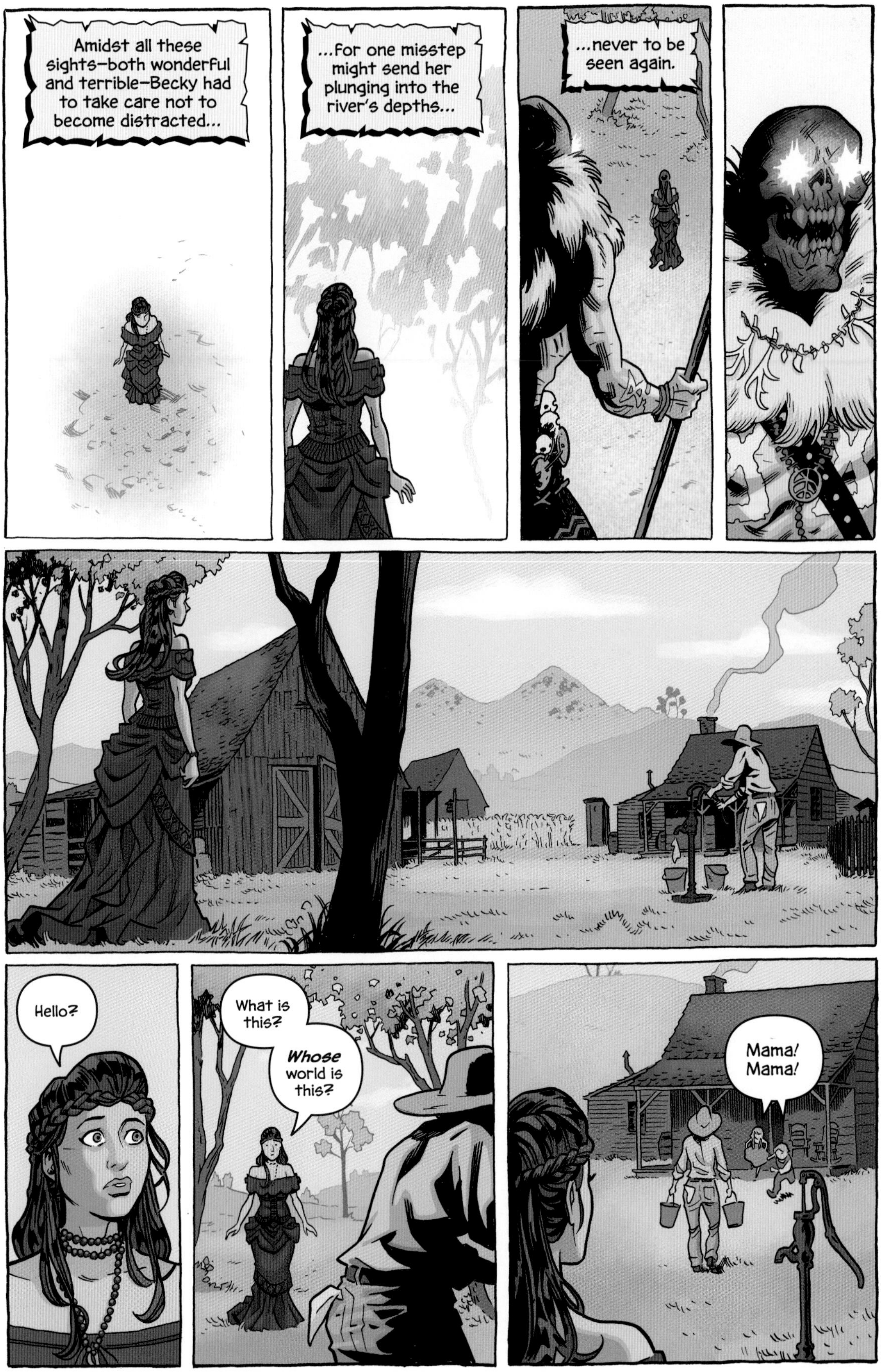

Amidst all these sights—both wonderful and terrible—Becky had to take care not to become distracted...
...for one misstep might send her plunging into the river's depths...
...never to be seen again.
Hello?
What is this?
Whose world is this?
Mama! Mama!

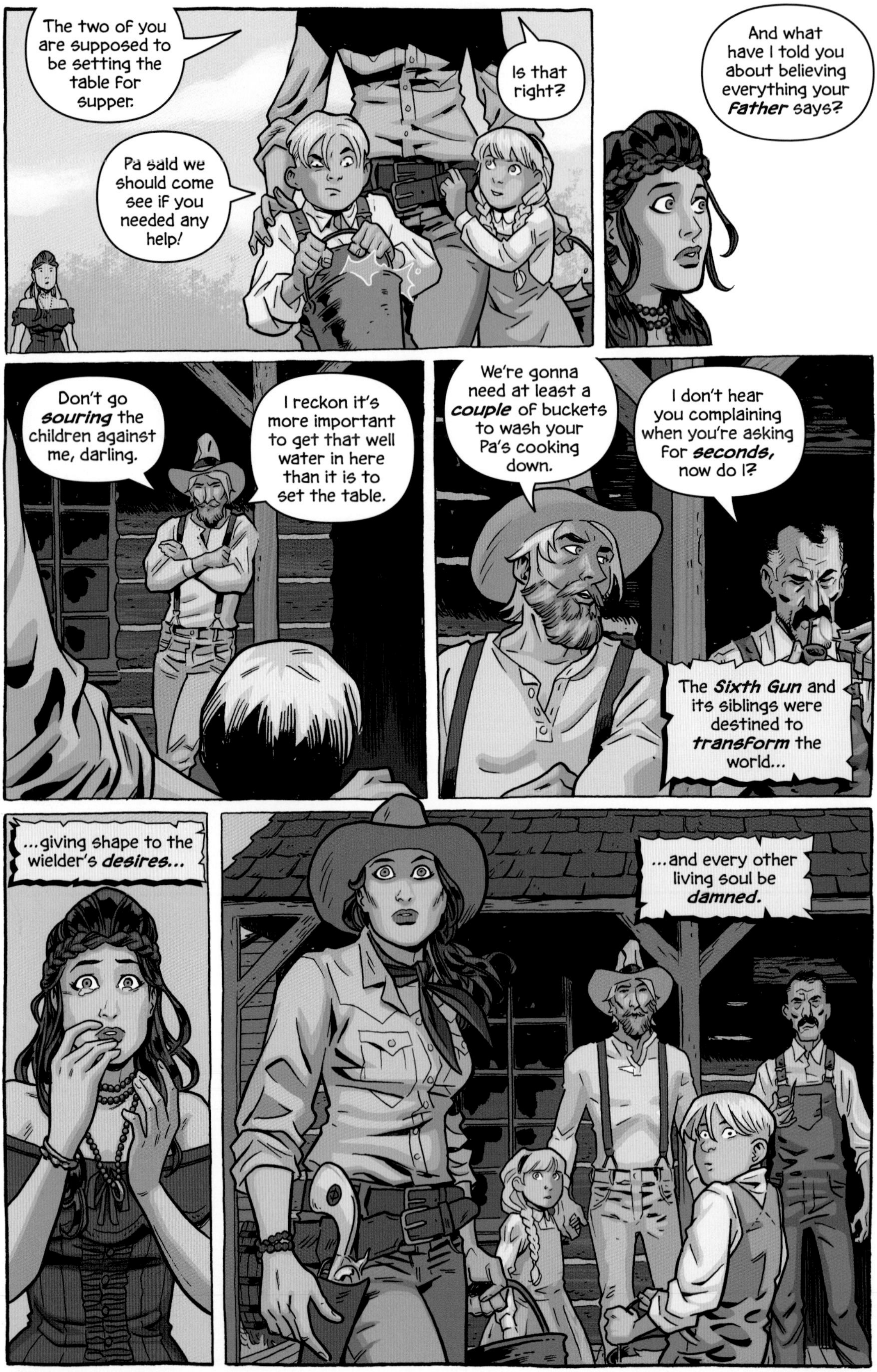

The two of you are supposed to be setting the table for supper.
Is that right?
Pa said we should come see if you needed any help!
And what have I told you about believing everything your *Father* says?
Don't go *souring* the children against me, darling.
I reckon it's more important to get that well water in here than it is to set the table.
We're gonna need at least a *couple* of buckets to wash your Pa's cooking down.
I don't hear you complaining when you're asking for *seconds,* now do I?
The *Sixth Gun* and its siblings were destined to *transform* the world...
...giving shape to the wielder's *desires...*
...and every other living soul be *damned.*

CHAPTER
SIX

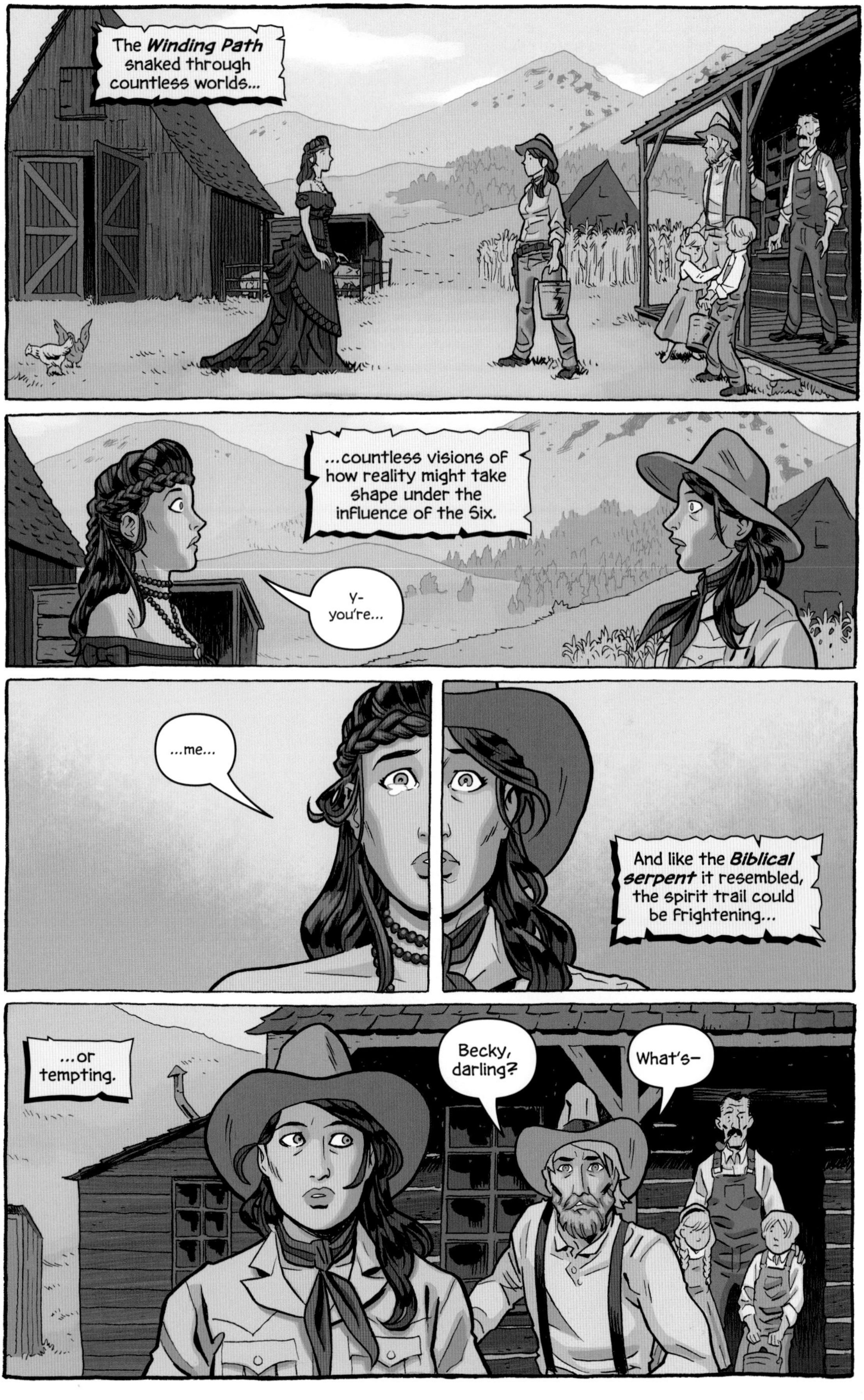
The *Winding Path* snaked through countless worlds...
...countless visions of how reality might take shape under the influence of the Six.
Y- you're...
...me...
And like the *Biblical serpent* it resembled, the spirit trail could be frightening...
...or tempting.
Becky, darling?
What's–

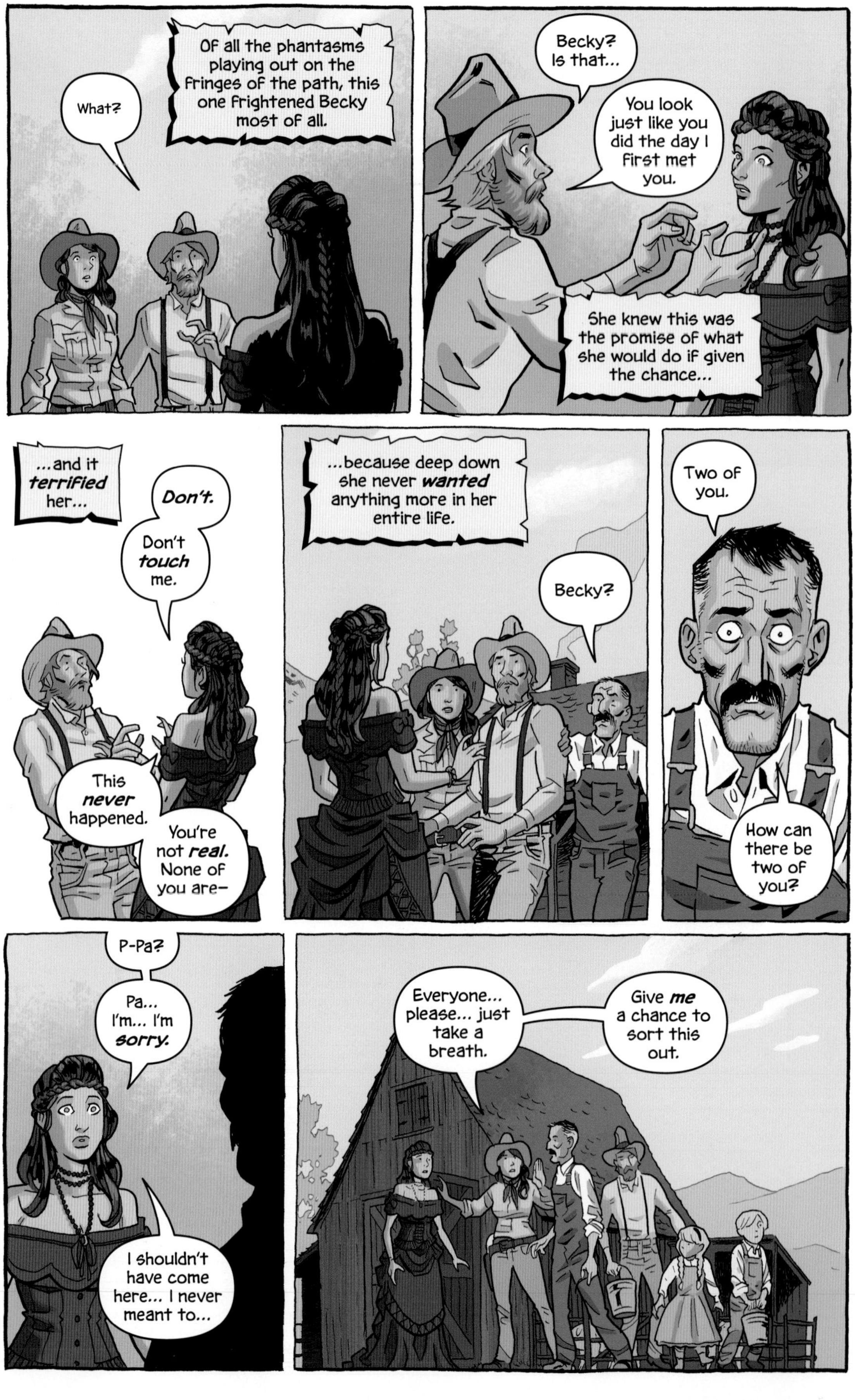
What?
Of all the phantasms playing out on the fringes of the path, this one frightened Becky most of all.
Becky? Is that...
You look just like you did the day I first met you.
She knew this was the promise of what she would do if given the chance...
...and it *terrified* her...
Don't.
Don't *touch* me.
This *never* happened.
You're not *real.* None of you are–
...because deep down she never *wanted* anything more in her entire life.
Becky?
Two of you.
How can there be two of you?
P-Pa?
Pa... I'm... I'm *sorry.*
I shouldn't have come here... I never meant to...
Everyone... please... just take a breath.
Give *me* a chance to sort this out.

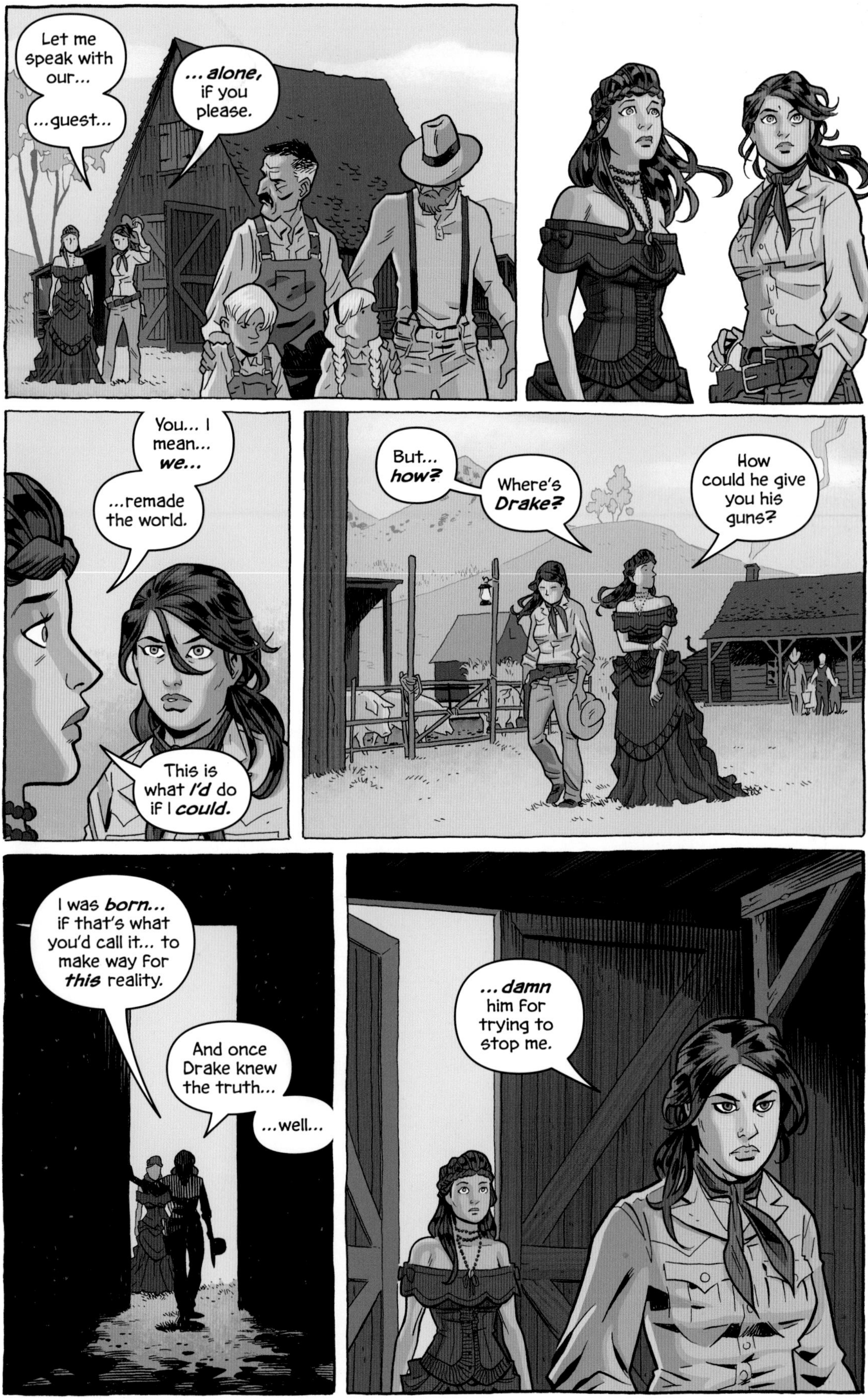

Let me speak with our...
...guest...
...alone, if you please.
You... I mean... we...
...remade the world.
This is what I'd do if I could.
But... how?
Where's Drake?
How could he give you his guns?
I was born... if that's what you'd call it... to make way for this reality.
And once Drake knew the truth...
...well...
...damn him for trying to stop me.

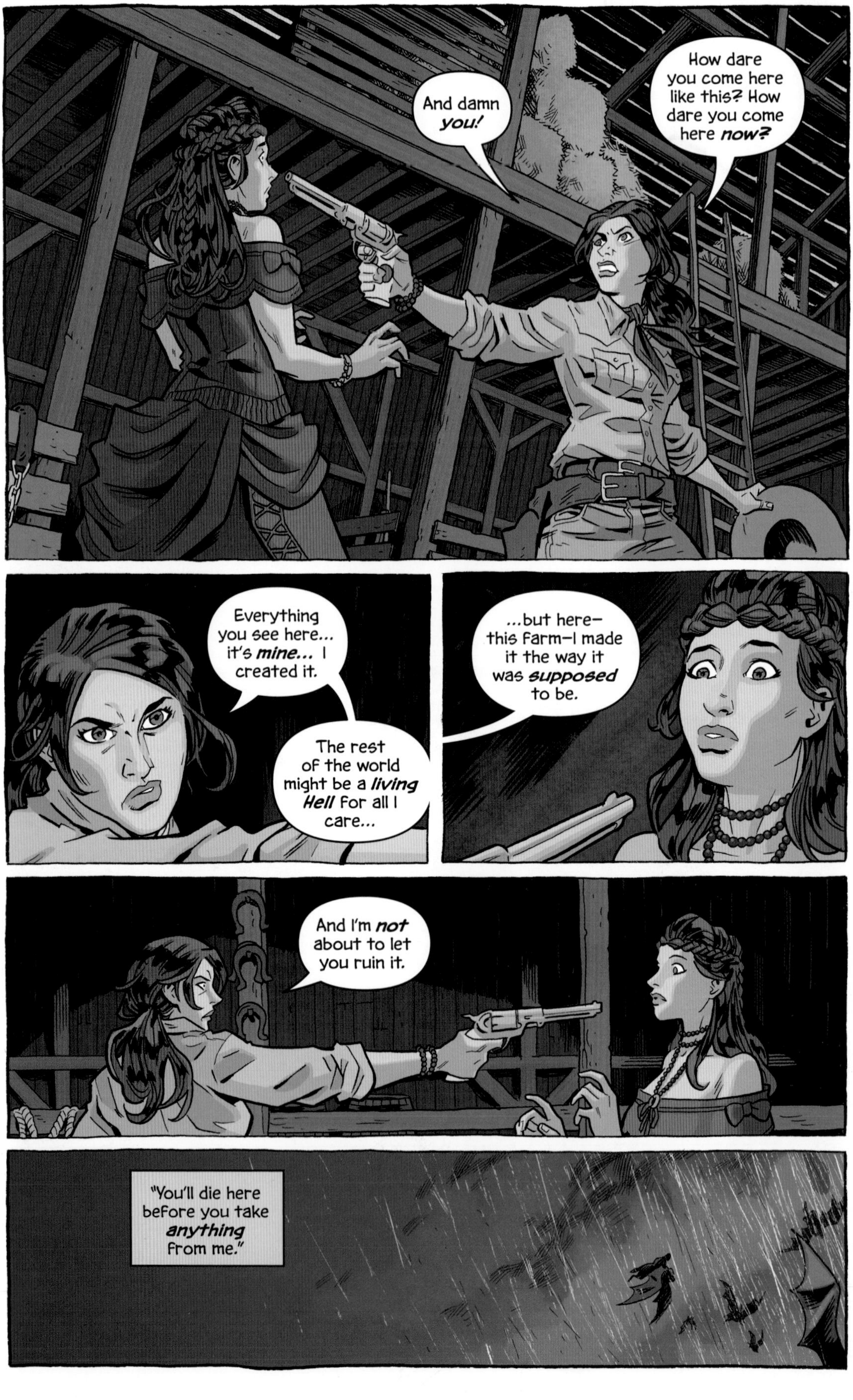
And damn *you!*
How dare you come here like this? How dare you come here *now?*
Everything you see here... it's *mine...* I created it.
The rest of the world might be a *living Hell* for all I care...
...but here— this farm—I made it the way it was *supposed* to be.
And I'm *not* about to let you ruin it.
"You'll die here before you take *anything* from me."

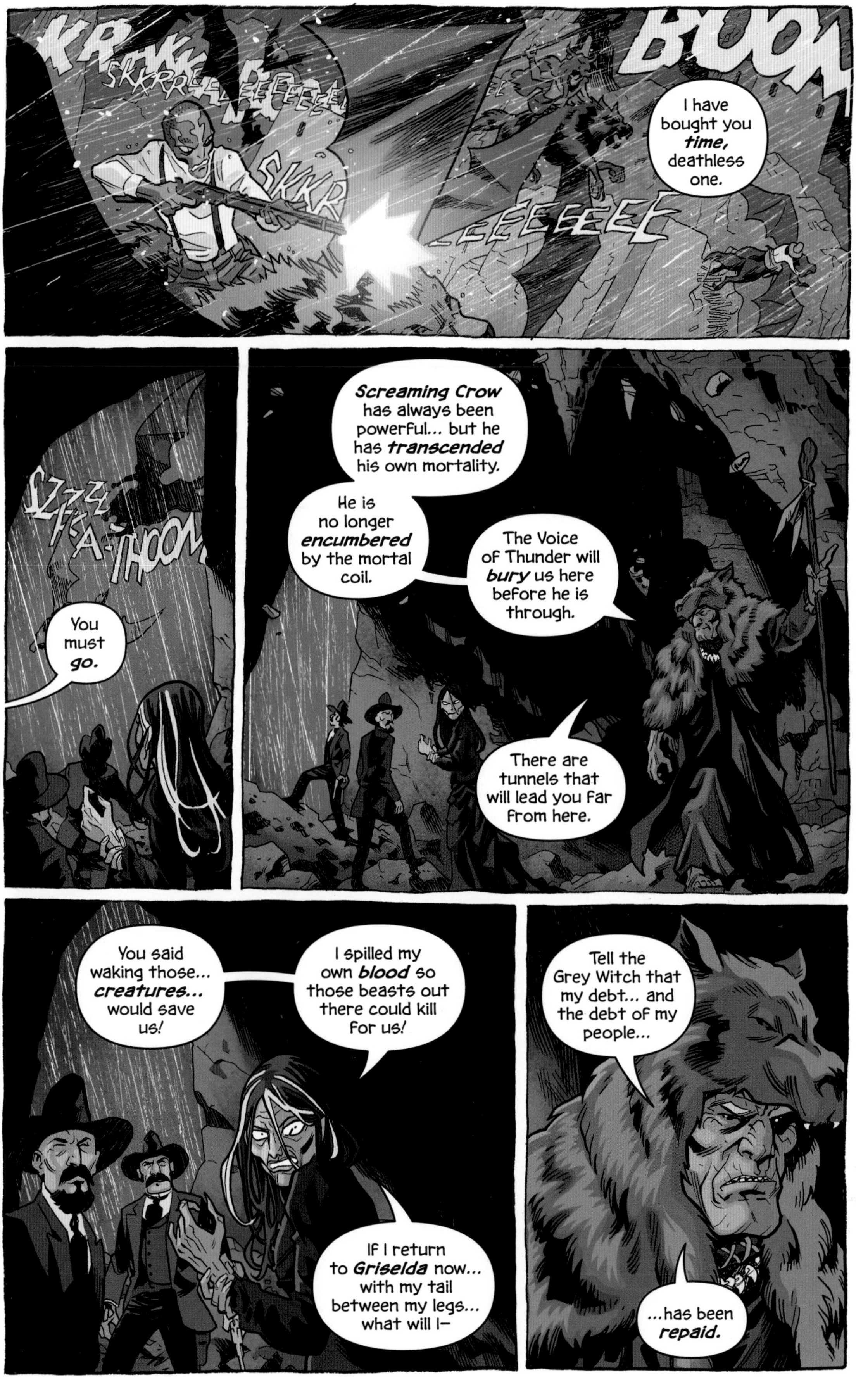

I have bought you *time,* deathless one.
Screaming Crow has always been powerful... but he has transcended his own mortality.
He is no longer encumbered by the mortal coil.
The Voice of Thunder will bury us here before he is through.
You must go.
There are tunnels that will lead you far from here.
You said waking those... creatures... would save us!
I spilled my own blood so those beasts out there could kill for us!
If I return to Griselda now... with my tail between my legs... what will I–
Tell the Grey Witch that my debt... and the debt of my people...
...has been repaid.

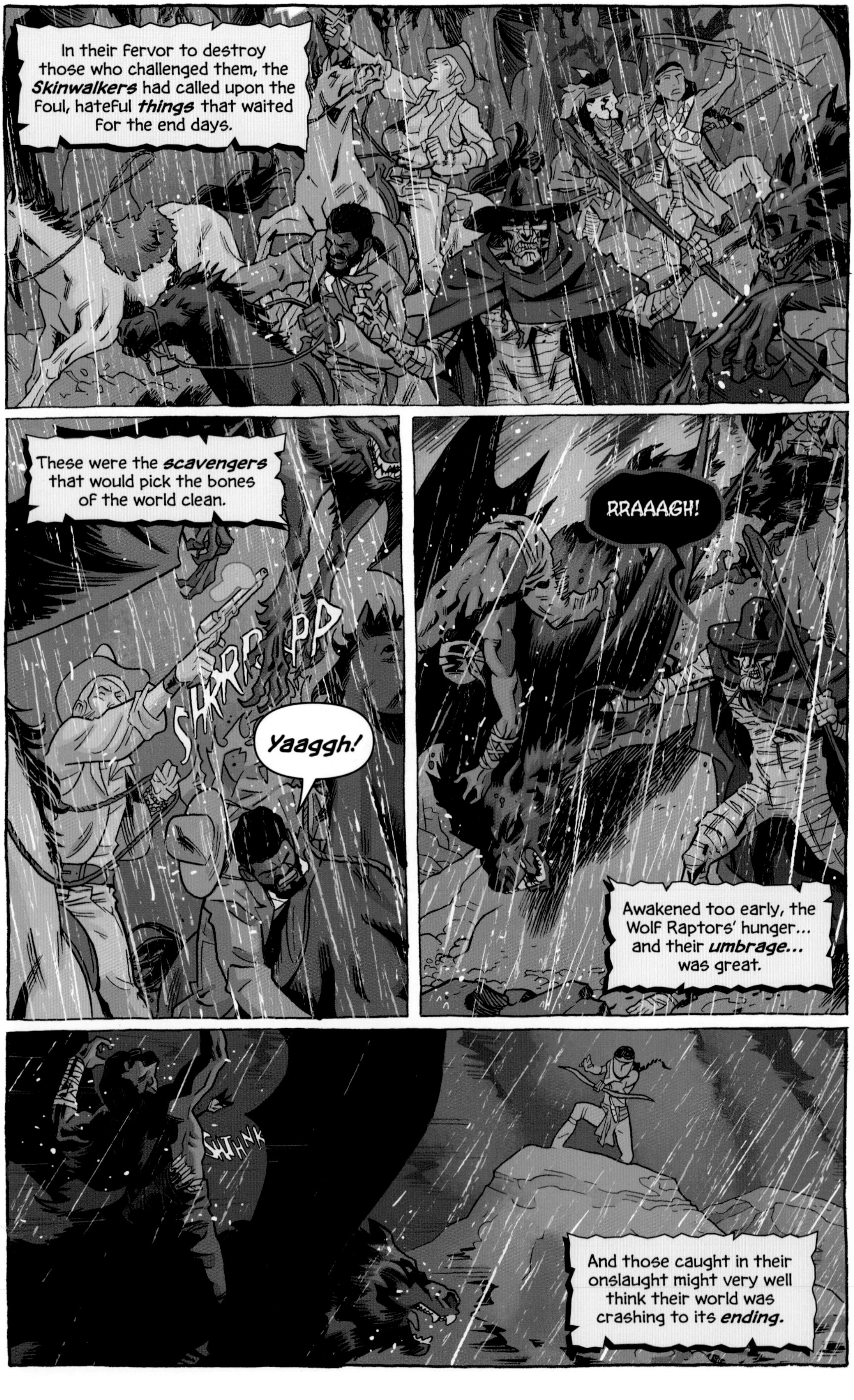
In their fervor to destroy those who challenged them, the *Skinwalkers* had called upon the foul, hateful *things* that waited for the end days.
These were the *scavengers* that would pick the bones of the world clean.
Yaaggh!
RRAAAGH!
Awakened too early, the Wolf Raptors' hunger... and their *umbrage...* was great.
SHTHNK
And those caught in their onslaught might very well think their world was crashing to its *ending.*

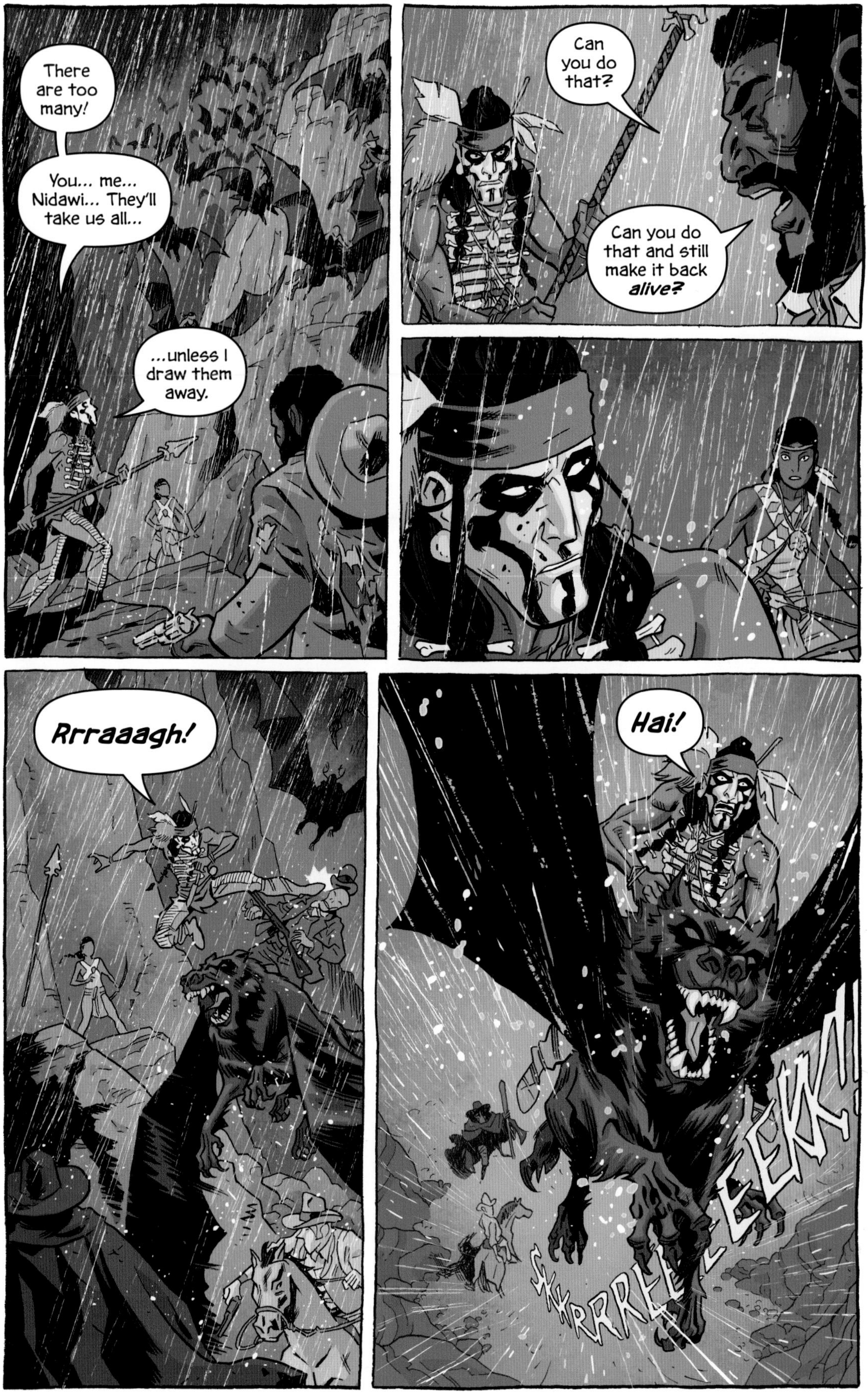
There are too many!
You... me... Nidawi... They'll take us all...
...unless I draw them away.
Can you do that?
Can you do that and still make it back *alive?*
Rrraaagh!
Hai!
SKKRRREEEEEKK!!

SKRT REEEEEEEEEKK!!

SKRT

Ammo's spent!

Same here!

We're in a **bad box** here!

CLIK

I can start kicking rocks at 'em, but that won't hold them off for long!

Nahuel.

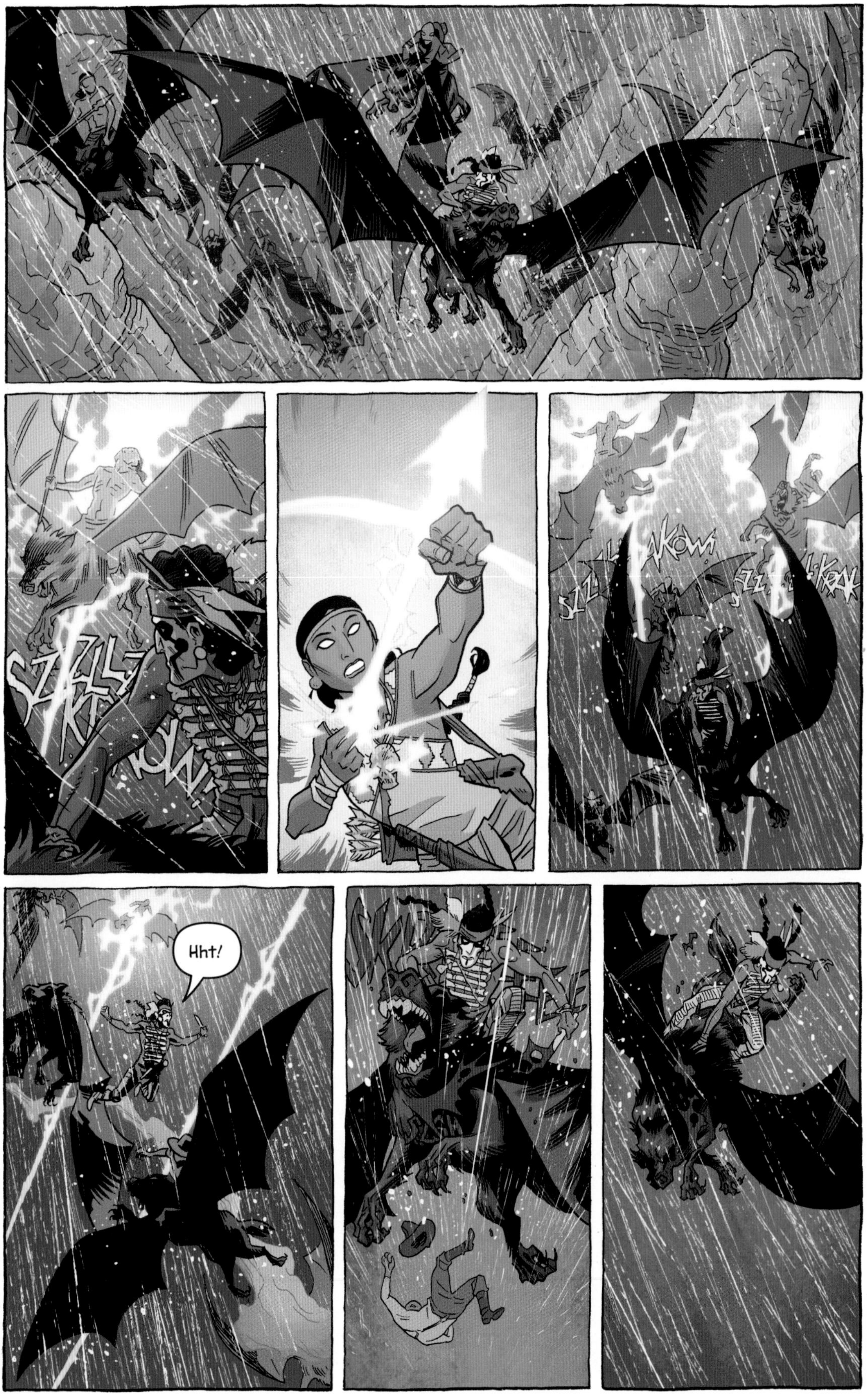
Hht!

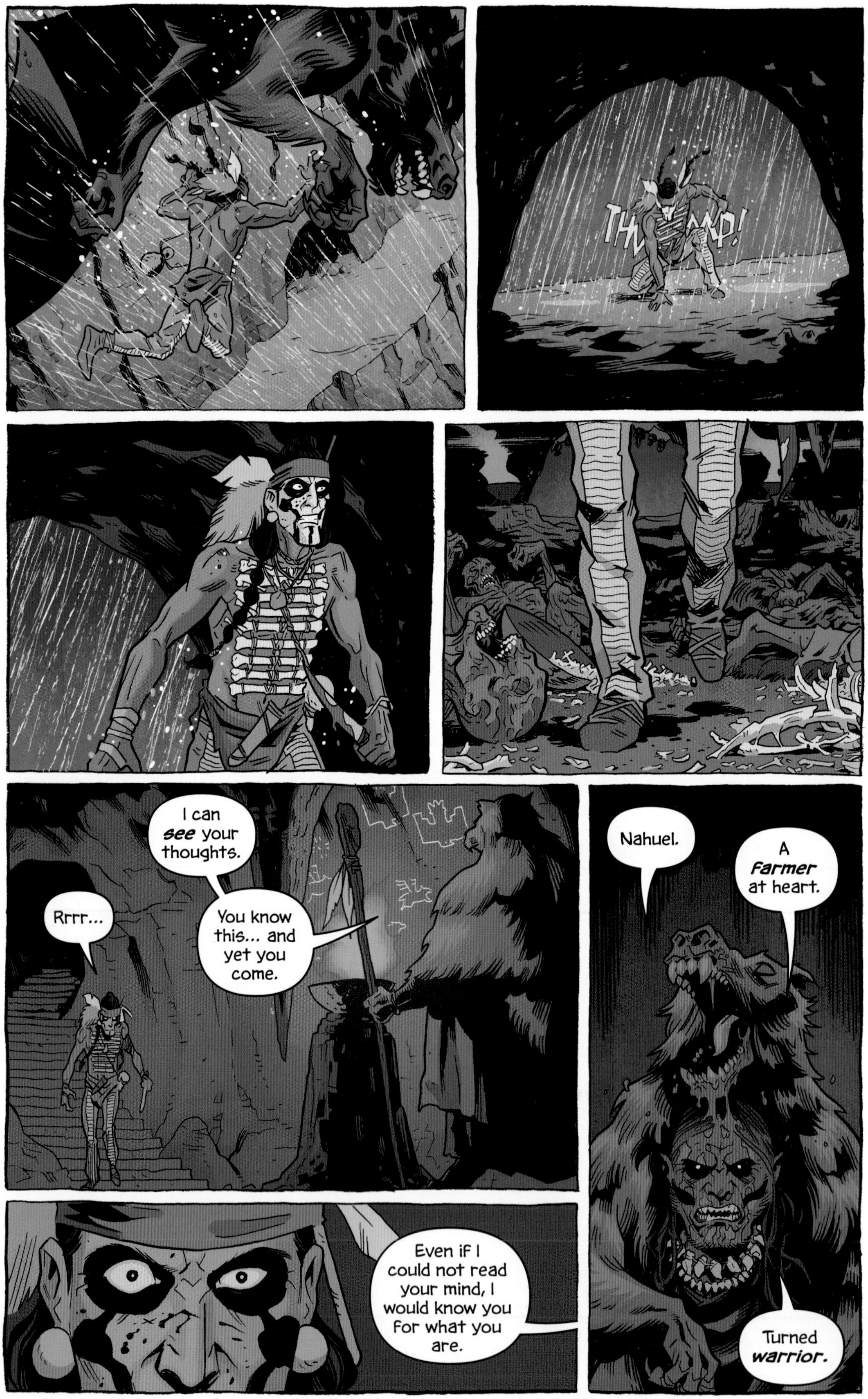
I can *see* your thoughts.
Rrrr...
You know this... and yet you come.
Nahuel.
A *farmer* at heart.
Even if I could not read your mind, I would know you for what you are.
Turned ***warrior.***

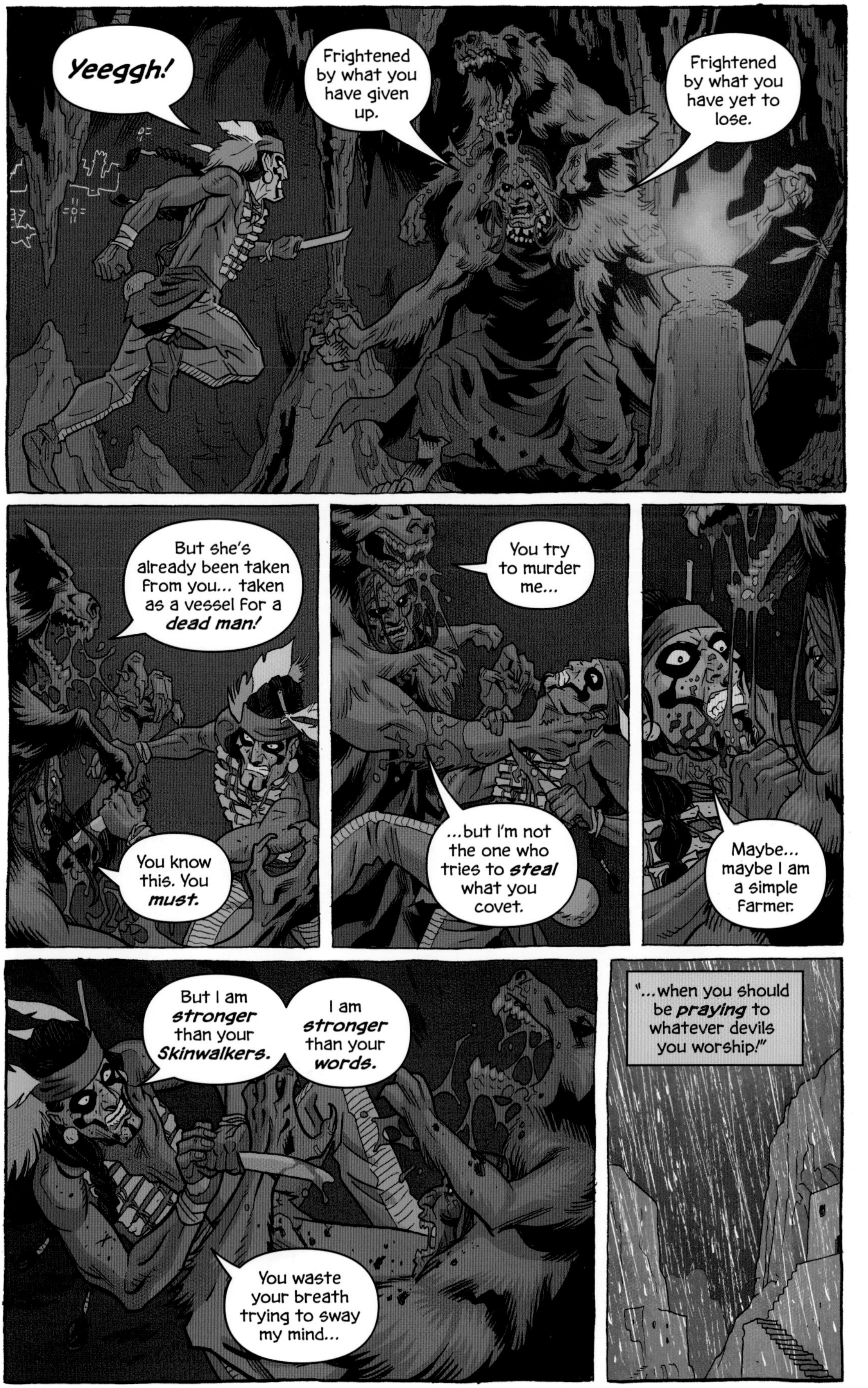
Yeeggh!
Frightened by what you have given up.
Frightened by what you have yet to lose.
But she's already been taken from you... taken as a vessel for a dead man!
You know this. You must.
You try to murder me...
...but I'm not the one who tries to steal what you covet.
Maybe... maybe I am a simple farmer.
But I am stronger than your Skinwalkers.
I am stronger than your words.
You waste your breath trying to sway my mind...
"...when you should be praying to whatever devils you worship!"

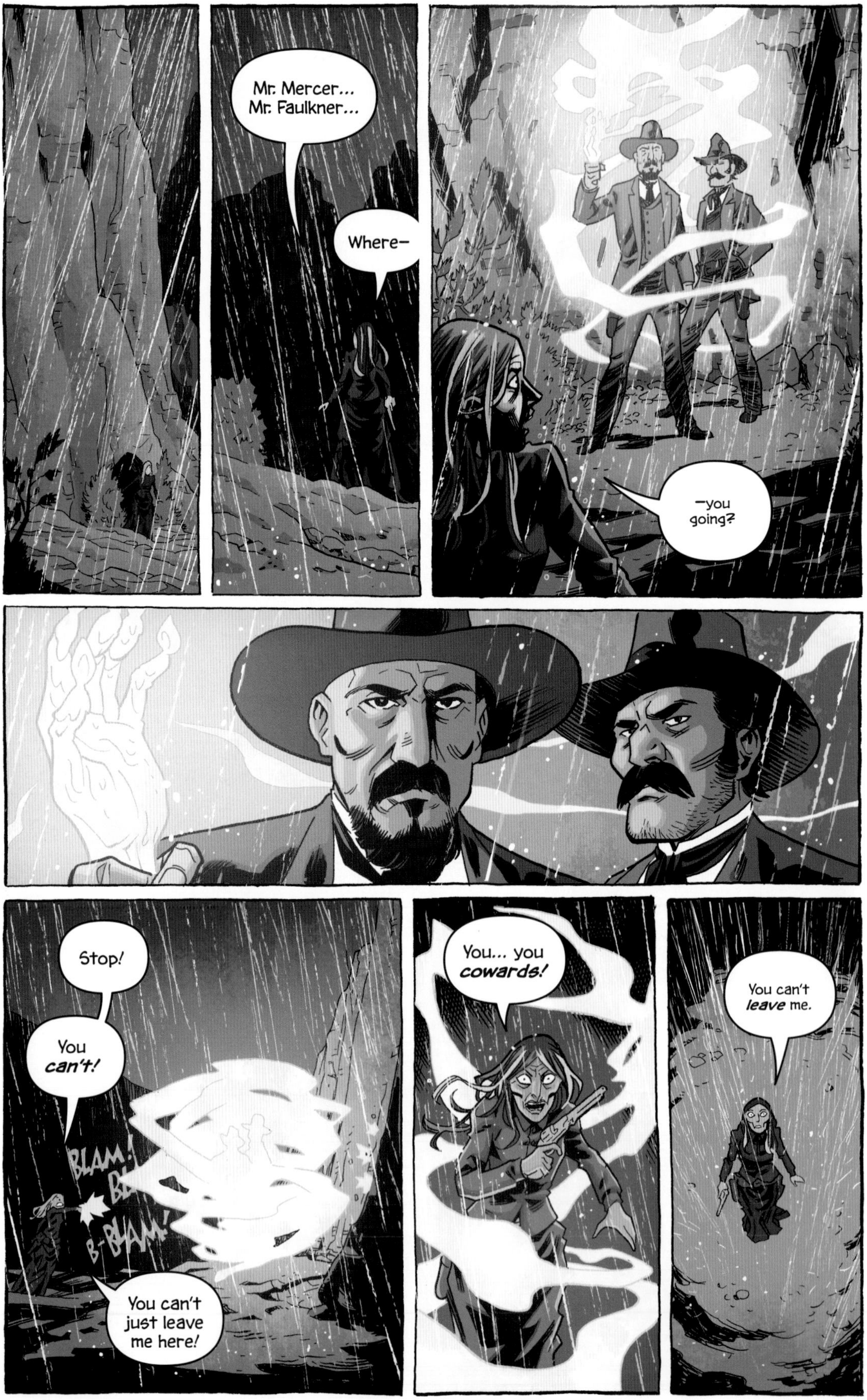
Mr. Mercer...
Mr. Faulkner...
Where—
—you going?
Stop!
You can't!
BLAM!
B-BLAM!
You can't just leave me here!
You... you cowards!
You can't leave me.

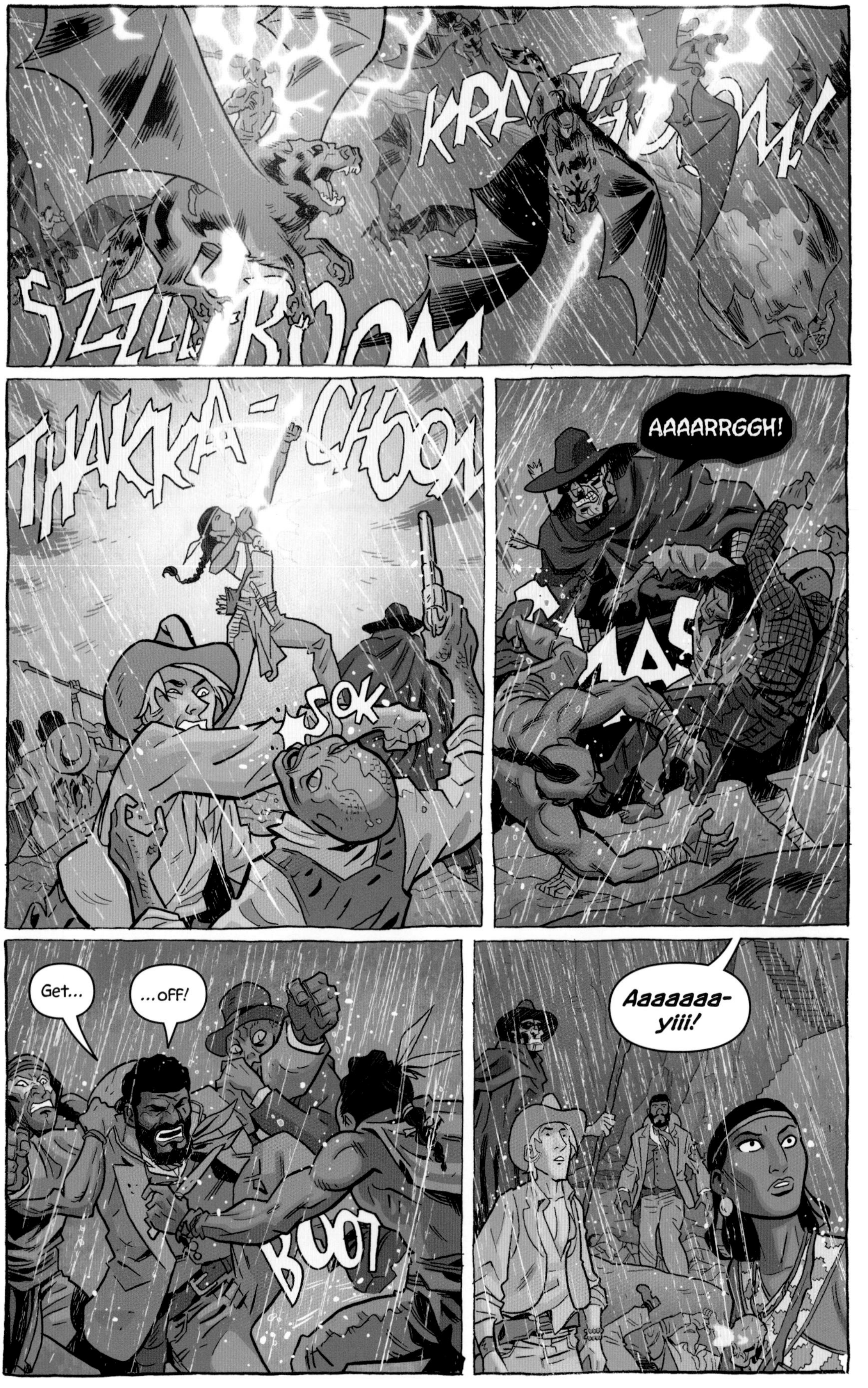
SOK
AAAARRGGH!
Get...
...off!
BOOT
Aaaaaaa-
yiii!

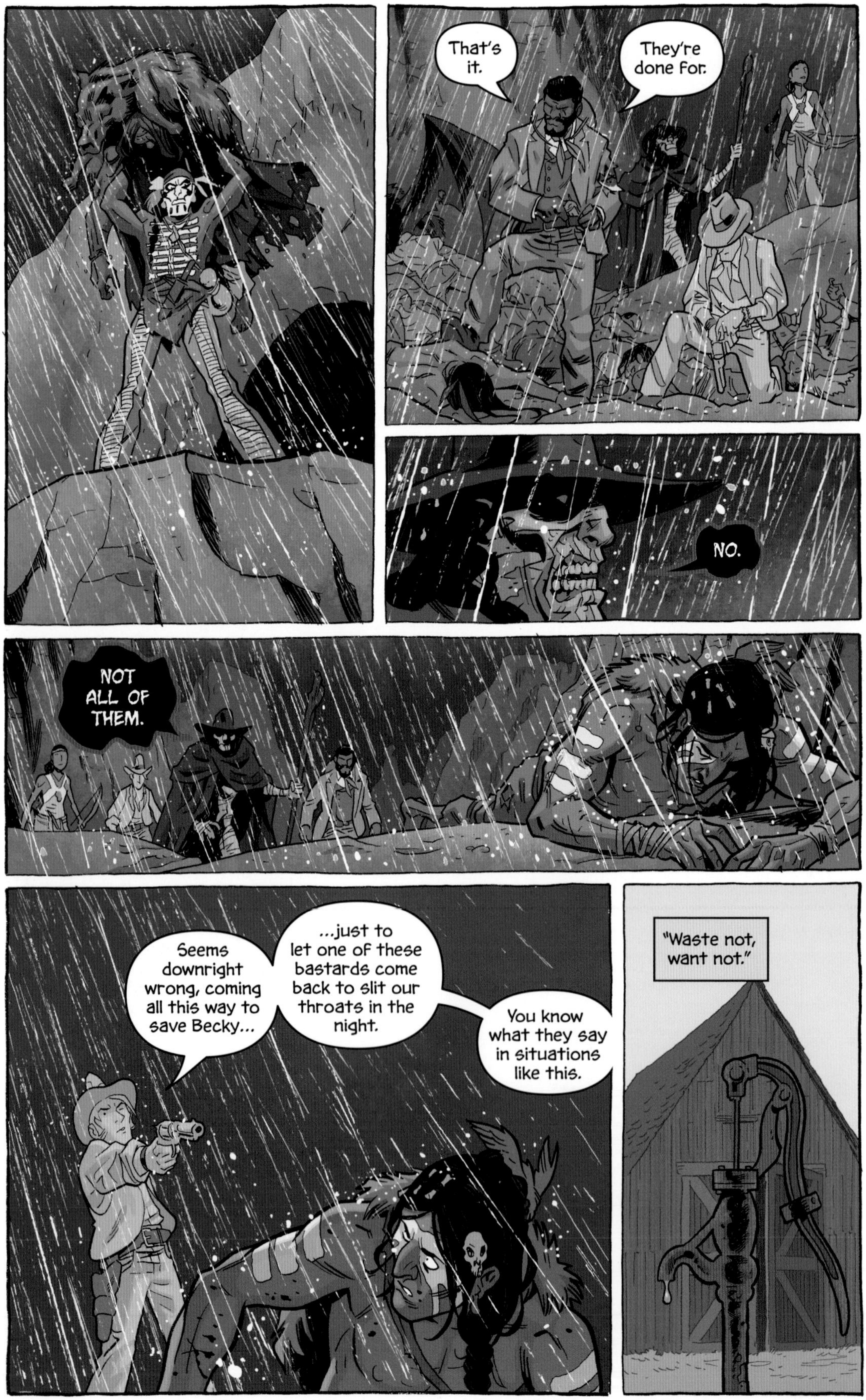
That's it.
They're done for.
NO.
NOT ALL OF THEM.
Seems downright wrong, coming all this way to save Becky...
...just to let one of these bastards come back to slit our throats in the night.
You know what they say in situations like this.
"Waste not, want not."

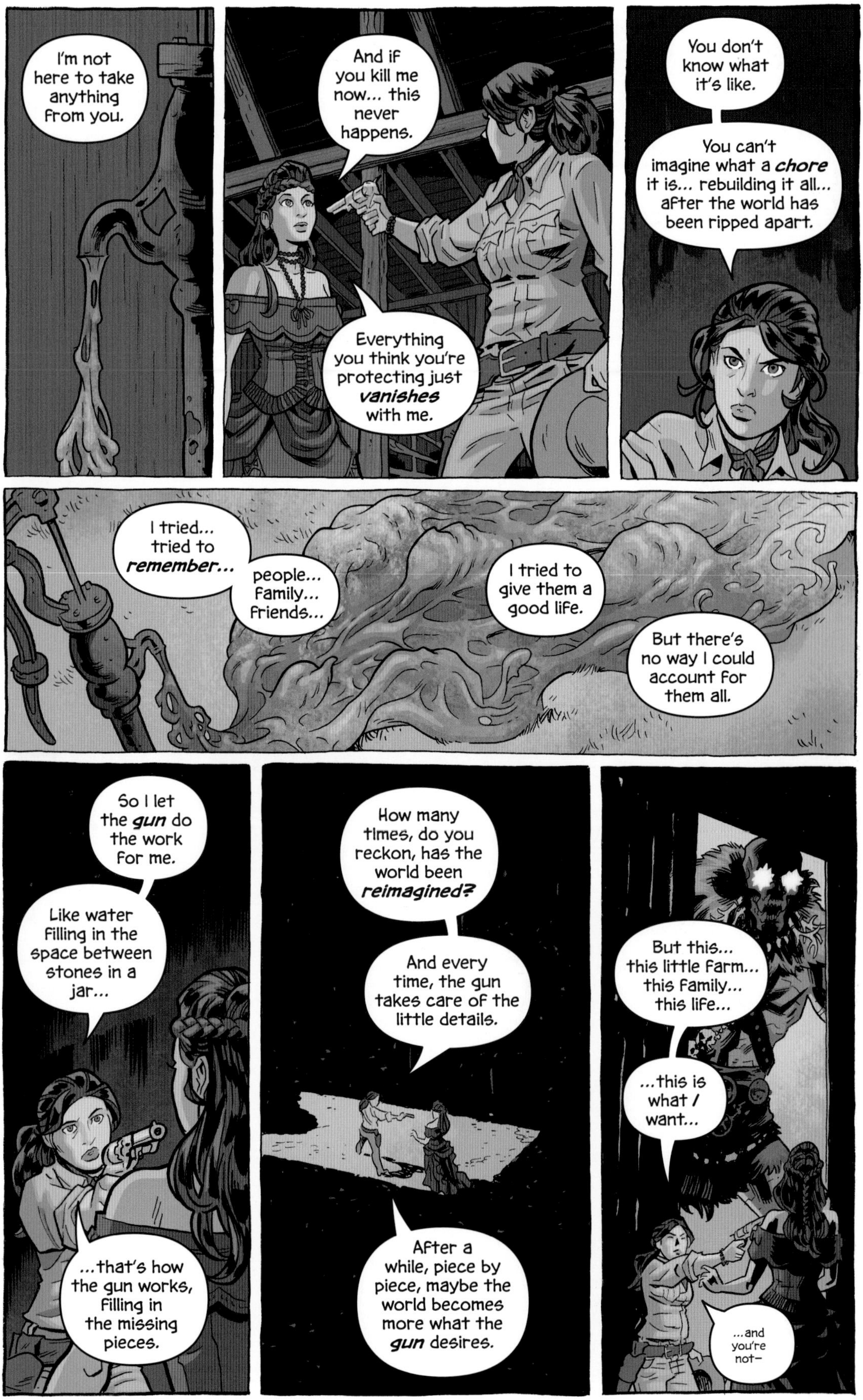
I'm not here to take anything from you.
And if you kill me now... this never happens.
Everything you think you're protecting just *vanishes* with me.
You don't know what it's like.
You can't imagine what a *chore* it is... rebuilding it all... after the world has been ripped apart.
I tried... tried to *remember...*
people... family... friends...
I tried to give them a good life.
But there's no way I could account for them all.
So I let the *gun* do the work for me.
Like water filling in the space between stones in a jar...
...that's how the gun works, filling in the missing pieces.
How many times, do you reckon, has the world been *reimagined?*
And every time, the gun takes care of the little details.
After a while, piece by piece, maybe the world becomes more what the *gun* desires.
But this... this little farm... this family... this life...
...this is what *I* want...
...and you're not—

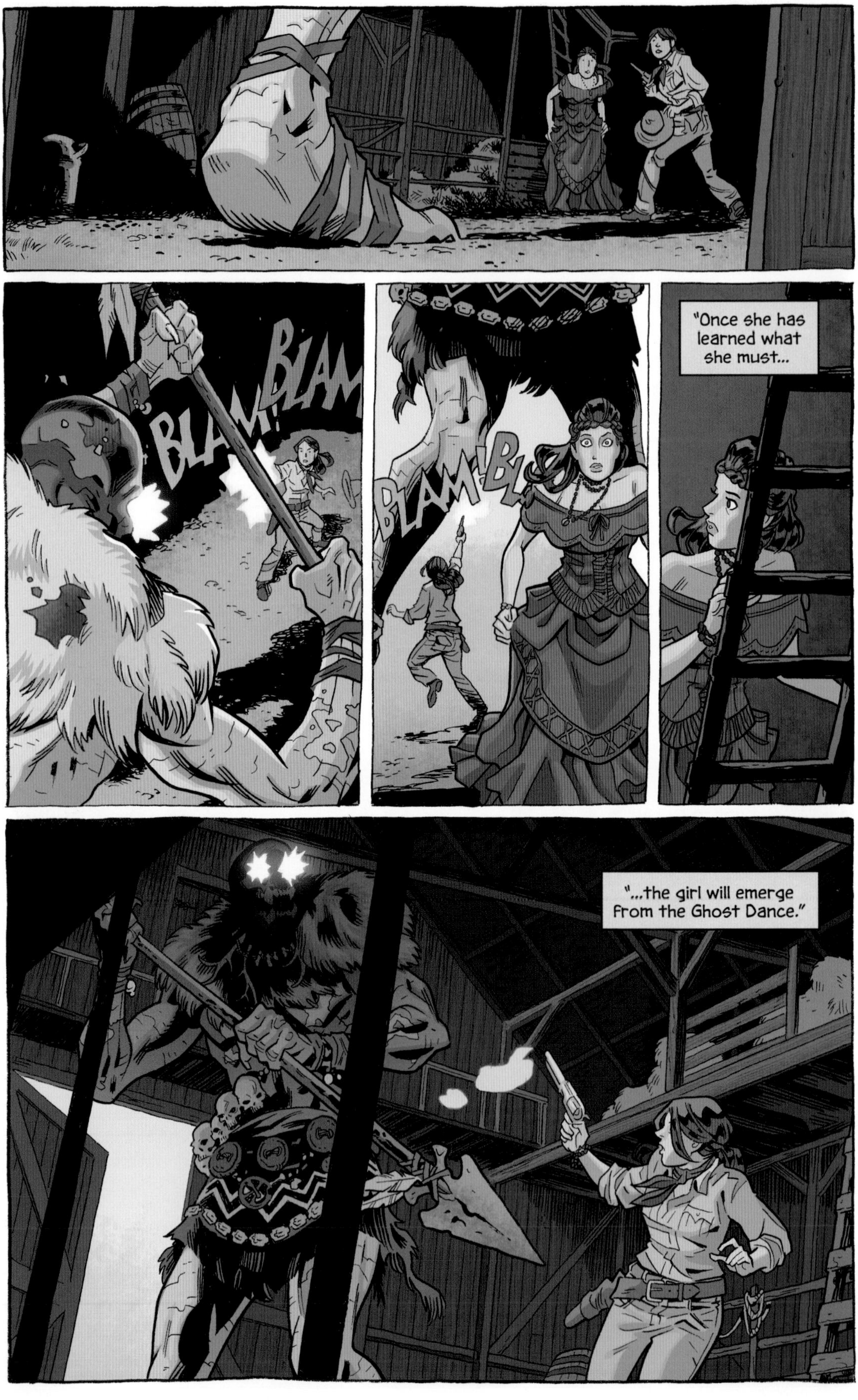
BLAM!
BLAM!
BLAM!
BLAM!BL
"Once she has learned what she must...
"...the girl will emerge from the Ghost Dance."

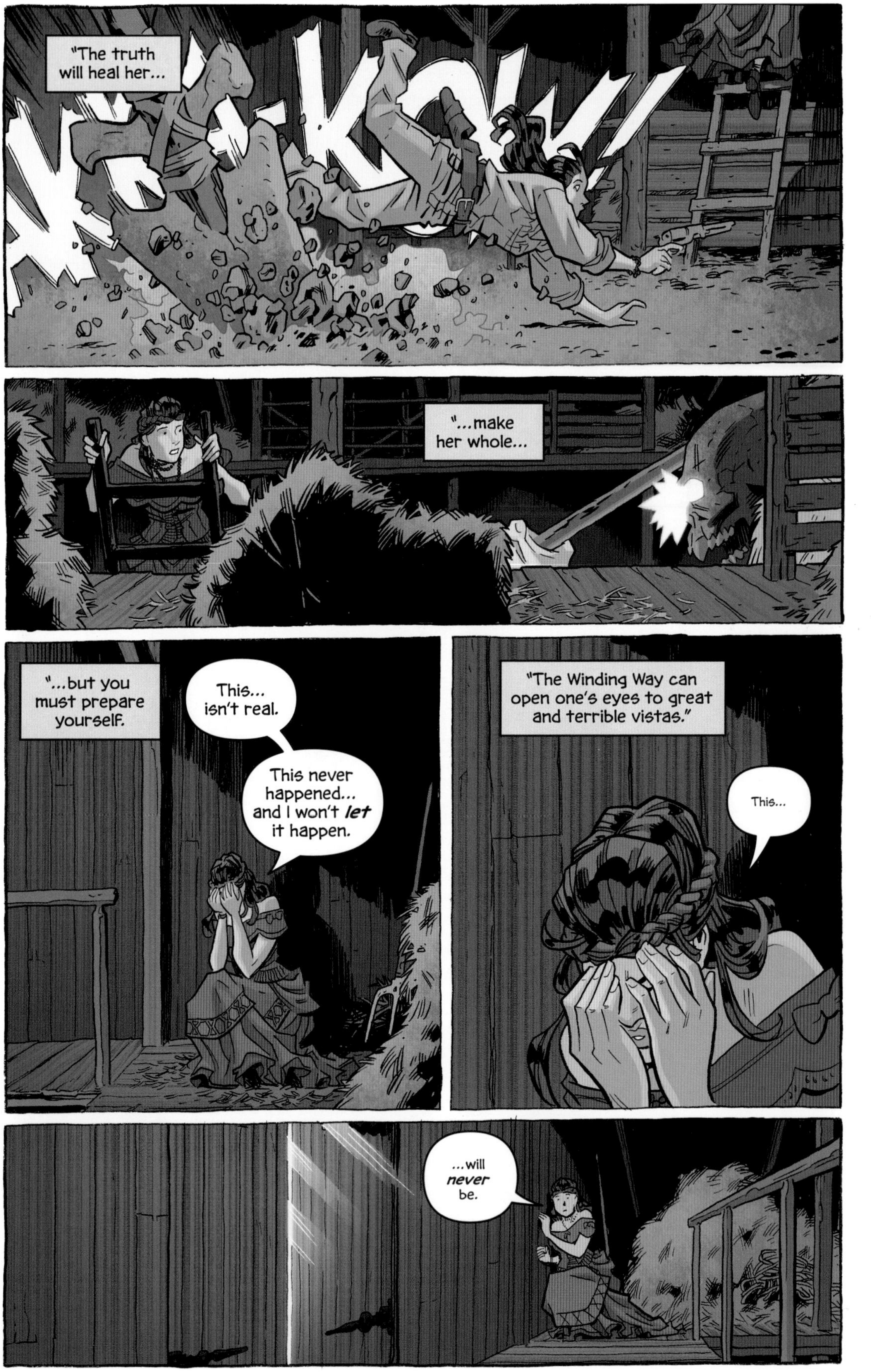
"The truth will heal her...
"...make her whole...
"...but you must prepare yourself.
This... isn't real.
This never happened... and I won't *let* it happen.
"The Winding Way can open one's eyes to great and terrible vistas."
This...
...will *never* be.

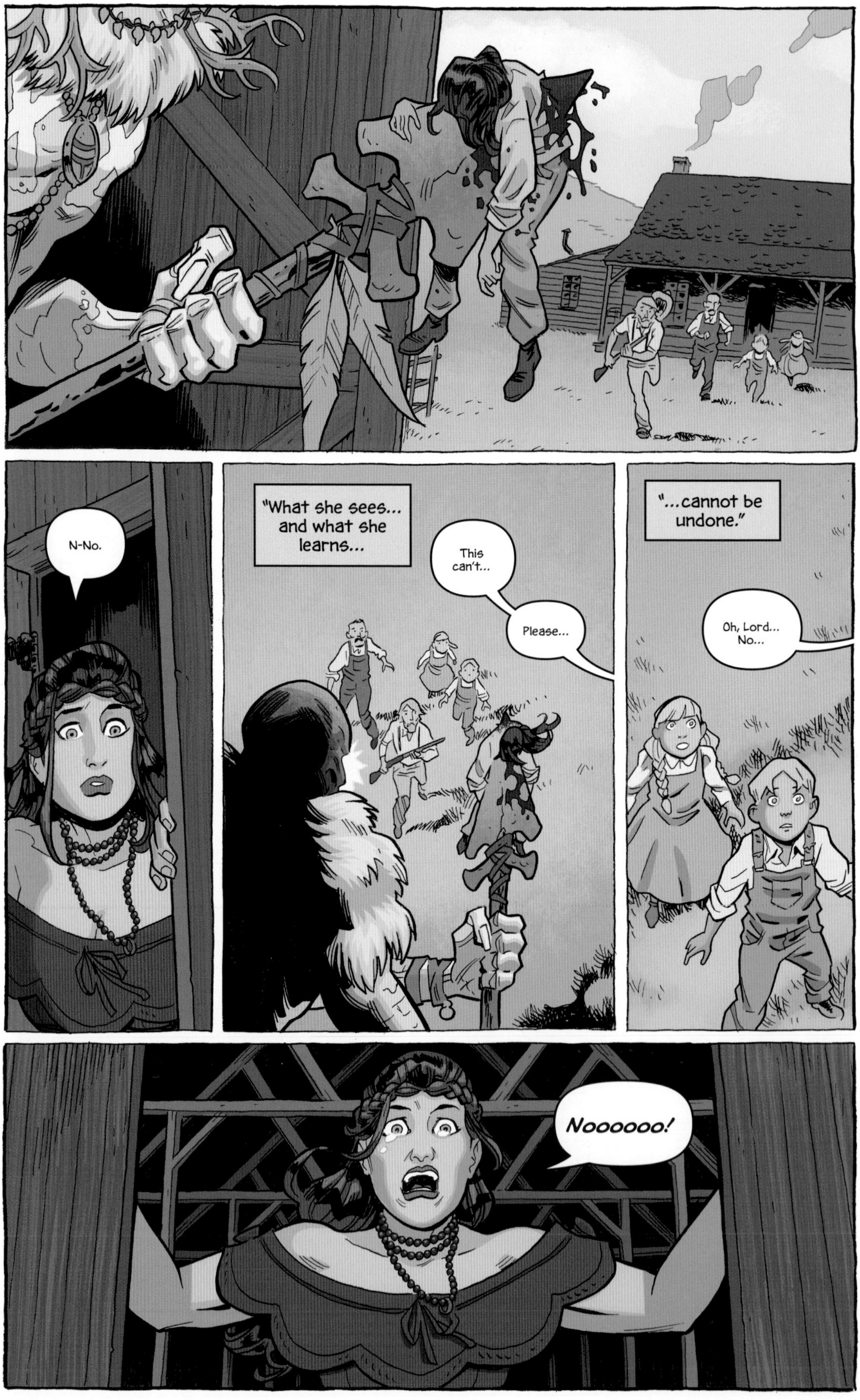
N-No.
"What she sees... and what she learns...
This can't...
Please...
"...cannot be undone."
Oh, Lord... No...
Noooooo!

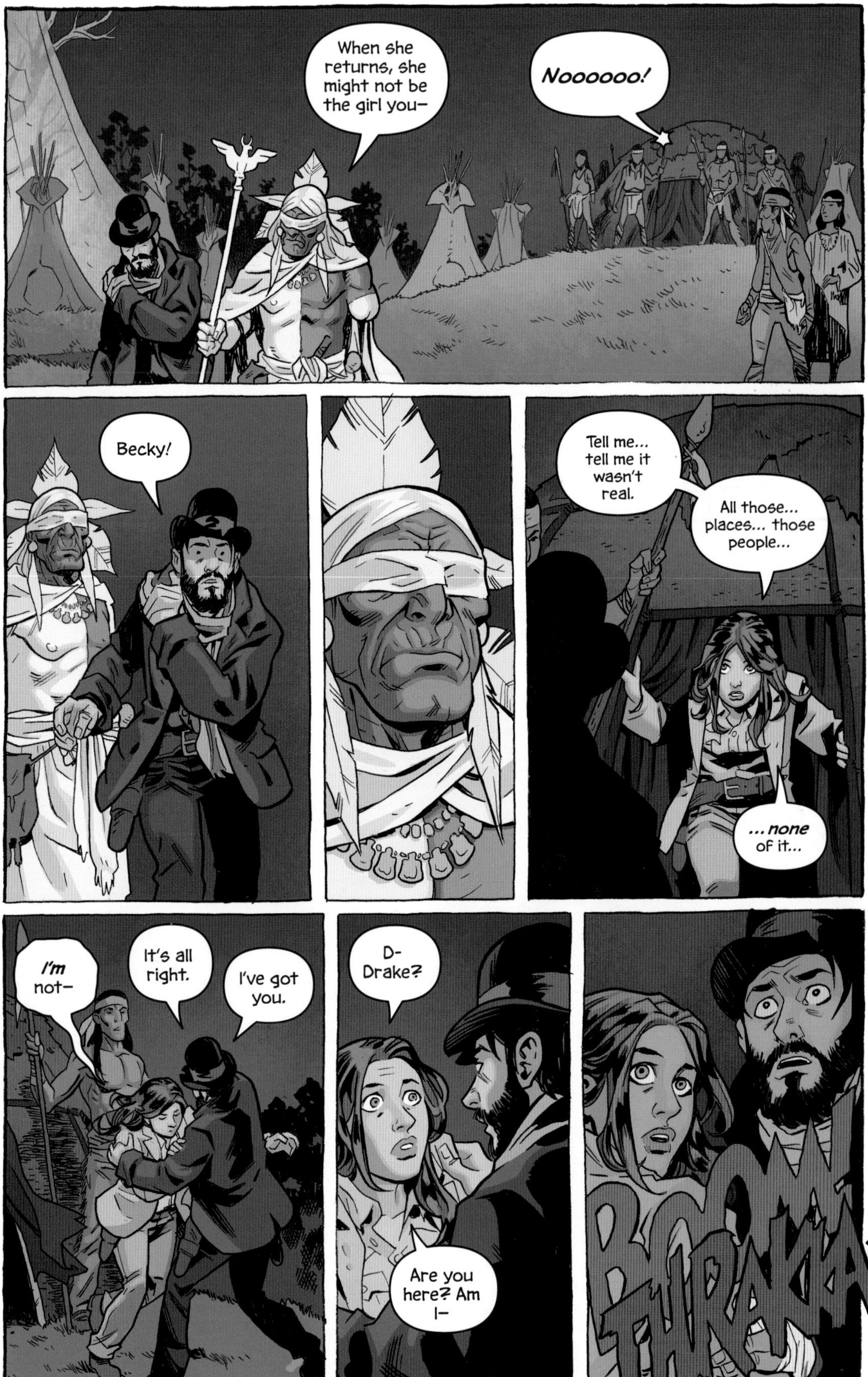
When she returns, she might not be the girl you–
Noooooo!
Becky!
Tell me... tell me it wasn't real.
All those... places... those people...
...none of it...
I'm not–
It's all right.
I've got you.
D-Drake?
Are you here? Am I–
BOOM
THRAKA

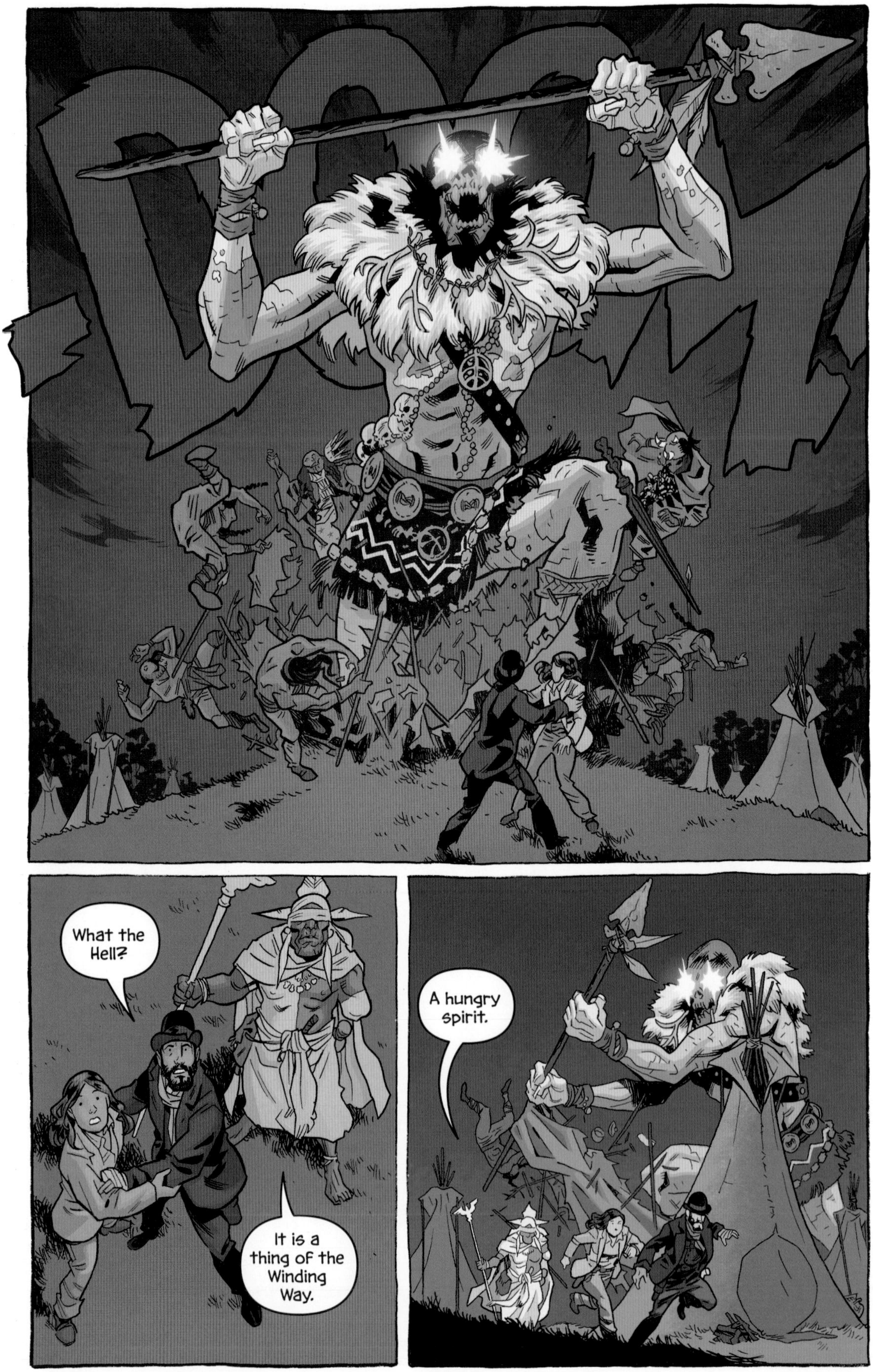
What the Hell?
It is a thing of the Winding Way.
A hungry spirit.

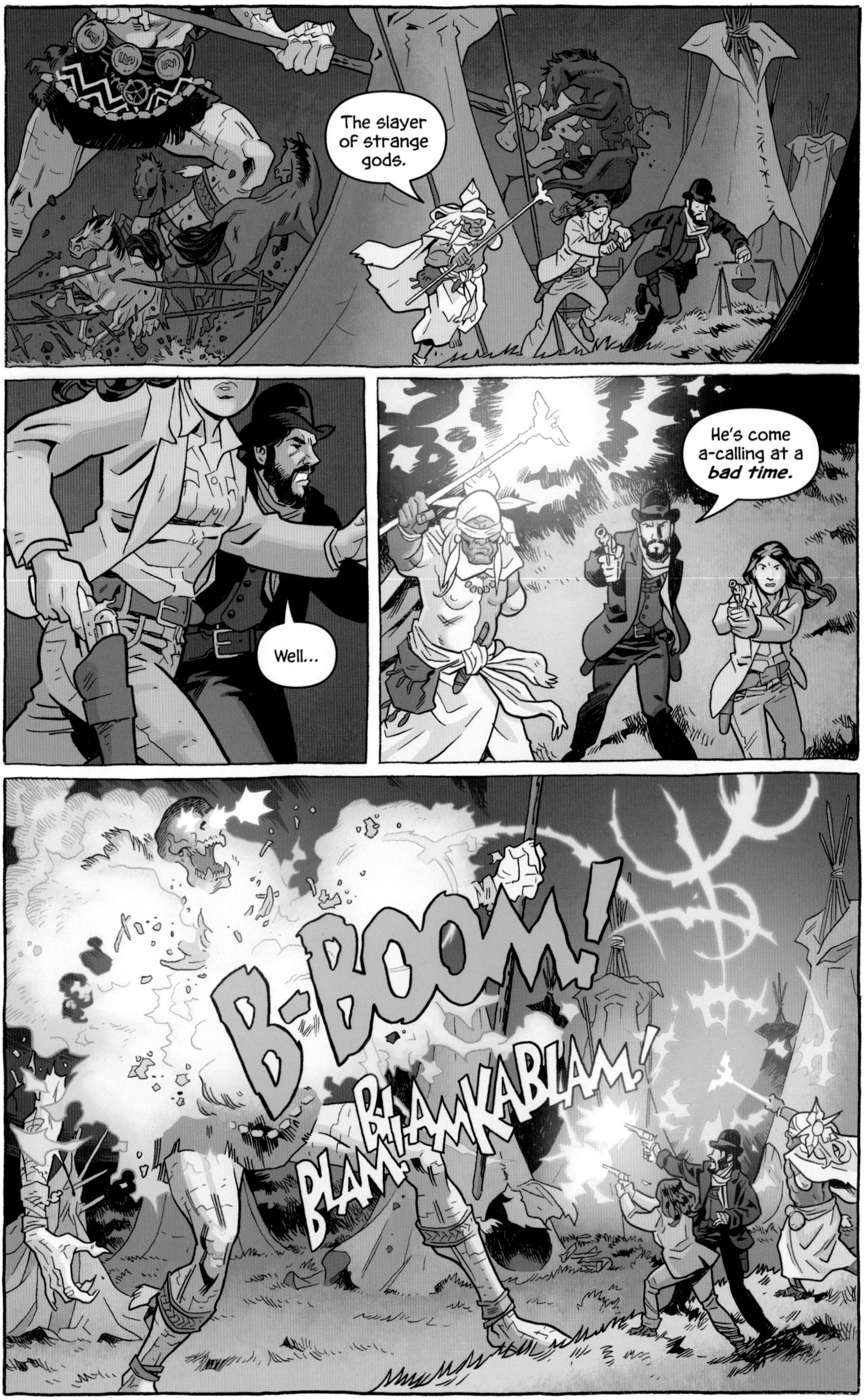
The slayer of strange gods.
Well...
He's come a-calling at a *bad time.*
B-BOOM!
BLAM!
BLAM!
BLAMKABLAM!

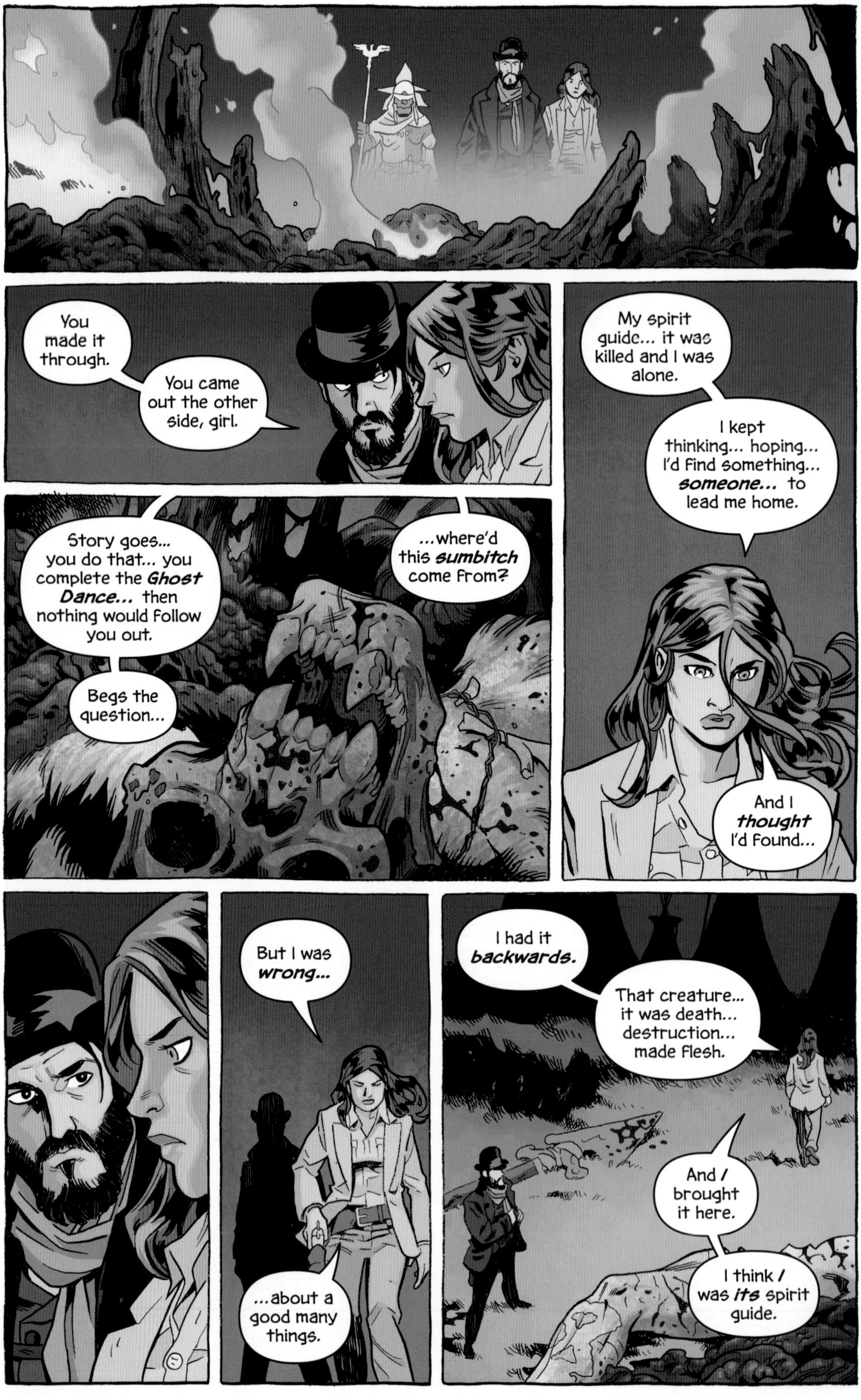
You made it through.
You came out the other side, girl.
My spirit guide... it was killed and I was alone.
I kept thinking... hoping... I'd find something... someone... to lead me home.
Story goes... you do that... you complete the Ghost Dance... then nothing would follow you out.
Begs the question...
...where'd this sumbitch come from?
And I thought I'd found...
But I was wrong...
...about a good many things.
I had it backwards.
That creature... it was death... destruction... made flesh.
And I brought it here.
I think I was its spirit guide.

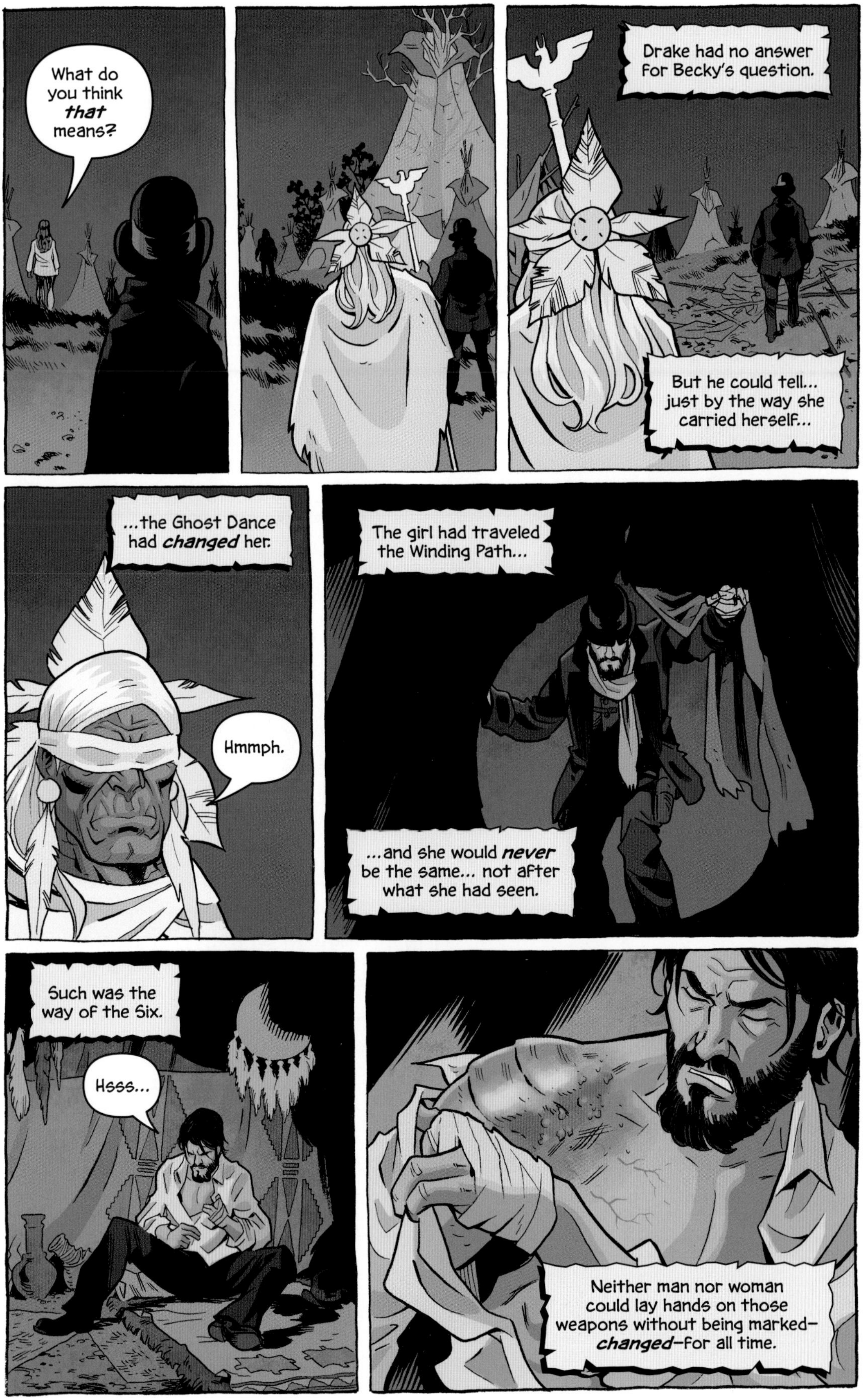

What do you think *that* means?
Drake had no answer for Becky's question.
But he could tell... just by the way she carried herself...
...the Ghost Dance had *changed* her.
Hmmph.
The girl had traveled the Winding Path...
...and she would *never* be the same... not after what she had seen.
Such was the way of the Six.
Hsss...
Neither man nor woman could lay hands on those weapons without being marked—*changed*—for all time.

EPILOGUE

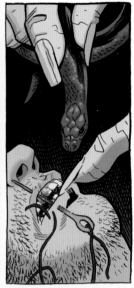

SKLLCH

CRKKK

Gr-Griselda.

They stopped us.

The girl's friends... They found us...

...and I fear they'll be *coming* for us next.

...*killed* so many...

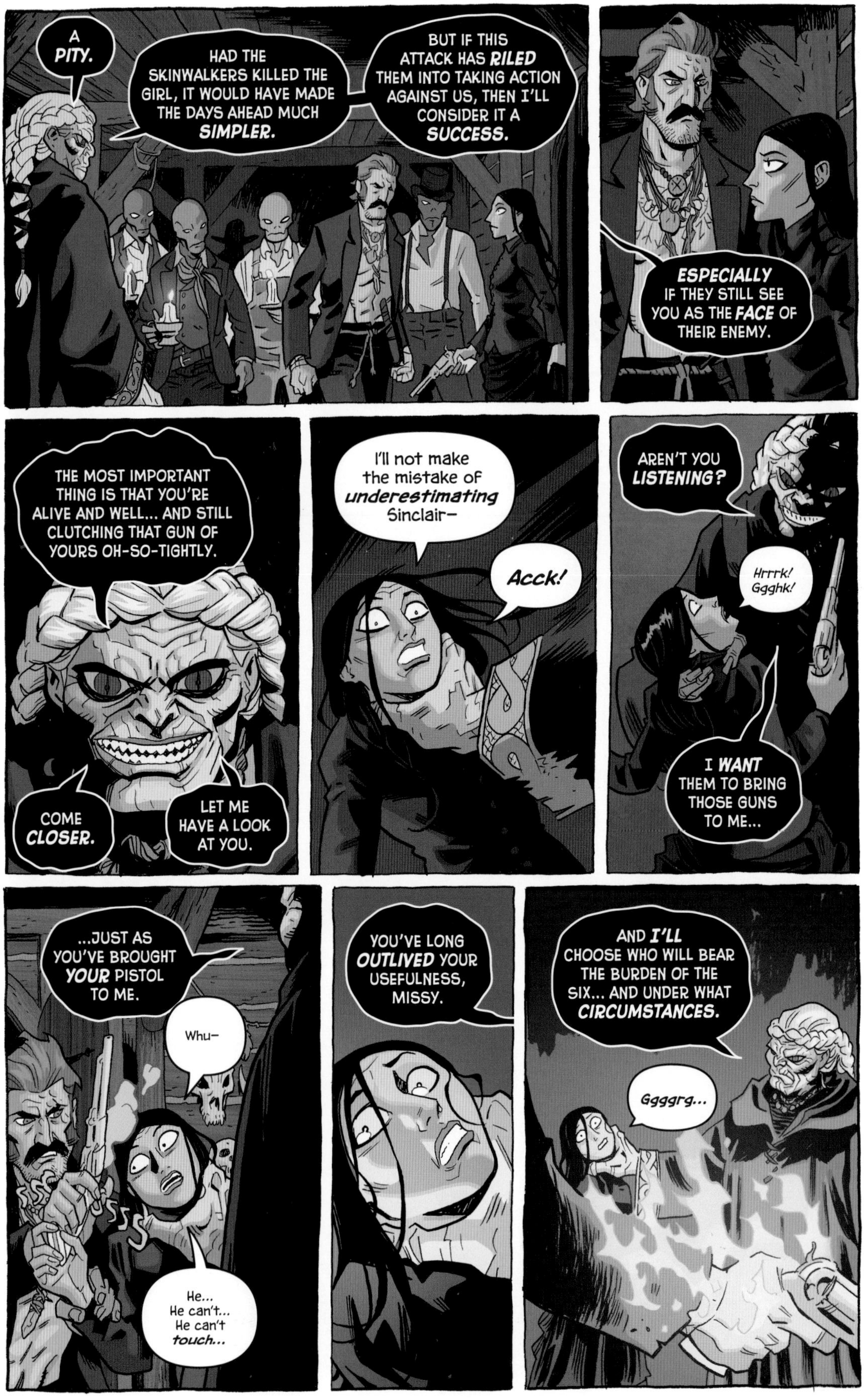
A PITY.
HAD THE SKINWALKERS KILLED THE GIRL, IT WOULD HAVE MADE THE DAYS AHEAD MUCH SIMPLER.
BUT IF THIS ATTACK HAS RILED THEM INTO TAKING ACTION AGAINST US, THEN I'LL CONSIDER IT A SUCCESS.
ESPECIALLY IF THEY STILL SEE YOU AS THE FACE OF THEIR ENEMY.
THE MOST IMPORTANT THING IS THAT YOU'RE ALIVE AND WELL... AND STILL CLUTCHING THAT GUN OF YOURS OH-SO-TIGHTLY.
COME CLOSER.
LET ME HAVE A LOOK AT YOU.
I'll not make the mistake of underestimating Sinclair–
Acck!
AREN'T YOU LISTENING?
Hrrrk! Gggghk!
I WANT THEM TO BRING THOSE GUNS TO ME...
...JUST AS YOU'VE BROUGHT YOUR PISTOL TO ME.
Whu–
He... He can't... He can't touch...
YOU'VE LONG OUTLIVED YOUR USEFULNESS, MISSY.
AND I'LL CHOOSE WHO WILL BEAR THE BURDEN OF THE SIX... AND UNDER WHAT CIRCUMSTANCES.
Ggggrg...

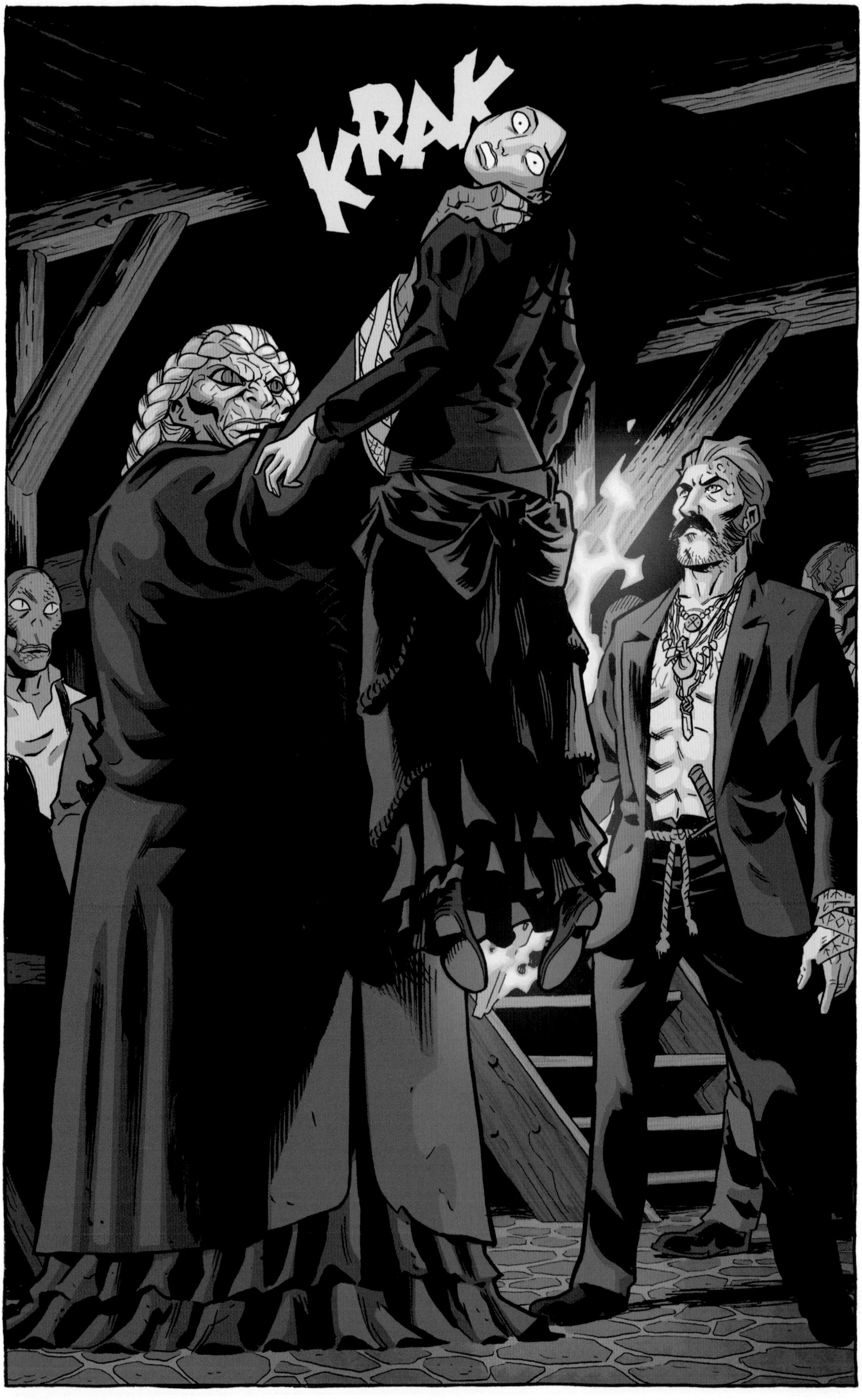
KRAK

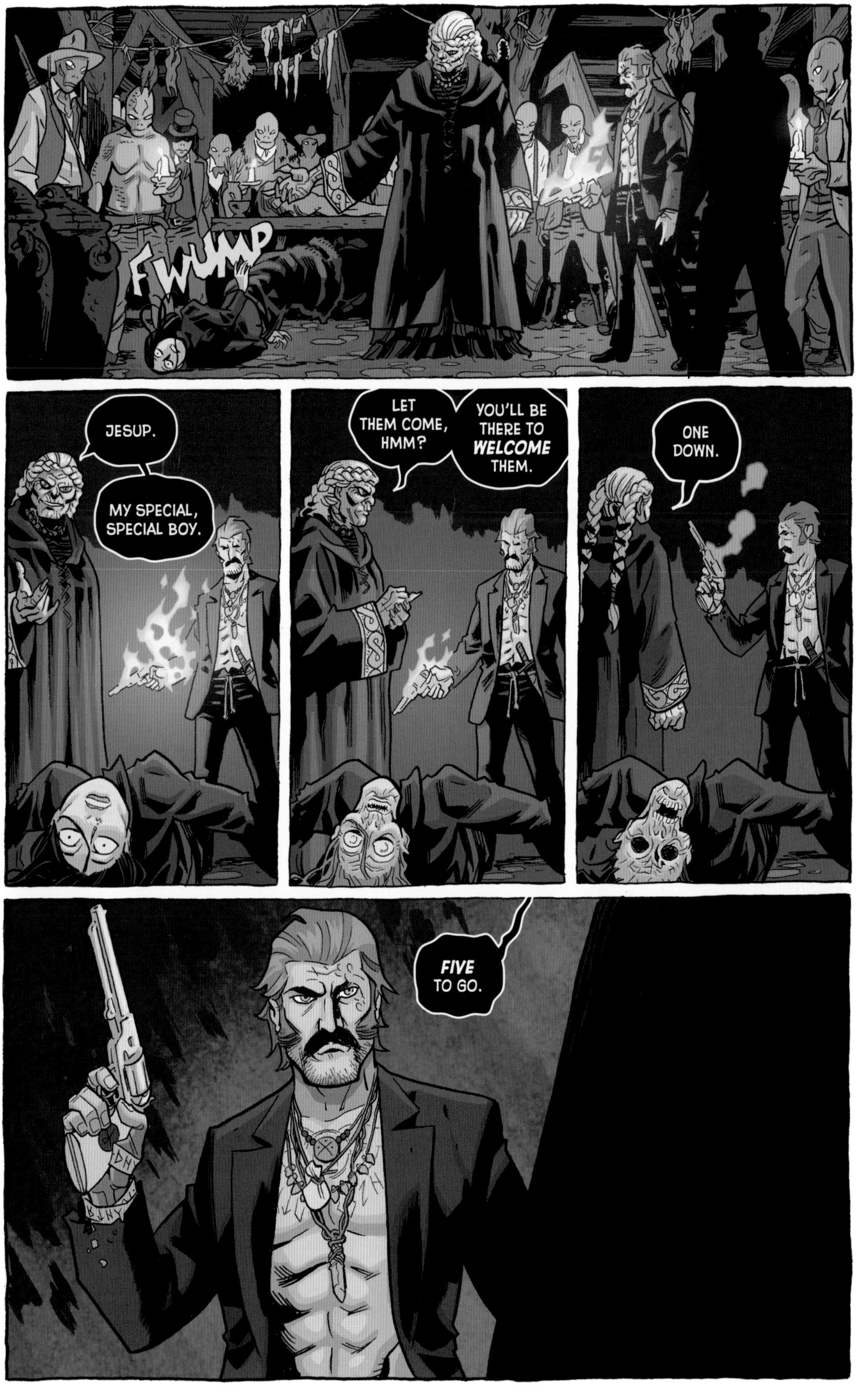
FWUMP
JESUP.
MY SPECIAL, SPECIAL BOY.
LET THEM COME, HMM?
YOU'LL BE THERE TO *WELCOME* THEM.
ONE DOWN.
FIVE TO GO.

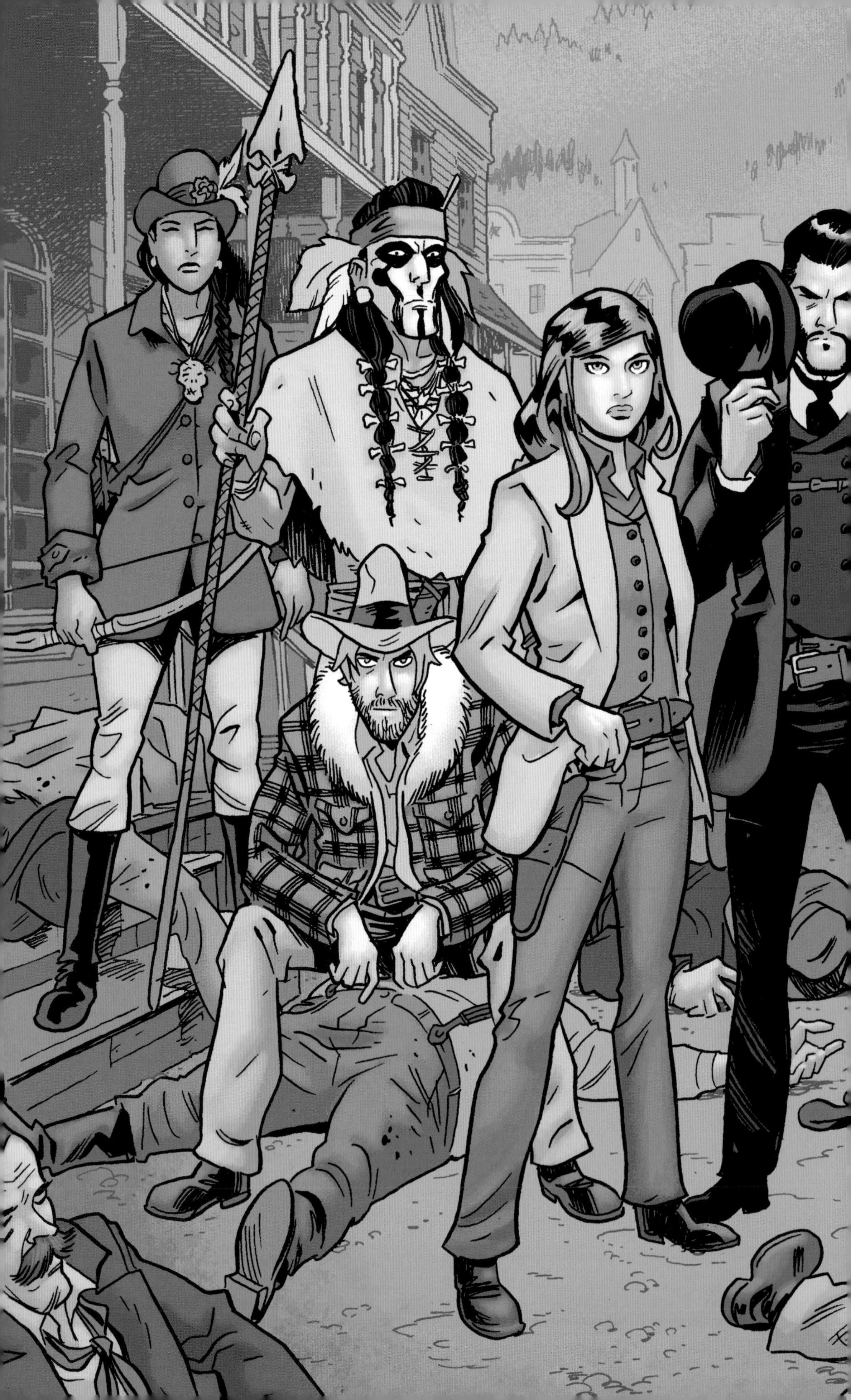

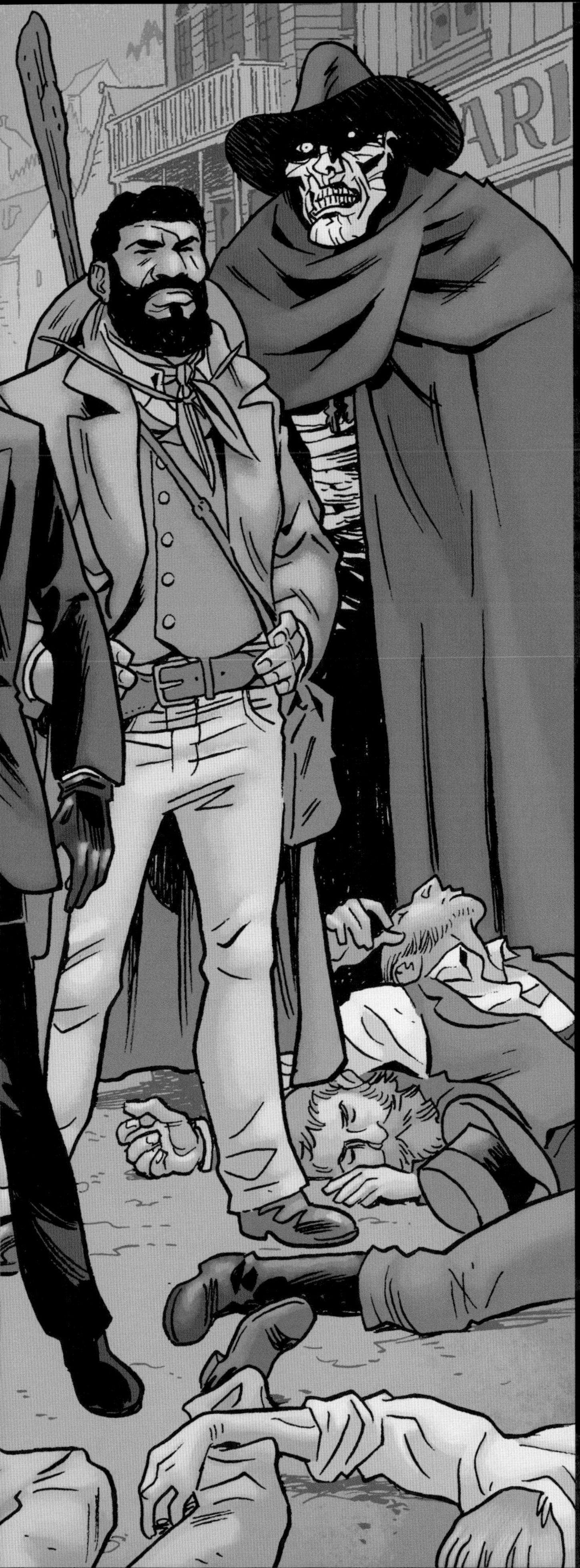

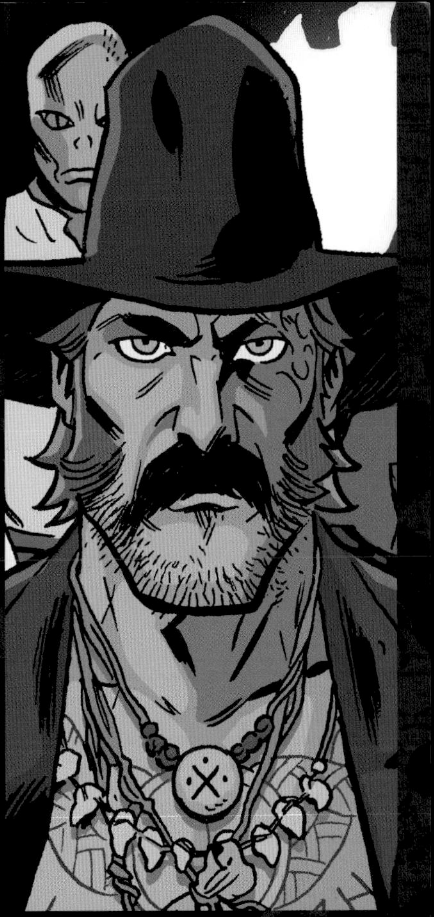

THE ADVENTURE CONTINUES EVERY MONTH!

The forces of darkness have hounded Becky Montcrief since she first placed her hand on the Sixth Gun. Now, Becky and her allies are taking the fight to their enemies. Their goal—destroy the cursed guns once and for all! The war for the Six starts here! This is the beginning of the end!

But the Grey Witch launches a devastating attack, and her forces are led by an old enemy. Jesup is back. He's been transformed into a vicious killing machine. And he's out for blood!

From the beginning, we've always said that no one is safe. Now we aim to prove it. Nothing can prepare you for the shocking events that are about to unfurl... or the climactic encounter that will change the fate of the Six forever!

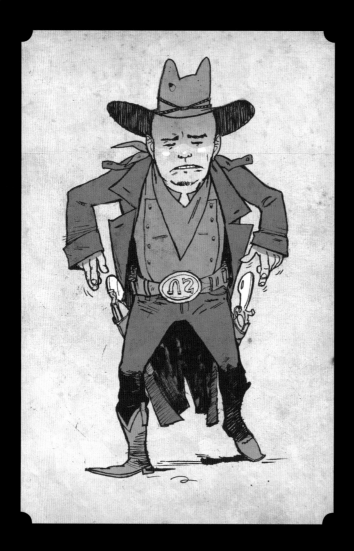

Cullen Bunn grew up in rural North Carolina, but now lives in the St. Louis area with his wife Cindy and Jackson, his son. His noir/horror comic (and first collaboration with Brian Hurtt), *The Damned*, was published in 2007 by Oni Press. The follow-up, *The Damned: Prodigal Sons*, was released in 2008. In addition to *The Sixth Gun*, his current projects include *The Tooth*, an original graphic novel from Oni Press; *Crooked Hills*, a middle reader horror prose series from Evileye Books; and various work for Marvel and DC. Somewhere along the way, Cullen founded Undaunted Press and edited the critically acclaimed small press horror magazine, *Whispers from the Shattered Forum*.

All writers must pay their dues, and Cullen has worked various odd jobs, including Alien Autopsy Specialist, Rodeo Clown, Professional Wrestler Manager, and Sasquatch Wrangler.

And, yes, he has fought for his life against mountain lions and he did perform on stage as the World's Youngest Hypnotist. Buy him a drink sometime, and he'll tell you all about it.

Visit his website at www.cullenbunn.com.

Author portrait illustrations by Jason Latour. jasonlatour.com

Brian Hurtt got his start in comics pencilling the second arc of Greg Rucka's *Queen & Country*. This was followed by art duties on several projects including *Queen & Country: Declassified*, *Three Strikes*, and Steve Gerber's critically acclaimed series *Hard Time*.

In 2006, Brian teamed with Cullen Bunn to create the Prohibition-era monster-noir sensation *The Damned*. The two found that their unique tastes and storytelling sensibilities were well-suited to one another and were eager to continue that relationship.

The Sixth Gun is their sophomore endeavor together and the next in what looks to be many years of creative collaboration.

Brian lives in St. Louis where the summers are too hot, the winters too cold, but the rent is just right.

He can be found online at thehurttlocker.blogspot.com.

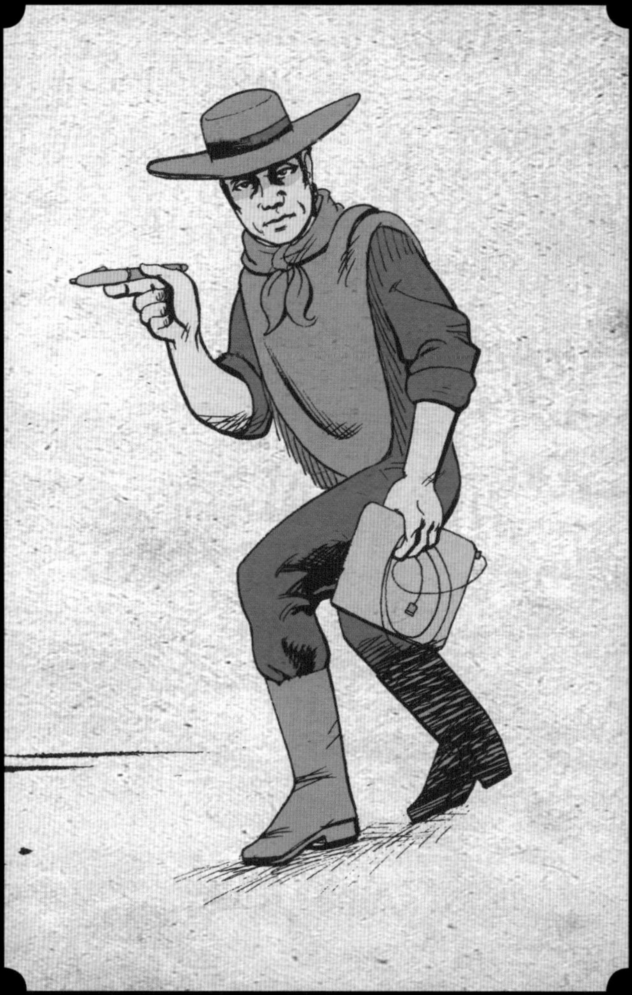

Illustration by Bill Crabtree

Bill Crabtree's career as a colorist began in 2003 with the launch of Image Comic's *Invincible* and *Firebreather*. He would go on to color the first 50 issues of *Invincible*, which would become a flagship Image Comics title, along with garnering Bill a Harvey Awards nomination.

He continues to color *Firebreather*, which was recently made into a feature film on Cartoon Network, as well as *Godland* and *Jack Staff*.

Perhaps the highlight of his comics career, his role as colorist on *The Sixth Gun* began with issue 6, and has since been described as "like Christmas morning, but with guns."

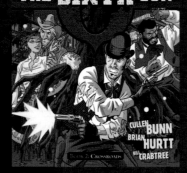

FROM CULLEN BUNN & BRIAN HURTT

THE SIXTH GUN, VOLUME 4:
A TOWN CALLED PENANCE
BY CULLEN BUNN, BRIAN HURTT
TYLER CROOK & BILL CRABTREE
168 PAGES • TRADE PAPERBACK
COLOR
ISBN 978-1-934964-95-8

THE SIXTH GUN, VOLUME 5:
WINTER WOLVES
BY CULLEN BUNN, BRIAN HURTT
& BILL CRABTREE
160 PAGES • TRADE PAPERBACK
COLOR
ISBN 978-1-62010-077-6

THE SIXTH GUN
SONS OF THE GUN
BY CULLEN BUNN, BRIAN HURTT,
BRIAN CHURILLA & BILL CRABTREE
136 PAGES • TRADE PAPERBACK
COLOR
ISBN 978-1-62010-099-8

ONI PRESS
REVOLUTIONIZE COMICS
www.onipress.com

"(Brian Hurtt) and Cullen Bunn deliver a real winner in The Damned."

— Kurt Busiek, writer of *Astro City* and *Trinity*

ONI PRESS

REVOLUTIONIZE COMICS

www.onipress.com

THE DAMNED

CULLEN BUNN / BRIAN HURTT

VOLUME ONE   "THREE DAYS DEAD"

"This is an absolutely terrific book. Tough guys, mobsters, and demons from hell. A bluesy, bitter mood and a fascinating, mysterious world. It's great to see Brian Hurtt back after the much-missed Hard Time, and it's even better to have him doing something beautifully realized. He and Cullen Bunn deliver a real winner in The Damned."
— Kurt Busiek (Superman, Conan, Astro City)

AVAILABLE NOW.

160 PAGES • 6"X9" TRADE PAPERBACK • BLACK & WHITE
ISBN 978-1-932664-63-8

Also Available From Oni Press...

THE SECRET HISTORY OF D.B. COOPER
By Brian Churilla
152 pages • Hardcover
Color
ISBN 978-1-934964-91-0

GHOST PROJEKT
By Joe Harris & Steve Rolston
152 pages • Hardcover
Color
ISBN 978-1-934964-42-2

GUERILLAS: VOLUME 1
By Brahm Revel
168 pages • 6"x9" Trade Paperback
B&W
ISBN 978-1-934964-43-9

PETROGRAD
By Philp Gelatt & Tyler Crook
264 pages • 6"x9" Hardcover
2-Color
ISBN 978-1-934964-44-6

QUEEN & COUNTRY DEFINITIVE EDITION: VOLUME 1
By Greg Rucka with Steve Rolston, Brian Hurtt, and Leandro Fernandez
366 pages • 6"x9" • Trade Paperback
B&W
ISBN 978-1-932664-87-4

STUMPTOWN: VOLUME 1
By Greg Rucka & Matthew Southworth
144 pages • Hardcover
Color
ISBN 978-1-934964-37-8

WASTELAND: VOLUME 1
By Antony Johnston & Christopher Mitten
160 pages • Trade Paperback
B&W
ISBN 978-1-932664-59-1

ONE SOUL
By Ray Fawkes
176 pages • Hardcover
B&W
ISBN 978-1-934964-66-8

ONI PRESS
REVOLUTIONIZE COMICS
www.onipress.com

THE SECRET HISTORY OF
D.B. COOPER
BY BRIAN CHURILLA

GHOST PROJEKT
VOLUME ONE

GUERILLAS
INTRODUCTION BY JACKSON PUBLICK (CREATOR OF THE VENTURE BROS.)
VOLUME 1
BRAHM REVEL

PETROGRAD
PHILIP GELATT • TYLER CROOK

GREG RUCKA
QUEEN & COUNTRY
DEFINITIVE EDITION
VOLUME 01

"STUMPTOWN IS, FOR MY MONEY, THE PERFECT RUCKA BOOK."
STUMPTOWN
GREG RUCKA • MATTHEW SOUTHWORTH

WASTELAND
ANTONY JOHNSTON
CHRISTOPHER MITTEN
BOOK 01
CITIES IN DUST

Ray Fawkes
ONE SOUL

For more information on these and other fine Oni Press comic books and graphic novels visit www.onipress.com. To find a comic shop specialty store in your area visit www.comicshops.us.

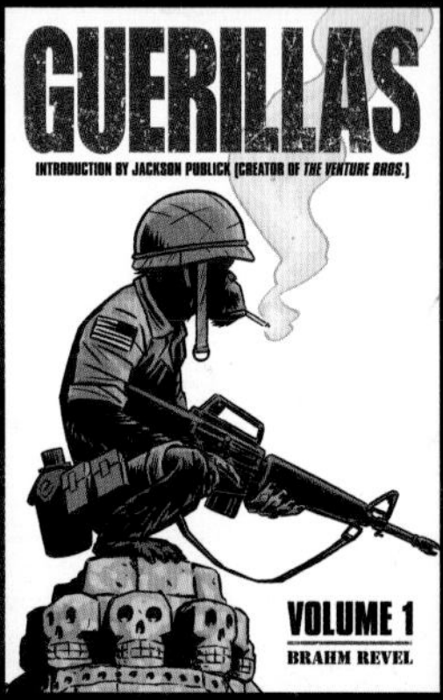